A successful physician, mother and community leader, Jennifer Schneider had everything—or so it seemed. Then her husband told her that he had been having an affair and that he wasn't sure it wouldn't happen again. After months of blaming herself, Jennifer began to learn slowly that her husband was a sexual addict, she a coaddict and that recovery for both of them was possible. At the same time in her professional practice, Dr. Schneider began to explore the dynamics of addiction in the couple relationship. Based upon interviews with patients and other women who have experienced the pain of discovering their husband's or lover's secret lives, she wrote this powerful book.

BACK FROM BETRAYAL

Recovering from His Affairs

Jennifer P. Schneider, M.D.

A Hazelden Recovery Book
BALLANTINE BOOKS • NEW YORK

The following publishers have generously given permission to use extended quotations from copyrighted works: From *The New Celibacy*, by Gabrielle Brown. Copyright 1980, published by Ballantine Books, a division of Random House, Inc. Reprinted by permission of McGraw-Hill Book Company. From *Diagnosing and Treating Co-dependence*, by Timmen L. Cermak, M.D. Copyright 1986, published by Johnson Institute Publications. Reprinted by permission of the publisher. From *Love Must be Tough*, by James C. Dobson. Copyright 1983, published by Word Books. Reprinted by permission of the publisher. From *The Feminine Mystique*, by Betty Friedan. Copyright c 1983, 1974, 1973, 1963 by Betty Friedan. Reprinted by permission of W. W. Norton & Company, Inc. From *The Second Stage*, by Betty Friedan. Copyright 1981. Reprinted by permission of Summit Books, a division of Simon & Schuster, Inc. From *The Art of Loving*, by Erich Fromm. Copyright 1956, published by Harper & Row, from 1974 Perennial Library Edition. Reprinted by permission of Harper & Row. From *How to Break your Addiction to a Person*, by Howard Halpern. Copyright 1981, published by Bantam Books. Reprinted by permission of McGraw-Hill Book Company. From *WE: Understanding the Psychology of Romantic Love*, by Robert A. Johnson. Copyright 1983, published by Harper & Row. Reprinted by permission of the publisher. From *Stranger on the Square*, by Arthur Koestler and Cynthia Koestler. Copyright 1984, published by Random House, Inc. Reprinted by permission of the publisher. From *The Booze Battle*, by Ruth Maxwell. Copyright 1976, published by Ballantine Books. Reprinted by permission of Henry Holt & Co. From "Avoiding the Scarlet Letter," by Dr. Louis McBurney, M.D. Published in *Leadership Magazine*, 1985. Reprinted by permission of the author. From *The Total Woman*, by Marabel Morgan. Copyright c 1973 by Marabel Morgan. Published by Fleming H. Revell Company. Reprinted by permission of the publisher. From *Co-dependence: Misunderstood / Mistreated*, by Anne Wilson Schaef. Copyright 1986, published by Winston Press. Reprinted with permission of Harper & Row. From "Co-dependency: A Paradoxical Dependency," by Robert Subby, in *Co-dependency: An Emerging Issue*. Copyright 1984, published by Health Communications, Inc. Reprint courtesy Robert Subby: CODEPENDENCY, 1984, Health Communications, Pompano Beach, Florida. From *A Loss for Words*, by Lou Ann Walker. Copyright 1986, published by Harper & Row. Reprinted by permission of the publisher. From "Sexaholic: Addict of Infidelity," by Bob Womack. From the *Arizona Daily Star* 5 May 1985. Reprinted by permission of the *Arizona Daily Star*.

Library of Congress Catalog Card Number: 87-82519

ISBN 0-345-36786-3

This edition published by arrangement with the Hazelden Foundation

Manufactured in the United States of America

First Ballantine Books Edition: July 1990

CONTENTS

ACKNOWLEDGMENTS

Many people have assisted me in the preparation of this book. Because I have promised to preserve their anonymity, I cannot publicly thank the men and women whose stories appear here, but I have expressed my gratitude to them individually.

The following people read parts or all of the manuscript in various stages and gave me helpful suggestions: Sheila Tobias; Mary McCarthy, C.A.C.; Richard Tanner, M.D.; Lindsey Busch, M.Ed., C.A.C.; Judy Nevin, M.Ed.; Donna Reed; Cynthia Arem, Ph.D.; Arnold Arem, M.D.; Richard Mandel, M.D.; Stuart Gellman; Raphael Patai, Ph.D.; and Daphne Patai, Ph.D. Roxanne Kibben, C.A.C., gave me her insights on treatment of codependency. I am particularly grateful to Robin Martin for many helpful discussions, excellent suggestions, and critical perusal of the manuscript at every step.

My husband gave me his unfailing support during the writing of this book, reviewed the manuscript, and had many important suggestions.

My five children and stepchildren got used to finding me deep in thought at the word processor or else involved in endless discussions about sex addiction, coaddiction, and codependency. I appreciate their patience and support.

Finally, I want to thank my editor, Kerry Finn, for her encouragement, enthusiasm, and belief in the book.

PREFACE

In 1983 I was a happy woman. I was a successful physician, had two healthy and bright children, and I was in a relatively new marriage with a man I loved very much. My husband and I had spent the preceding year learning how to make a success of our stepfamily, and we were doing well. We had just bought a new house that could accommodate his three children and my two, and our hard work with our new family was beginning to pay off.

Then something happened that turned my life upside down: My husband, in great distress, told me he had been having an affair for some months. Despite the pain we were both feeling and his guilt over hurting me, he wasn't sure it would not happen again. He realized he was addicted to the excitement of the chase.

I thought back to our stormy courtship, to the several times he had backed out of a commitment, saying we both "needed to meet other people" (which I knew meant *he* wanted to meet other women). I knew he had not been faithful during his first marriage either, but I had naively assumed that monogamy would not be a problem for him this time. Now he was telling me he had so little control over his actions that he couldn't promise fidelity in the future, no matter how much he wished he could. I felt devastated; our marriage seemed headed for divorce.

Several weeks later, he read a letter to "Dear Abby" in the newspaper. A woman stated that although she loved her husband and did not want to destroy her marriage, she kept getting involved in meaningless affairs. She didn't know how to stop. Abby referred her to a self-help recovery program for people whose lives are out of control because of their compulsive sexual activity. My husband joined the same self-help program and suggested that I also attend a program based on the Twelve Steps of Alcoholics Anonymous. I had attended Alcoholics Anonymous (A.A., a self-help group for alcoholics) and Al-Anon meetings (for families of alcoholics) during medical school, but felt they had no relevance to my situation. My husband recognized the similarities between alcoholism and other addictions and advised me to attend Al-Anon, the only program for families of addicts available in our city. I went reluctantly and resentfully at first, but eventually I learned I was a codependent (someone who looks to others for validation of her self-worth) and a coaddict (a person who is in an addictive relationship with an addict).

I soon realized that it was no accident I had chosen to marry the man I did—that all of my previous important relationships had also been with men who were emotionally unavailable in one way or another. My childhood experiences were typical of women who become coaddicts, and even my choice of career was logical in view of the caretaker role I had when I was growing up.

I found I subscribed to a set of irrational beliefs typical of the coaddict: I was fearful of abandonment, I felt my real worth came from validation by another person, and I thought I could control my husband's behavior. If I were more attractive, or kept a neater house, or were more understanding and unselfish, he would be satisfied to stay home.

Through attendance at a self-help program for spouses of sex addicts, I came to understand that I was powerless over my husband's behavior, and that my self-esteem did not depend on him or anyone else. I became able to set limits on what is acceptable for me within a relationship.

My husband has had no affairs since his participation in a Twelve Step program. I am grateful that he and I are sharing the path of recovery. Even though we married ''for

the wrong reasons,'' as he has told me, we are now together for the right reasons—out of choice, not addiction,
because our lives are enriched by each other.

Fifteen years ago when I entered medical school, my
goal seemed simple: I would learn all I could about the
human body and its disorders, about how to diagnose and
treat each ailment. Basic information about the healthy
body came from my anatomy, biochemistry, histology, and
physiology courses. I learned about disease by studying
pathology. Knowledge about diagnosis and treatment came
primarily from years spent on hospital wards as a student
and later as a resident in internal medicine.

By the 1970s, medical school curricula included consideration of social problems. A Human Behavior and Development course included lectures on suicide, sexuality,
and alcoholism. For those of us who were interested, the
school arranged visits to Alcoholics Anonymous meetings. Having had no exposure to chemical dependency
among my own family or friends, I would otherwise have
never attended such meetings and would have graduated
from medical school, as did most of my classmates, with
no knowledge of the valuable resource for recovery that
A.A.'s Twelve Step program provides.

My professor gave me the name of a recovering alcoholic to contact. I phoned her, and a few evenings later I
was taken by an attractive, articulate woman to a large
meeting hall where a clergyman and a physician told of
their struggles with alcoholism and their subsequent recovery. As I looked around the room, I noticed not only
chain-smoking, crusty, old men (who fit my preconception
of the hard-core alcoholic), but also well-dressed men and
women and, surprisingly, quite a few young people. Their
faces projected hope and a sense of belonging. The Twelve
Steps of the A.A. program had clearly made a big difference in their lives.

This was an unknown part of society to me, and I decided to learn more. My next step was to find out what

life was like for the spouses of alcoholics. My guide suggested I attend an Al-Anon meeting. I did and found it very different from the inspirational A.A. meeting I had observed the week before. At the Al-Anon meeting, a dozen women listened to a crying newcomer describe how her life was totally out of control because of her husband's drinking.

"I know how you feel, because I was once there too," confided a member. Several of the women described similar situations they had been through and how their program helped them deal with each problem. By the end of the meeting, the newcomer felt much better and left the meeting with some hope. I still knew nothing about the program, but I could see these women were helping each other. I made a mental note that if, in my practice, I were to encounter a patient who was living with alcoholism, I would tell her about Al-Anon. In my naiveté, I did not really expect this to happen very often.

By the time I began private practice, I was in my new marriage. My husband, a graduate student in counseling, would bring home books and articles about psychotherapy. I read them with interest, and I began attending workshops with him on individual, family, and sexual counseling. He spent some months working at a chemical dependency treatment unit for adolescents, which led to my increased awareness of the pervasiveness of alcohol and other drug addiction. This awareness was reinforced by lectures and workshops on addiction I attended with him. I frequently heard A.A. and Al-Anon mentioned at these talks, and remembered the meetings I had attended as a medical student.

I began to question patients more extensively about their use of alcohol and other drugs. Not surprisingly, I soon learned that many of my patients, especially those I had been treating for hypertension, insomnia, headaches, fatigue, and vague gastrointestinal symptoms, had excessive use of alcohol as their underlying disease. I learned how to recognize the clinical and biochemical signs of early alcohol dependency and began referring patients to alcohol recovery programs.

As a female internist, I am often sought out by women who want to have the sympathetic ear of another woman. As I began talking with them, I was struck by how often they were dealing with very difficult situations: husbands who drank excessively, who were rarely at home because their jobs were all-consuming, who were demanding and jealous, or who were engaged in sexual affairs. Some women held full-time, demanding jobs and then came home to housework, meal preparation, and child care, as well as providing a sounding board for their husbands' problems and complaints. They had grown up so firmly entrenched in caretaker roles that they didn't feel they had the right to ask their spouses to share in the work. Moreover, they felt unable to let go of any of the responsibilities they had assumed.

These women had not come to see me because of their relationship problems; rather, they were in my office because of headaches, backaches, insomnia, fatigue, or stomach pains. In the past, I had approached each symptom individually, ordering various tests and prescribing appropriate medications. At times the particular symptom would improve, but the patient would be back a few weeks later with a different complaint. Often, nothing really seemed to help. Eventually, I recognized that the physical symptoms were manifestations of the depression, anger, resentment, and helplessness they were feeling about their circumstances at home. They were caretakers in the family, trying their best to make things better, trying to change their husbands' drinking, overworking, gambling, or other destructive behaviors. They were stuck and didn't know how to improve the situation. They were so committed to a relationship that they couldn't imagine getting out. They stuffed their feelings—often literally. In fact, when I started asking obese women about their home lives, I discovered they were frequently in alcoholic or otherwise unhealthy relationships or had grown up in dysfunctional families.

The women I saw seemed to share a common affliction which was at the source of their varied symptoms. The disease was codependency, and I was learning about its insidious nature by observing my patients. Not until codependency suddenly became personal for me did I realize I was suffering from the same problem. My experience made me much more attuned to my patients' problems, and more able to intervene effectively by referring them to appropriate counseling and to self-help programs.

In my own recovery group and in my office, I have become aware of the deep shame we feel when our husbands have had affairs. Believing that our husbands' behavior is a reflection of our own inadequacy, we blame ourselves, convinced that if we were sexier or more supportive they would not have strayed. We are deeply ashamed to tell what is happening in our marriages. It took me a long time to be comfortable about admitting to others my husband's affairs. Until then, I always worried about what others would think of me. Now I recognize that my husband's affairs reflected only on him.

Yet there is justification for our reluctance to admit our husbands' affairs. Many people do automatically blame the wife. This was evident on a television program I saw in 1984. Phil Donahue interviewed Patrick Carnes, author of *Out of the Shadows*, and a married couple who were in treatment because the husband was a compulsive masturbator. The audience reaction was particularly hostile. Several women seemed threatened, asking the wife if she didn't agree that if she had been more sexually available to her husband he would not have had to resort to frequent masturbation. (This is the same line of reasoning frequently used to blame the wife for her husband's affairs.) There was little understanding that the husband's behavior was caused by an addiction, not by his wife. This man had learned to medicate his emotional pain with the es-

cape and relief he got from compulsive masturbation, just
as other people alleviate their emotional pain by drinking
alcohol to excess. In neither case is the wife to blame, and
in neither case can she control her husband's activity.

The most important element of maintaining addictive
behavior is secrecy. To be able to talk about a problem
openly is the first step toward resolving it. For a woman
to become healthy she needs to understand she is not responsible for her husband's affairs and that he has a disease which causes him to behave in hurtful ways. Many
women can now state that their spouses have an alcohol
addiction without feeling they are responsible for the
drinking or that they are unworthy. It is my hope this book
will hasten the day when a woman is more willing to talk
about her husband's sexual addiction and get help for herself, whether he is still acting on his sexual compulsions
or whether he believes he has a problem.

In being open about my own family problems, I risk
being accused of sensationalism. Some may ask why I
don't simply write this book as a professional, without
owning up to my personal involvement. My answer is I
am following the tradition of counselors in the chemical
dependency field. Open any brochure for a chemical dependency treatment program and you will find that most
staff members list their own recoveries from alcohol or
other drug abuse as part of their credentials. Likewise,
those who counsel family members admit their experiences in alcoholic families. In the chemical dependency
field it is considered an asset to have experienced and
grappled with the problem. When a counselor can say, ''I
know what you're going through—I've been there myself,'' he or she can cut through the isolation that is part
of addictive behavior. This powerful therapeutic tool enables the client to feel that the counselor can really understand.

This, of course, is very different from the traditional
approach of the psychiatrist or psychologist, whose role is

to listen to the client, supply insights where they are deemed helpful, and make suggestions for better ways of coping. Therapists are very careful to provide a minimum of personal information, even about their marital and family status. They want to project to the client the image of a healthy person, one who has no significant emotional problems.

Therapists have not always been able to openly admit to their own chemical dependency. Fifty years ago, when the Alcoholics Anonymous movement first began, alcoholism was considered as shameful as sexual addiction is today. Very few people were willing to speak openly about their own alcoholism or their involvement in an alcoholic family. It took many years for chemical dependency to be considered a disease and for the medical and psychotherapeutic community to acknowledge the validity of the A.A. approach as a road to recovery. When the first edition of *Alcoholics Anonymous: The Story of How More Than One Hundred Men Have Recovered from Alcoholism*[1] appeared in 1939, a review of the book in the *Journal of the American Medical Association*[2] described it as ''a curious combination of organizing propaganda and religious exhortation'' and concluded, ''The one valid thing in the book is the recognition of the seriousness of addiction to alcohol. Other than this, the book has no scientific merit or interest.'' However, this book, which lists the Twelve Steps and describes the recovery program that has been successful for so many years, is still the basic text for members of A.A. and is the model for all other self-help recovery programs based on A.A.

At this time, the sexual addiction and coaddiction field is where the alcoholism field was in the early days of A.A. Like the chemical dependency and codependency fields, it is likely that many workers in the sexual addiction area are in it because of personal as well as professional interest. Few, however, are acknowledging it.

I had the option, when I began this project, of writing

it strictly as a physician and portraying that I had only a professional interest in the subject. I felt my husband should make the final decision, since he, even more than myself, is likely to get negative comments from members of the community who may think that in describing his affairs as an addiction I am merely trying to excuse his behavior. He opted for honesty, and for this I owe him the greatest respect and love.

Some readers may contend that a man who is addicted to affairs is not in the same category as one who is addicted to alcohol. They may argue that pursuing women is more of a voluntary activity, and calling it an addiction or compulsion may serve only to absolve a man of responsibility for his actions. I would ask such readers to keep an open mind. It is not my intent to provide any man with an excuse for hurtful behaviors, nor to urge his wife to go along with it on the basis that her husband has an illness. On the contrary, a major emphasis in this book is to show wives how to stop the enabling behaviors that protect the addict from experiencing the unpleasant consequences of his acts, thereby encouraging the behavior to continue.

It is my hope that this book will reach the many women who are suffering silently and alone as their husbands repeatedly connect with others, who are too ashamed to talk with anyone except perhaps their closest friend about what is happening in their lives, and who feel that somehow their husbands' affairs are their fault and an indication of their inadequacy.

Section One:

The Problem

CHAPTER ONE

The Problem of Addiction to Affairs

What is life like for a woman married to a sex addict? Each relationship is different, of course, but here is the story of one woman who was unable to change her very unsatisfactory life.

Beth's Story

There were what Beth calls signs she would have spotted when they were dating, but it wasn't until four years after they were married that Beth discovered she had an unfaithful husband.

She had noticed that Barry was spending less and less time at home. One day she asked a neighbor if he had seen Barry. Yes, he responded, he had seen him loading a woman friend's bicycle into the back of his car and driving off with her.

Beth drove over to the woman's house and spotted her husband's car parked there. She drove home, telephoned the woman and asked to speak to Barry. She recalls:

I told him I thought it would be real swell if he got home right away and he did. He told me their friendship was real important to him and it had nothing to do with us. Then he told me he was going to Mexico with her, which he did.

A dozen years later, separated but still married to Barry, Beth says she was devastated at the news of his trip, yet was able to rationalize it this way:

I told myself he had never made a decision on his own and this was a decision he had made. So it was okay. I just waited at home for him. I wasn't sure he was ever coming back.

But Barry returned and his fling seemed to have been just that—an isolated incident frozen in Beth's memory but fading into the past. He went into business and became a workaholic. She devoted herself to the tasks of a homemaker.

They had two children, and Beth was pregnant with their third child about four years ago when Barry left one evening for a baseball game and didn't come home until the next morning.

I called the police and the hospitals—I thought something had happened to him. Then I thought maybe he had gone back to work after the game and fallen asleep at the office. I put the kids in the car at 3 A.M. and drove over there, but he wasn't there.

She did that, she thinks, because she had to have reality ''slap'' her in the face. The reality became even sharper that morning at six when Barry called her and asked if he could come home.

She had been slapped into the realization that she was married to a philanderer. Or, as she prefers to call it, a sexaholic.

She remembers a feeling of terror.

This time it was not just me—I would be left with two small children—more than I thought I could handle. And I was pregnant, and I was feeling fat and ugly. I felt my responsibilities were overwhelming.

She began trying to "catch" her husband and confront him with evidence of his infidelity. She stooped to actions she concedes were not only degrading but useless: smelling his clothing, going through his car.

"Your clothes smell like perfume," she would say. Or, "How can a normal person come home at four in the morning and just have taken a shower?"

Each time, however, Barry had an excuse. And he would add, in an accusatory tone, "Look how suspicious you've become!"

Each time he would flip things around to where I felt like I was a bad person, a bitchy wife. How could I be making his life so miserable?

He would call her about 5 P.M. and say he had a few more things to do at the office and that he would be home about six-thirty. One day she decided to find out just how busy he was so she drove over to his office and parked so she could see his door. It wasn't long before a girlfriend drove up and ran into Barry's office.

I was furious. I went home and called him. I asked the kids, "Wanna talk to Daddy?" and I put them on the phone. I couldn't think of what else to do.

She once followed him after he left home for work. He stopped at one girlfriend's house on the way to work and had a lunch date with another. When he came home, he and Beth had a fight, and he left at 11 P.M. and returned at 2 A.M. freshly showered.

Why did she spy on him? What good did it do? No more good than something she witnessed her mother doing in a vain way to "control" Beth's alcoholic father by marking the levels on his liquor bottles.

Beth and Barry began seeing a counselor once a week, after, she says, Barry convinced her she was "crazy." He quit going, Beth said, after the counselor understood what the real problem was.

One day the counselor asked me, "Do you realize this person you're married to is compulsively sexual?" I didn't know what that meant. I felt it must be something I'm doing—maybe he sees other women because they have jobs, because they're prettier than I am, because they're more intelligent than I am.

A year later, still feeling responsible for their problems, still spying on Barry, and fighting almost constantly with him, Beth decided to leave. He wasn't pleased at the news, but she took the kids and left town.

When she returned three weeks later, he greeted her warmly with a cake that said, "Welcome Home." Beth was still angry and she and her husband went into their bedroom to talk. Exhausted from her trip, she lay down on her bed. Her pillow reeked of perfume. "It was like aaaarrrruuuugggghh," says Beth, emitting a strangled exclamation.

Shortly afterward, Barry moved out. Since then, they have had numerous short-term reconciliations, but the only time he moved back in was the next Christmas. A day or two afterward, he stayed out late, returning at 3 A.M. freshly showered.

Barry told Beth how badly he felt about himself, about the "pressure" he was under. She thought she must have been "pretty rotten" to accuse him of sleeping around.

As for herself, she insists:

I feel really strong about myself. I feel it's okay that I don't know what will happen. I think there's a fairly good chance we will reconcile.[1]

Beth's passivity in the face of her husband's multiple affairs may be difficult for some readers to understand. Her fear of losing her husband, her attempts to spy on him, her willingness to take the blame for her husband's behavior, and her wishful thinking that things were likely to improve despite all the evidence of his ongoing affairs, are typical of the coaddict.

Here is Carmen's account: her husband, unlike Beth's, had just two affairs, but eventually identified himself as a sex addict.

Some people have told me, "So your husband had a couple of affairs! So do the majority of married men at some time. What makes his situation different? Why does he consider himself an addict?"

The essential problem was not that he had two affairs, but rather that his preoccupation with connecting with women interfered with all other aspects of his life. Wherever he went his roving eye would pick out a potential connection—usually someone whose appearance or body language suggested vulnerability or lack of self-confidence. He would then begin planning how to meet her and would fantasize what the meeting might lead to. His original purpose for attending the meeting or the class would be forgotten. He would arrange to have coffee or lunch with her. Even if she didn't accept, the emotional high he got from the experience of pursuing her made our home life dull by comparison. He would return home and walk around with a long face, finally confessing to me his unhappiness with the lack of excitement in our life. At times he would pick an argument with me so as to justify (in his mind) connecting with someone who would be more understanding or less demanding. Of course, I didn't understand this at the time; I just knew that he seemed terribly unhappy for no particular reason. I tried my hardest to make him happy, but nothing worked.

We would get into a vicious circle—I would feel rejected by his statements of boredom with our life and I would respond by shutting down communication with him. He would then feel justified in concentrating on his latest fantasy. Eventually we would make up and things would be okay for a while, until just when our life seemed to be going very well, he would come home and tell me how unhappy he was. I felt I was on a roller coaster. I could never predict what state of mind I'd find him in when I got home from work. And since my sense of well-being depended on him, my moods also kept swinging widely.

I kept expecting something bad to happen. Several times he stayed out late and wouldn't tell me why; he said he was helping someone and had promised secrecy. When he finally told me about an affair he'd been involved in for months—and a briefer one that had happened a year earlier—I realized that I had suspected it all along.

Beth's and Carmen's suspicions are shared by millions of women in the United States. About half of all men have at least one affair during their marriage, according to Dr. Alfred Kinsey's classic study, done in the 1940s, of sexual behavior in American men.[2] Sociologist Morton Hunt's survey in the 1970s showed no significant change in that behavior pattern.[3] This was confirmed in 1981 by Shere Hite, whose survey found that 72 percent of men married two years or more had extramarital sex.[4] Certainly most of these men were not addicts! Rather, the fact that affairs are so prevalent indicates that the needs of many people are not being met within the marriage. Traditionally, marriage was viewed as primarily an economic arrangement, designed to insure financial security and a stable environment for the children. In cultures as diverse as China, India, and the Jewish ghettos of Europe, arranged marriages were accepted because they fulfilled the purpose of marriage as a practical, functional arrangement. In these cultures, marriages were not expected to fulfill the partners' emotional needs, nor their longing for romantic love. Only in modern Western society have we made romantic love the basis of marriage and the cultural ideal of "true love."

What is "Romantic Love"?

According to Robert A. Johnson:

> Romantic love doesn't just mean loving someone; it means being "in love." This is a very specific psychological phenomenon. When we are "in love," we believe we have found the ultimate meaning of life, revealed in another human being. We feel we are finally completed, that we have found the missing parts of ourselves. Life suddenly seems to have a wholeness, a superhuman intensity that lifts us high above the ordinary plane of existence. For us, these are the sure signs of "true love." The psychological package includes an unconscious demand that our lover or spouse always provides us with this feeling of ecstasy and intensity.[5]

The tradition of romantic love endows the lover with the power and responsibility to make the life of the loved one whole, meaningful, happy, intense, and ecstatic.

What are the elements of romantic love? A pamphlet entitled, *So Your Happily Ever After Isn't* contrasts the myth of living "happily ever after" with the reality of being "comfortable" in a marriage. It lists the criteria for romance: (1) To feel a romantic "high" with another person, you have to feel somewhat insecure with him, not totally sure that he cares. (2) You have to not know him well; he must be a little strange, unpredictable. (3) There must be barriers to your encounters, such as physical distance between you or the need for secrecy. (4) There must be limits on the time you can spend together.[6]

Strangeness, insecurity, barriers, and limits are clearly not the components of a stable relationship. According to this theory, a romantic relationship can flourish only when the partners don't know each other very well. The barriers assure one does not get to know the partner well enough to learn about his faults and to know him as a real person. When they do get to know each other, the thrill of the romance diminishes.

As *So Your Happily Ever After Isn't* tells us:

> The truth about all highs is that they gradually fade. You gradually get to know the guy and he becomes predictable. Or you get to feeling overly secure. . . . The barriers fall. The limits are exceeded. The tingle fades, and there you are wondering where your "happy" went, and if you really want the tingle, the tension, the "high," then you have to go looking for another Prince. And another one after him, and another one after him. There's nothing wrong with wanting highs. The only problem with it is that if you only get sexual romantic highs and that's *all* you want, you're probably going to spend a lonely and disastrous old age. Princes get few and far between when you're forty. . . . Remember: some women only think they're "happy" when they're "in love." Which means that some women are really fouled up with the Wretched Habit of Romance.[7]

As the marriage partners get to know each other better, the mystery dissolves and the idealization of the loved one yields to reality. Frequently boredom follows, and with it the longing to recapture, with another person, the intensity and ecstasy once felt with the spouse. In a long-term marriage, few of these criteria for romantic love survive.

What Keeps Some People Happily Married for Many Years?

According to Francine Klagsbrun, author of *Married People: Staying Together in the Age of Divorce*,[8] the key to keeping a relationship going is commitment. Commitment is giving up something of ourselves to help our partner grow. It may be willingness to give up our protective shell and leave ourselves vulnerable to hurt.

Most people will not allow themselves to be vulnerable unless they are accepted by another person. According to Klagsbrun, acceptance is a prerequisite for intimacy, and from acceptance grows trust. Acceptance and trust are both most likely to occur when the marriage is monogamous.

> The reason marriage provides the greatest possibilities for intimacy is because marriage is predicated on the idea of exclusivity. And one of the differences between marriage and other friendships is the importance of exclusivity.[9]

Based on the couples she interviewed, Klagsbrun compiled a list of characteristics of successful long-term marriages:

- an ability to change and to tolerate change;
- a willingness to live with the things one can't change;
- an assumption of permanence in the relationship;
- trust between the partners;
- a balance of depending on one another;

- a balance of power;
- enjoyment of each other; and
- a shared history that is cherished.

What is absent is any mention of romantic love or of lasting ecstasy and intensity.

Nonetheless, according to sociologist Morton Hunt, nearly all American husbands and wives at some point in their marriage find themselves wishing for an affair and imagining it in their minds.[10] The intensity of falling in love is not easily forgotten, and it is natural to want to experience it again. Unlike the greylag goose and several other animal species, people are not naturally monogamous.

Monogamy is a social institution which developed primarily for economic reasons. The moral condemnation of extramarital involvements is a legacy of the Judeo-Christian tradition and is far from universal. On the contrary, in a study cited by Hunt,[11] only 16 percent of 185 societies studied by anthropologists insisted on lifelong monogamy, and 39 percent actually approved of extramarital liaisons of specified types. Because men wanted to be sure that their sons were their biological offspring, and because women were often considered the property of their men, women in most societies were denied sexual freedom.

In the United States today, while lip service is paid to the desirability of monogamy, affairs are widely tolerated. For many people, an affair is a way of having one's cake and eating it too. It is a way both to participate in a stable, long-term marriage and its economic and social benefits, and at the same time to enjoy the excitement of romantic love and reexperience the ecstasy of a new sexual involvement. For those who perceive stability in a relationship as boredom, an affair is a way of escaping the boredom and adding a measure of variety and excitement. An affair is generally rationalized as a way of fulfilling needs not being met in the marriage.

Not all affairs are the same. An extramarital liaison can consist of a visit to a prostitute, a casual sexual encounter with someone whose last name is not known and who will never be seen again, or it may be an all-consuming passion that goes on for years. Even imagined affairs can be harmful or beneficial. Hunt says:

> Occasional fits of fantasized infidelity usually indicate nothing more than the normal human desire for variety, which they partly satisfy; continual obsessive fantasies of infidelity are more likely to indicate severe frustration and marital discontent, which they cannot alleviate but which they may prepare the daydreamer to relieve by means of actual extramarital relationships.[12]

In other words, for some dissatisfied people, fantasizing about affairs is the first step to a real affair, and the whole process occupies such a large part of a person's inner world that little energy is left for the marital relationship. This is what happens to the man who is addicted to affairs.

Consequences of Affairs

Even when there is no question of addiction, affairs are harmful. A major element is the dishonesty that is usually necessary. Affairs are usually carried out in secrecy—at least they're kept secret from the spouse. A recent survey of female readers of *New Woman* magazine revealed that whereas 41 percent of the married (or otherwise involved) women had participated in one or more affairs, only 19 percent of the readers knew for certain that their husbands or lovers had cheated on them.[13] In view of the results of the surveys of men conducted by Kinsey and Hunt, what the *New Woman* survey tells us is that many men are successfully concealing their affairs from their wives. Most people who have extramarital affairs apparently still believe that their actions would be unacceptable or threatening to their spouse.

The dishonesty that is involved in most affairs leads to guilt. The greater the emotional investment in the extramarital relationship, the more the married lover is likely to feel guilty. Even if he believes his wife does not suspect, he knows he is lying to her, and his self-esteem is likely to suffer.

Decreased attention to the marital relationship is another likely consequence of the affair. In his mind, the marriage relationship appears dull in comparison to the excitement and novelty of the affair, and his wife cannot hold a candle to his new, exciting lover. The husband's energies are focused outside the marriage, and problems within the marriage are likely to be avoided rather than dealt with. Time and energy that might be spent with the spouse and the children are devoted instead to the affair.

In addition to these costs, there are other potential consequences:

- the possibility of contracting a sexually transmitted disease;
- the risk of losing one's job if an affair with a co-worker comes to light;
- potential physical retaliation by an irate spouse;
- the emotional and financial trauma of divorce; and
- the possibility of an unwanted pregnancy.

Many men interviewed in Morton Hunt's 1970s survey of extramarital behavior felt that their affair did not affect their marriage adversely; some, in fact, said their sexual relationship with their wives had improved as a result of the affair. But this may be little more than a rationalization or a failure to acknowledge the harm done. The author of the survey concludes: "Many supposedly unharmed or even benefitted marriages suffer unseen emotional decay as a result of the external intimacy, and later collapse with a suddenness that takes the partner by surprise."[14] Many people who believed their affairs were harmless forms of recreation that added variety and zest to their lives have found themselves in a major marital crisis when they were discovered.

While extramarital sex is very common in the United States, it is even more prevalent in other societies where there is a greater acceptance of a "division of labor" between wife and mistress. Because cultural norms differ, this book primarily addresses those who live in the United States; however, extramarital sex is likely to be applicable to several other countries including Germany, Canada, and Iceland, where an increasing number of men have identified themselves as sexual addicts and formed self-help recovery groups.

Many married men in the United States have had an occasional affair. For some, this caused no problem; this book is not about them. It is not about men for whom an affair is an expression of a desire for variety. Rather, this book is for the woman whose husband has a *pattern* of affairs. Instead of dealing with problems in his marriage, this man will escape from one relationship into another. When things go bad at work he soon finds a new romance to distract him. The romance may be real or it may be imaginary. He may have had two or three actual affairs during his marriage. When not involved in an affair, he may be preoccupied with imagining it or planning for it. The excitement of the chase is to him what a drink is to the alcoholic. It is useful in terms of diagnosis, and approach to treatment, to regard him as addicted to affairs. I use the terms addiction and compulsion interchangeably in this book, although some researchers split hairs over the meaning of addictive versus compulsive sexual behaviors.

How likely is a man who has an affair to be an addict? Patrick Carnes, Ph.D., author of *Out of the Shadows: Understanding Sexual Addiction* (formerly *The Sexual Addiction*), believes that about 6 percent of the population is sexually addicted.[15] In a survey, reported in 1953, of married women who have had affairs, Kinsey found that 41 percent had only one affair, 40 percent acknowledged two to five affairs, and 19 percent reported more than five.[16] Twenty years later, in 1972, a different survey of married women gave very similar results—40, 44, and 16 percent respectively.[17] If these figures can be used as an estimate of married men who have affairs, and if we consider it likely that many of the men who have had more than five affairs during their marriage are engaging in affairs compulsively, then we may guess that perhaps 10 percent of married men who have affairs are sexually addicted. Another substantial proportion use affairs addictively at some time in their lives; at other stages, they will refocus their energies on their work and away from affairs.

A friend commented to me, "You make a good case for an affair being more exciting than monogamy. But how can you decide whether it is immaturity or compulsion that makes a man seek affairs?" I believe the answer lies in the man's ability to control his actions; loss of control is the primary characteristic of compulsive behavior. Should the sex addict's wife find out about an affair, he will probably admit only to that particular relationship, and may promise not to do it again. But sooner or later, despite his best intentions, he will once again find himself involved with another woman. He may make promises to himself—not to have an affair with someone in the same city, not to have an affair with another employee at his office, or with a student at the college where he teaches, or with one of his parishioners if he is a minister. He is like the alcoholic who tries to limit himself to drinking only beer, or to drinking only after 5 P.M., or only on weekends.

As his disease progresses, the alcoholic will break his own rules, and so will the man who uses affairs compulsively. This man has a disease very similar to alcoholism. Like the alcoholic, he has lost control over a problematic behavior. The specifics differ—instead of numbing his low self-esteem and his pain with alcohol, he forgets it temporarily through the "high" of the chase and the conquest. The addiction model has been very useful in understanding this behavior. Because the concept of chemical addiction is more familiar to most readers than is the idea of an addictive behavior, I frequently refer to alcoholism throughout this book to make a point about sex addiction.

I think it's important, however, for the reader to understand that recovery from sex addiction is more similar to recovery from compulsive overeating than from alcoholism. Most recovering alcoholics find they must abstain from alcohol to remain sober. Compulsive overeaters do not have the option of avoiding food; they must learn how to eat "normally" or in a more healthy way. Similarly, the goal of recovery from sex addiction is not to avoid sex; rather, it is to learn how to be a sexual person in a healthier way. Nonetheless, the analogy with alcoholism is useful in understanding the behavior of the sex addict and his spouse.

The sex addict's focus is not the sex act itself so much as it is all that precedes it: the feeling that accompanies the initial contact with a new woman; winning her over with his sensitivity, openness, and attention; and then, in some cases, getting her into bed.

The woman whose partner is such a man is in a no-win position. No matter how attractive or sexually available she is, she cannot provide him with the one thing he seeks—a new woman to conquer. She is doomed to failure in her attempts to keep him at home.

Look again at Beth's and Carmen's stories.

Do either of these stories sound familiar?

Does your husband or significant other have a pattern of affairs—or do you suspect that he does?

Do you tell yourself that if he really loved you he would change?

Do you believe, despite all evidence to the contrary, that things will somehow improve?

Do you blame yourself for not having tried hard enough to please him?

Do you make excuses for his behavior?

Do you believe that if you could only get his current girlfriend out of his life then all your problems would be over?

If you've answered ''yes'' to several of these questions, you may need help to feel less like a victim and more in charge of your life. Based on my experience, I hope to provide you with some answers.

Goals for This Book

- To help women married to sex addicts understand their own personality disorders and identify the denial and isolation.
- To provide therapists with a description of codependency as it relates to sex addiction in the hope that more affected families will find understanding and recovery when they come for counseling.
- To describe a pathway for recovery, with suggestions for women who are living with a recovering sex addict and for those who have separated from a sex addict.

I realize that there are many women who are struggling with their own sex addiction (the heroine of the book, *Looking for Mr. Goodbar*, is one), and that there are many men trying to cope with their wives' affairs. By limiting this book to the wives of addicts, I am not minimizing the very real pain of the male coaddict.

I have chosen to write about women for two reasons:

- I am more familiar with the experiences of female coaddicts. (I am very interested in hearing from men whose wives had affairs.)
- The problem for women coaddicts is somewhat different from that for men.

As will be shown in Chapter Six, there is much societal support for women's codependency and for men's affairs. Men who have affairs generally get approval from their peers; their wives don't get much sympathy. The wife is often blamed, and a conspiracy of silence exists among men to protect the promiscuous husband. Consequently, the wife feels shame and isolation, in addition to guilt at her wish for monogamy in the face of society's tacit approval of her man's affairs.

In contrast, a woman who has multiple affairs gets no approval from society, and her husband is regarded as the innocent victim. He is considered the wronged party and his wife is condemned. He has a special pain, the pain of fearing that he is "not really a man." More than this pain, he is probably obsessed about the specifics of his sexual technique and where he failed. Because of society's support, he may feel less isolated than a woman. Moreover, he does not "need" to feel as much guilt, since people agree that his wife is the one to blame.

There is a related area that will be addressed, and that is the woman whose husband acts out compulsively with other men. His interactions with them may range from emotion-laden affairs to casual sex in pornographic bookstores. Often, the wife who learns of these relationships will dismiss them with the consoling thought that "at least it's not another woman." To the husband, these relationships may be equivalent to an affair with another woman or a visit to a female prostitute, but the wife's denial system will not permit her to recognize this. The husband may encourage his wife in her denial, saying, "You're the only *woman* in my life," or "You're the only one who really counts."

The dynamics of marriage with a sex addict are similar whether his affairs are with men or with women. The feelings of the wives I interviewed were the same. The recovery process is also the same. There is one difference, and that is society's attitude toward the "wronged" spouse. To the extent that society is more tolerant of a man who has an affair with a woman than it is of a man who has an affair with a man, there is more support for the wife in the latter situation. The husband is perceived to be engaging in unacceptable behavior, and the spouse is encouraged to leave him. On the other hand, there is less support for the wife who chooses to stay married to a man who has homosexual affairs than for the wife who decides to remain with a husband who has heterosexual affairs. The woman whose husband has been involved with other men may feel more ashamed and isolated, or she may feel less threatened by another man than by another woman. Nonetheless, for those readers whose husbands have had homosexual relationships, I urge them to read this book and recognize that they have basically the same problem, and the same potential solution, as wives who have to cope with the "other woman."

Finally, I want to stress that this book is not written exclusively for married women. Many single women will recognize themselves in these pages. The important factor is not the wedding ring, but the nature of the relationship.

If you thought you were in an intimate, monogamous relationship, and suspected or learned that your partner was involved in multiple affairs, you may be a sexual coaddict.

If more than one of your relationships have been with men who cheated on you, you are most likely a sexual codependent.

If you're a single woman who keeps finding herself in relationships with married men who tell you that *you* are the most important woman in their life, but who somehow never leave their wives, this book may be about you.

Although I frequently use "married" for brevity rather than "involved in a relationship with," I am addressing unmarried relationship addicts just as much as married ones.

All the nonattributed quotations in this book come from personal interviews with men who acknowledged several affairs and with women who were involved with men who had affairs. The names have been changed, but their words and stories are real.

In addition to the formal interviews, my conclusions are based on conversations with many men and women in self-help groups for sexual addiction and coaddiction as well as on writings and lectures by experts in the field. The conclusions are not based on any type of scientific study. Researchers in the field of compulsive sexual behavior are just beginning to gather data, using tools such as questionnaires. Unfortunately, there is doubt about the validity of statistics based on self-reporting in an area where there is so much unconscious as well as conscious denial. For example, people often suppress memories of childhood sexual abuse, and may suddenly remember this after several months or years of counseling.

Thus, if 20 percent of a sample of compulsively sexual men answer "yes" to a survey question about any incest or molestation experience, this does not mean that only 20 percent of the men were in fact abused. All it tells us is that at the time of the survey, 20 percent of the men *remember* being abused; the actual figure may be much higher. An integral part of addiction and codependency is the suppression of feelings, and this is often accomplished by ''forgetting'' troublesome experiences. Much of one's childhood is often buried in the unconscious mind. This important fact must be remembered before drawing any conclusion about factors that explain the development of addiction and codependency in any particular person.

CHAPTER TWO

"I can't give up on him—he's been my whole life"

Characteristics of the Coaddict

When I had my first baby my husband enlisted in the Army. Then when my son was four years old Jack had an affair. For the next eight years I knew he was seeing other women because of the lipstick and makeup on his clothes. I was afraid to say anything, and he would always deny anything was going on. When my daughter was born, Jack re-enlisted in the Army and was gone for a year. My little girl was sick for much of that time, but Jack wasn't around to help. Now he has a new girlfriend, and if he would just stop seeing her I know everything would be so much better. He's told me he can't guarantee he will be faithful next week or even tomorrow. He said he's a sex addict, but I told him, "Oh, baloney, that's just an excuse men use." When he isn't running around, he's a wonderful husband, so supportive of me. I can't give up on him—he's been my whole life.

—Irene

Patrick Carnes, Ph.D. says:

> The coaddict is the loved one or friend who becomes so involved in the life of the addict that he or she truly starts to participate in the same impaired mental processes of the addict. Coaddictive behavior is behavior that the coaddict uses to attempt to change the addict, but that in reality contributes to the addiction. The alcoholic, sex addict, or other addict is not the only troubled one in his family. His spouse, for one, can develop behaviors that are designed to help her cope but often work to maintain the addictive cycle. She usually subscribes to a set of irrational beliefs long before she marries, but being in the addicted family situation accentuates them.[1]

The sexual coaddict's belief system is very similar to that of her spouse. This is not surprising, since the coaddict is herself an addict—to the relationship. In addition, she often develops other addictions to help her cope with the unmanageability of her life. These include problems with food, compulsive housekeeping, compulsive shopping, workaholism, dependency on alcohol or other drugs, or over-involvement with her children.

The wife of an alcoholic may drink to keep her husband company—and eventually may find herself addicted to alcohol. Such a sequence was beautifully portrayed in the classic film, *Days of Wine and Roses*. Similarly, the wife of a sex addict who takes part in his sexual adventures may come to enjoy them and may herself become compulsively sexual. The primary addiction of these wives, however, is to their husbands. If the couple gets into a recovery program, the wife will usually find the relationship addiction more difficult to give up than the alcohol or sex. This is because the alcoholic drinking or the compulsive sexual activity has as its main goal to hold on to the partner; the drinking or the sex itself is not the wife's preferred addiction.

What is addiction? It is "a pathological relationship with a mood-altering substance or experience."[2] The experience to which the sexual coaddict is addicted is the relationship with the sex addict. The coaddict is preoccupied with the addict; he is the center of her conversations with her friends. She fantasizes about him when she is alone. She plays out, in her imagination, scenarios of conversations they might have. She thinks of good and bad outcomes of actions she is considering taking, and of ways she can influence his behavior. At times she is so focused on her inner thoughts that she fails to notice what is happening around her.

Jeannie, an attractive 37-year-old dress shop owner, says:

Last month I got into my first car accident. As I was driving the kids home I started thinking about the extra motel charges on Paul's MasterCard. The longer I thought about it, the angrier I got—not just at the idea that he was obviously again involved with another woman, but also that he thought I was so dumb that I wouldn't even notice that it was right there on the MasterCard bill. I was considering how best to confront him—and then suddenly I heard a loud crunch and felt a jolt! I had simply not noticed that the car in front of me had stopped, and I piled right into it at 30 miles per hour. Thank heavens the kids and I were wearing seat belts! We were all bruised, but nothing worse. The kids started crying and I felt terribly guilty. Our car was nearly totalled, and our insurance rates are going up. I told Paul I'd been distracted by the kids and turned around to look at them; he believed me. He was really very understanding. I decided to say nothing about the MasterCard.

The sexual coaddict is also addicted to the excitement of the relationship. The guesswork, the obsession, and the constant turmoil keep her very involved and prevent her from having to deal with her own negative feelings. Of course, she is usually not aware that she needs turmoil in her life. On the contrary, her fondest wish is for a loving, caring, consistent husband who is always emotionally available to her. She frequently believes that it was an unfortunate quirk of fate that put her in a marriage with a man who keeps her guessing.

If there was a high level of tension in a coaddict's family of origin, she most likely has become ''comfortable with the uncomfortable.'' She has no real sense of what it's like to live without tension. By the time she reaches adulthood, the intensity of the feelings evoked by her reactions to her spouse *are* in a sense her feelings; she has never experienced a significant relationship that does not include extreme highs and lows. She confuses the biochemical reactions she experiences from stress, shock, or fear with emotions. She perceives the tension in her primary relationship as love or sexual attraction. A relationship lacking such tension is felt as boring and lacking in love. For the coaddict, the experience of tension is familiar, similar to what was often experienced while growing up in a dysfunctional family.

When the coaddict leaves her family of origin and marries, external events look different and she is unable to relate them to her past. In order to feel really alive, she needs to have a certain level of tension in her relationship. She confuses the intensity of her body's reactions with love. If things get too calm, she may provoke an incident or create a crisis in order to get a dose of the natural high that stress creates. This may be one reason for returning to the spouse after a separation or getting involved in another, similar relationship. For the coaddict, to feel intensely is to be vital and directed; not to feel intensely is to be bored or even depressed.

Alice is a 42-year-old research scientist whose husband, after a series of affairs, is now in a recovery program. She says:

When I left home in the morning I never knew how things would be when I got back. I always tried to phone Alan during the day to get some idea of how he was feeling. If he sounded angry, I tried to figure out how I might have caused it and what I might do to improve things. I tried to relate his moods to what was happening with us, but usually there seemed to be no connection. My moods depended on his moods, and I would find myself swinging from a real high to a real low without understanding why. Life was never boring—we had a very intense relationship. Our sexual relationship was very intense too.

For such a couple to develop a healthy relationship, they *both* need help. "Otherwise," as Robin Norwood pointed out in *Women Who Love Too Much*, "should her man begin to seriously address his own problems in a healthier way, she suddenly may find herself yearning for someone more exciting, more stimulating, someone who enables her to avoid facing her own feelings and problems."[3]

Life with a man who is addicted to affairs can be particularly exciting because unlike alcoholism, which can be a solitary pursuit requiring no social skills, the man who is successful at attracting women has learned how to romance a woman and how to appear caring and tender. At times, he will turn these charms on his wife.

Beverly, a 35-year-old mother of three who is now divorced, says:

Our relationship was always exciting. He would bring me flowers unexpectedly, with a romantic card. He told me once that when he had been with another woman, he would come home very late so I wouldn't be mad anymore, but worried and glad to see him.

In our early years together, I never dreamed that a compulsively sexual man could be sensitive, tender, and loving and at the same time be lying, cruel, and unfeeling. A Jekyll and Hyde. Sometimes he used to tell his girlfriends

*he couldn't see them because he had the kids for the day—
and they would call me to see if he really had the kids or
if I did. I understood why they called—they couldn't believe that such a "nice guy" could lie through that sincere
smile.*

Several of the women I interviewed alluded to the intensity and excitement of their relationships. Clarissa and
her husband, a sex addict, are also recovering alcoholics.
Clarissa remembers, "Our relationship was always very
intense. There were no peaceful moments. We drank together and we had intense sex." As Patrick Carnes points
out, the coaddict mistakes *intensity* for *intimacy*.[4]

The chaos and drama in the life of the sexually addicted
couple can prevent them from dealing with their bad feelings, irrational beliefs, and the general unmanageability
of their lives. The tension creates the illusion of intense
involvement in life.

The sexual coaddict has a set of deep-rooted beliefs
about herself, about her relationships, and about sex.
These beliefs are interrelated, and each supports the others. She believes she is not a worthwhile person, no one
would love her for herself, she can control other people's
behavior, and that sex is the most important sign of love. (A
similar set of beliefs is discussed by Carnes.[5]) We will explore these beliefs and their consequences for the coaddict.

1. *She is not a worthwhile person.* The coaddict believes
that she is not a worthwhile person and therefore doesn't
deserve to be happy. She believes that, inside, she is deeply
flawed.

One recovering coaddict states:

*I believed that there was something missing in my emo-
tional and spiritual makeup. What would be considered
the essence of my personality or personhood, the core of
my character, simply wasn't there. I wasn't a whole person. My shame stemmed from my belief that I was wrong*

*as a human being, with no possibility of being fixed. My
fear was being discovered and dumped, and my defense
was to construct a chameleon-like personality adaptable
to all situations and people. My irrational thinking allowed me to believe that my personality, which people responded to and that men were attracted to, was fake, not
a real part of me. I could neither see nor appreciate the
special and extensive talent, skills, and abilities I had and
used in order to interact with a variety of situations and
a variety of people.*

The coaddict fears that she may be seen as bad or unacceptable by others. She feels different from other people, and to her, different is equivalent to bad. She feels a
wide gulf between the outside she presents to others and
the inadequate person she really is. Not wanting to let
others learn about the real person inside, she covers up
her feelings and doesn't let people get too close to her.
She will not allow herself to feel vulnerable. She believes
that if people knew what she was really like they would
not want to be with her.

A sense of isolation and loneliness is commonly felt by
the coaddict. Diane, a quiet, soft-spoken schoolteacher
who is the mother of a little boy, explains:

*I was the typical oldest child, the good child, mommy's
helper, a perfectionist, very quiet and shy and good. I was
in honors classes at school, but I didn't have many friends.
In junior high we moved to a different community, and
after that I never got into any circle of friends. I remember
feeling very lonely and isolated and turning to books, going for long walks with my dog, not dating, just being off
by myself. I thought I didn't have friends because I lived
so far out of town. But now I see that my younger siblings
grew up in the same house and had all kinds of friends
over all the time. So it was me, not where we lived. I've
always felt like I didn't quite fit in, kind of lonely.*

Diane remained isolated as she grew up, but often lonely young women learn to exchange sex for attention, and become quite sexual at an early age.

Jean Harris, former headmistress of a prominent girls' school, is currently in prison for the shooting of her long-time lover, Herman Tarnower, an acknowledged womanizer. Harris did not have women friends. She felt uncomfortable around women, suspecting they knew something she didn't.

Because the coaddict feels so worthless, she believes she has to acquire her worth from the outside, from other people. Anne Wilson Schaef calls this *external referenting*.[6] The coaddict needs outside approval even to exist. She believes, I am nothing without a man, and may attempt suicide if her relationship ends. She doesn't trust her feelings and reactions, and does not value her opinions. Very skilled at seeing things from the other person's perspective, she doesn't really have a point of view herself. She doesn't believe that her feelings are valid to her or acceptable to others. She may suppress her feelings so that much of the time she doesn't feel anything. She may constantly apologize, even when it isn't her fault. She is always ready to take blame for what goes wrong in the family.

Alice, a scientist married to a man who had several affairs, says:

When Alan first asked me out, I was overjoyed. He was by far the most handsome man I had ever dated. A few weeks later we visited a girlfriend of mine in Washington, D.C. She pulled me off into a corner and said, "Wow! Where did you ever find such a gorgeous guy?" That was the ultimate in validation for me. If a gorgeous guy like Alan was interested in me, that meant I must be a really worthwhile person. Somehow that meant more to me than the fact that I had a Ph.D. and was making a success of my life! None of that really mattered.

Alice's feelings are typical of the woman who measures her worth by what other people think.

Ellen is a self-confident, assertive, well-dressed 40-year-old administrator who is now in a recovery program for partners of men who have affairs. She recalls how she used to be:

I didn't know who I was without a male to tell me. I was always trying to be cute so that a man would take care of me. I didn't believe that I, a woman, could function without a man.

Jean Harris also measured herself by what others thought. What was important was to live up to other people's expectations of her. She sought her self-esteem in others rather than within herself. Harris did not believe she deserved much in her relationship with Tarnower. Because he was a bachelor, she felt she was in a no-win situation. Believing she was only one of many women in his life, she would not permit herself to think he needed her. Harris kept apologizing for her lover's insensitivity and for the poor way he treated her. Her low self-esteem led her to believe that she didn't deserve any better. When Tarnower made it clear that he was losing interest in her, she decided to pay him a final visit and then commit suicide by shooting herself. In the struggle for the gun, Tarnower was killed and Harris was convicted of murder. Her book, *A Stranger in Two Worlds*, written from prison, reaffirms her love for him.

Clarissa and Charlie were an alcoholic couple who began having problems in their marriage after becoming sober. They separated over the issue of his affairs. Clarissa says:

After he moved out I felt like nobody. I felt empty. I couldn't even get the kids to school. We just stayed home and I cried. I started going to A.A. (Alcoholics Anony-

mous) meetings every day because I didn't know what else to do. I stopped eating and lost weight.

For Clarissa, life was hardly worth living without Charlie. Eventually they reconciled, but he was unable to remain monogamous and they separated again. Clarissa went through another depression, and though it wasn't as bad as the first one, she says, "I lost myself again." She and Charlie are still on an emotional roller coaster today.

Faith, an attractive redheaded 32-year-old mother of a small child, is married to a wealthy businessman who does not bother to hide his affairs. He is so preoccupied with his outside involvements that he has very little emotional energy left for his wife. Faith has learned to cover up her feelings. She tolerates behavior from her husband that would make other women furious. She is proud of her ability to control her emotions. "Henry has told me he really admires me for knowing when to make a fuss and when not to." She rarely makes a fuss.

Another aspect of the coaddict's need to look outwards for validation of her existence is her lack of boundaries. To have a boundary means to have a sense of being separate, of having separate feelings and a separate reality from others. The coaddict who doesn't know how she feels because she hasn't yet talked with her husband today does not have healthy boundaries; she doesn't know where she begins and another person ends. Physical abuse constitutes invasion of one's boundaries, and so does emotional abuse. The coaddict is so dependent on another person that she has no sense of self.

The coaddict is a very needy person. Having "been there" so long for so many people, she desperately wants someone else to be there for her—she needs someone to rescue her from her loneliness and isolation. This other person is expected to make up for all that's missing in the coaddict's interior, to calm her hunger, thirst, and all other needs. The trouble is that the coaddict is so needy that she's willing to settle for nearly anyone. And once that person is in her life, she may even convince herself that she literally cannot live without him.

2. *No one would love her for herself.* The consequence of the coaddict's second belief, that no one would love her for herself, is that she must *earn* his love. She confuses being needed with being loved. If he accepts her caretaking, she thinks it means he loves her—even if he does not act kind or caring or loving. She believes that if someone is in a relationship with her, it's because he wants something from her—that there's always a price to pay.

People cannot be depended on or trusted. She is drawn to a man who is needy, who she believes needs fixing, and she makes herself indispensable to him. Believing that the more she can do for him, the less likely he is to leave her, she assumes increasing responsibility for his life.

Faith is the slender redhead who lives with her wealthy husband and small daughter in a luxurious house on a well-cared-for estate by the seashore. Her husband has not made love with her for several years, ever since the birth of their child. She knows that he has affairs, and that this pattern began long before her daughter was born. Faith is grateful that she has the house and that she and Henry are friends, but she sorely misses the intimacy their marriage is lacking. Why, then, does she stay in the relationship? "He needs me and he's afraid of losing me." Faith does not believe she is entitled to happiness and is willing to settle for being needed rather than loved.

Gillian, a 44-year-old lawyer, met her husband in college when he was dating someone else seriously. He was very good-looking, but what really appealed to her was that "he had a lot of problems and he needed to be taken care of." Her husband went to medical school while she stayed home and took care of him and the children. He had several affairs, but she didn't confront him. Instead, she felt guilty for complaining to him about his frequent absences; her complaining made her think of herself as a bitch.

Gillian not only pretended she didn't know about Gerald's affairs, she also was so out of touch with her feelings that she didn't even feel concerned about his deception or his inattentiveness to her—until the day she went to his office with her ten-year-old daughter to surprise him for lunch and found him having sex with his nurse. She recalls, "I didn't really feel anything until I caught him in his office." Then she experienced "incredible pain and a need to find out why it happened." Now divorced, she is in S-Anon, a Twelve-Step recovery program for sexual coaddicts, still trying to understand her life.

The coaddict is terrified of abandonment, and will do anything to keep the man in the relationship. For the sake of the relationship she ignores her own feelings and needs. She excuses his behaviors even though they may hurt her deeply. She avoids conflict and smooths things over. She is afraid of arousing his anger or of showing her own. An argument awakens her fear of abandonment, so she avoids discord. She needs frequent reassurance that she is loved; her husband may end up feeling smothered. Layers of anger and resentment over repeated hurts, real and imaginary, are buried inside her with no healthy outlet. She will deny experiencing these feelings rather than risk showing them.

To prevent conflict, the coaddict uses denial, the pretense that a problem does not exist. The denial may be unconscious, as when the wife ignores what is happening around her; or it may be conscious, as when she is aware of her husband's activities but finds excuses to rationalize his behavior or her failure to take action to change the situation.

For example, she may ignore evidence of an affair rather than confront her husband. She will pretend to her friends and family that her marriage is fine at a time when things are falling apart. She continues to believe that if she only hangs on long enough, he will change for the better. Unfortunately, one consequence of denial is *enabling*; that is, at a time when a marital crisis may be the only way to get the husband to look realistically at his destructive behavior, the wife's failure to take action in the face of an unacceptable situation enables the addict to continue the same behavior.

A woman who has written a book with her husband about how they dealt with his multiple affairs recalled that once when he came home from a trip she found a long blond hair in his suitcase. Since she was a brunette, her first impulse was to cry and scream. She knew on one level what was going on, but had to find a way to deny it. She finally recalled that the wife of one of the men he worked with went on the trip, and she had a blond wig. She tried to tell herself that it was a wig, ignoring a lot of obvious clues in trying to reassure herself.

Helené, a 38-year-old recovering alcoholic who is now divorced from her husband, says, "He had repeated affairs, but it was okay, because he had a tremendous sex drive and I just wanted to be left alone." Years later she is still excusing his behavior.

Clarissa tolerated her husband's affairs for a long time for fear of losing him.

We had always worked together at home. I knew what Charlie did every moment of the day. He was always home at night. So when he started not coming home nights, I knew he was having affairs. I let it go on. We never even talked about it. I would fix him sandwiches when he got home and say nothing.

Eventually Clarissa was unable to keep up the pretense, and they separated temporarily. Charlie is still very much in Clarissa's life, and she admits that she is still afraid of his anger and of not pleasing him.

Irene, whose husband told her he is addicted to affairs,

took an active role in getting rid of Veronica, Jack's latest girlfriend. She called up Jack's sister and told her about the affair. Jack's sister then called up Veronica and "really told her off." Jack's sister also called Veronica's husband and told him what was going on. The affair was soon over, and Irene is convinced that things are much better now. "We're working together again. He's smiling and laughing again. He's so relieved that Veronica is out of our lives."

Irene believes that eliminating Veronica from Jack's life has solved her problem. Despite Jack's long history of affairs and admitting to her that he can't promise fidelity even as long as next week, she continues to deny that there is an ongoing problem.

Beverly, who was married for many years to a man who eventually recognized that he was addicted to affairs, says:

When we went into counseling, I was so afraid to say anything that might anger him (and therefore risk losing him to one of his girlfriends) that we spent three months talking about everything except his affairs. Until he finally yelled at me in utter frustration after a therapy session, "When are we going to talk about the affairs, the sex?" I realized it had been too scary for me.

Currently in a Twelve-Step recovery program for families of sex addicts, Beverly understands the fear of anger that she experienced in her marriage.

3. *She can control other people's behavior.* The coaddict believes that she can successfully manipulate those around her to accomplish her goals. To illustrate the concept of control, let's consider the mother who, in order to get her 15-year-old son to school on time in the morning, wakes him up, nags him to get dressed, and keeps reminding him that he is running late. Every day the two go through the same ritualistic tug-of-war—the mother nagging and prodding, the son procrastinating. Ask the mother why she doesn't just let her son get himself off to school,

and she will answer, "If I didn't get involved he would never get to school on time." She is unable to let go and to let her son experience the consequences of his behavior. The way out of her bind is to remove herself from the situation. Her son might oversleep and arrive late at school. If this were to happen more than once he might get detention after school or some other unpleasant discipline. It is likely that he would then modify his behavior and learn to get himself to school on time.

By her continued involvement with her son's morning routine, the mother's controlling behavior only succeeds in enabling her son to continue oversleeping and depending on her to get him off to school. In other words, rather than encouraging change, trying to control the actions of another's behavior perpetuates the status quo. It prevents him from experiencing the consequences of his behavior and thereby learning a new behavior.

To argue that one person cannot control the ongoing behavior of another is not to deny that one person can influence another. Television advertisements can influence us to buy a certain product or vote for a certain candidate. Letters to politicians may influence their views on given issues. It is often possible to get other people to behave as we like them to—all we have to do is set up the consequences so that the outcome we want is a lot more attractive to the other person than any other outcome.

For example, you may be able to get your daughter to clean up her room by promising her a dollar if she cleans it up, a spanking if she doesn't. If your daughter then cleans up her room, you may delude yourself into believing that it was because you asked her to; the reality, however, is that she decided it was in her best interest to do so. The fallacy of control is in not realizing that people act in certain ways because they have decided it is in their best interest, not because you told them to do so.

The coaddict's erroneous belief that she can control other people's behavior is actually a defense against her feelings of helplessness and powerlessness. In childhood she often felt helpless to influence events around her. This led to great insecurity. In adulthood she tries to control and manipulate her environment in order to avoid feeling helpless. Unfortunately, the ability to control another person's actions implies great responsibility. She believes that she is responsible for the success or failure of her relationships. As Robin Norwood points out, "Help is the sunny side of control."[7] The coaddict will "help" her husband and friends to do things they should do for themselves, just like the mother who "helps" get her son off to school on time.

By her controlling behavior, the spouse enables the addict to continue in his addiction, as is described dramatically by Ruth Maxwell in her book, *The Booze Battle*. Although she is illustrating alcoholism, the same can be said for the sexually addicted husband and his wife.

The wife will hide her husband's own behavior from him (if she can) because she does not want him to suffer the consequences of his drinking. She reasons this would be so upsetting to him that he would then have further justification to drink. She is quick to pick up the pieces after her husband, to reduce his need to drink. As he drowns his pains in alcohol, she surrounds him with a blanket of comfortable unreality. Instead of making it increasingly difficult for the husband to accept his behavior and seek help, she makes his drinking increasingly easier for him to tolerate.

While the wife is busy making changes in her husband's environment to reduce his reasons for drinking, she eliminates his incentive to make the *one* change that is needed: the treatment for his addiction.[8]

Keeping silent about her feelings is another enabling behavior; this keeps the sex addict from feeling uncomfortable about how his affairs may be hurting his wife. The coaddict keeps silent for fear of a confrontation, or because she truly doesn't believe that she deserves to have her needs met, or because she is afraid of driving her spouse further away with her negative comments. She is always waiting for the "right time" to talk to him. The right time is not when he is angry or preoccupied—this is too scary. But when he is in a good mood, she wants him to feel good about their relationship rather than spoil it with complaints and demands.

Because she believes erroneously that her words and actions have a significant impact on her husband's sexual behavior with other people, she doesn't want to risk saying or doing the wrong thing. Unaware that her husband's affairs were caused not by her inadequacies but rather by his own addiction, she covers up her doubts and pain and attempts to present her best side to her husband. She thereby denies him needed feedback that might make him realize sooner that his marriage relationship is in trouble. Consequently, the husband is able to continue longer with his affairs, believing that his wife doesn't suspect and that "what she doesn't know won't hurt her."

For the spouse of the sex addict, attempts to control her husband center on his sexual behavior. If the wife suspects that her husband is interested in a particular woman, she may turn down a party invitation if she knows the other woman will be there. She does not even consider whether she would enjoy going to the party; it is more important to her to keep her husband from seeing the other woman. She forgets that she can't *always* prevent her husband from seeing the other woman. For example, a businesswoman may give up a travel opportunity that might be professionally advantageous to her because she doesn't want to leave her husband home alone.

A housewife who suspects her husband of playing around calls him at work twice a day to be sure that he's there. Her husband, meanwhile, feels increasingly tied down. He loses credibility with his staff because it's clear his wife doesn't trust him. His resentment against his wife provides him with the excuse he seeks to spend more time with the understanding young lady he met on the elevator.

I interviewed men who admitted they needed excuses to justify their cheating and to assuage their guilt feelings. At times they deliberately engaged the spouse in an argument to create emotional distance between them. In this way, these men could justify seeking emotional closeness elsewhere. But frequently the spouse, by her own actions, gives her husband the excuse he's looking for. If she calls him at work, looks through his belongings, smells his clothing, and in other ways puts herself in the role of a controlling mother, the husband may feel like a little boy who has a right to rebel. Thus, the wife's attempts to control her husband's behavior merely succeed in encouraging his addictive behavior.

A common way for a wife to attempt to control her husband is through her sexual behavior. She will dress seductively, buy special nightgowns or flimsy underwear, learn new sexual techniques, or threaten or hint at having sex with others in order to make him jealous. She may even engage in sexual activities that she considers immoral to please him and to keep him at home.

The coaddict will try to manipulate the environment in every possible way to control her husband. She usually fails, as Beverly relates:

I wanted so badly to make him happy, but every time I did something to please him he was more critical, so I tried harder. When I found out about his affairs, I offered to have any kind of sexual relations he wanted, and the requests got more and more uncomfortable for me. I yelled at my kids, I cried, I begged, I bullied—nothing worked.

A terrible consequence of the coaddict's belief that she can control her partner's behavior is that if her attempts to change him do not succeed, she feels she has personally failed. She blames herself, feels guilty, and determines to try even harder. Her self-esteem (which is low to begin with) descends further. One woman who was beginning to understand her relationship addiction, asked, "Why, when I've had no success at controlling his behavior, do I feel compelled to keep trying?" The answer is, because the alternative is to admit that she *cannot* control his behavior—and this is too frightening a realization for many people.

4. *Sex is the most important sign of love.* The coaddict's belief that sex is the most important sign of love leads her to confuse sex with love. If a man is sexual with her, she takes it as evidence that he loves her.

Jessica, a 45-year-old intensive care unit nurse recalls:

There were many times when I was unsure of how Bill felt about me. He would act distant, or seem preoccupied, or we'd have a disagreement. At those times I felt that if I could just get him to go to bed with me, then everything would be all right. The physical intimacy was reassurance to me that he still loved me. My fear that he would leave me was temporarily gone after we'd make love.

Because she believes that sex is the most important sign of love, the coaddict feels a terrifying personal rejection when her partner has sex with someone else. Her fear of abandonment looms large and her self-worth plummets. She may feel that her life is at an end.

Helen, a counselor who is now divorced from her sex addict husband, writes:

Because my "man" was the vehicle with which I gained acceptance in society and personal validation of being capable, lovable, and needed, his affairs endangered my very existence as a functioning part of the human race. Therefore I tried to look and behave with him in such a way that he could see that, indeed, I was worth "keeping." The other side of this precariously balanced, irrational belief system was that in keeping him I would maintain my place of value with the "others." The fear which provided motivation to continue this balancing act was that both my man and society would discover I was a "fake"—that they had been misguided—and would dump me.

The coaddict also believes that sex is the price for love. She uses sex to get her man to love her more. Fearful of refusing him sex even if she is not in the mood, she believes that if she is always available he will be less likely to stray. New lovemaking positions or techniques may become part of her repertoire. If she is not sexually satisfied she is likely to pretend that she is, in an attempt to make her spouse feel good.

In the sex addict's ongoing quest for novelty, he frequently attempts to enlist his wife's participation. She may find herself involved in sexual activities that are against her values. She may take part in humiliating or degrading sexual behaviors in order to control and please him, believing that participating in these activities will keep him interested in her. She will usually guard them as shameful secrets that she is reluctant to reveal.

One 22-year-old woman, a mother of two infants, sat in silence through several meetings of a self-help group. Dressed in a leather skirt and vest, draped in beads and long earrings, and sporting a short, punk-style haircut, she seemed out of place among the older, more conservatively dressed women. Only after hearing several other stories did she explain why she was there: Her marriage was in crisis because she no longer was willing to agree to her husband's wishes. What he wanted her to do, and what she had been doing for several months, was to go out alone at night to a nearby convenience store, pick up a stranger, bring him home, and have sex with him while her husband watched. Her husband had also been having extramarital affairs, and she had believed that participating in her husband's voyeuristic activities would keep him at home. But now she was too scared to continue.

Another woman in the same group admitted:

My husband was always telling me I was very narrow-minded for insisting on monogamy. He said I was preventing him from expressing his full sexuality, that sex with other people would have nothing to do with our relationship. He kept pressuring me but I wouldn't change my mind. I told him I was willing to do anything he wanted me to sexually, but I couldn't deal with affairs.

Then he suggested, if I was so threatened by the idea of him making love with another woman, how about if I choose the woman, someone I knew and liked, and that the three of us have sex together. He was really turned on by the idea of two women working on him at the same time. I was very anxious to please him, and felt guilty at how unhappy I was making him. So I said I'd consider the threesome idea. He and I actually talked about various "candidates" among my single girlfriends. Looking back on it, I must have been crazy! Just as I was about to sound out one of my friends, my husband told me it wasn't such a great idea after all. I found out later that the real reason was that by then he was involved in another affair.

Because both sex addicts and coaddicts have sexual issues as well as irrational beliefs about the role of sexuality in their lives, their behaviors may be similar. The sexual history of the coaddict can at times sound exactly like the history of the sex addict. For example, Marisa, a sophisticated 28-year-old brunette recounting her past described how she spent many evenings in bars hoping to meet a man. She had many sexual partners, some never to be seen again after one night, others present for weeks or months. When she married, she became involved in increasingly violent sexual behaviors with her husband, and also participated in group sex and in sex with other men while her husband watched. When the marriage finally fell apart, she returned to the bar scene and to one-night stands.

Was she a sex addict? There is often an overlap between the sexual behavior of addicts and coaddicts. Indeed, some women ultimately identify themselves as both addicts and coaddicts. I believe the answer can usually be found by examining the *goal* of the behavior. Further discussion with Marisa revealed that she believed sex was the way to obtain love. What she hoped to find in the bars was not just a sex partner, but rather someone to love her and nurture her. When she did finally marry, she engaged in unorthodox sexual activities to please her husband, even though she was frightened by some activities and uncomfortable with others. And when the marriage ended, she returned to the only way she knew to "catch" a man—the bar scene. Whereas the addict's goal is sexual gratification, Marisa's use of sex to obtain love and to satisfy another person's needs identified her as a coaddict rather than an addict.

In summary, the sexual coaddict has several basic irrational beliefs: She is not a worthwhile person, no one would love her for herself, she has the power to control people, and sex is the most important sign of love. Married to a sex addict, she is in a vicious circle in which her beliefs support her spouse in his addictive behavior, and his behavior validates her erroneous beliefs. Her efforts to get him to change inevitably fail, and she responds by trying harder.

The more out of control her life becomes, the harder she tries to control and fix things. As she continues to fail in her efforts, her self-esteem slides ever downward and she becomes more resentful and angry. Fearful of expressing her anger, which she is convinced will drive her husband further away, she turns her anger inward and may become depressed. Feeling helpless and powerless, she may cope by overeating, drinking excessively, or becoming addicted to Valium or other sedatives. Some women respond by becoming compulsive housekeepers, or by taking on so many workplace or volunteer responsibilities that they don't have time to think. Others focus all their attention on the children, becoming "supermoms." Still others bury themselves in work, becoming the valued administrator who does the work of three people and never takes a vacation.

The wife may take on the role of martyr. She will entertain (or bore) her friends endlessly with tales of her husband's outrageous behavior. To every suggestion her friends make, she will reply, "Yes, but . . ." When they say, "Your husband doesn't deserve such a good, understanding wife," she feels vindicated. When her neighbor asks, "How can you put up with the rat?" she feels rewarded. Meanwhile she continues in the vicious circle of enabling.

Finally, the coaddict's anger, resentment, and depression are frequently expressed in physical symptoms. This is the woman who visits her doctor because of fatigue, lack of energy, insomnia, headaches, backache, vague abdominal discomfort, or weight gain "although I hardly eat anything." Unwilling to admit what is going on at home—and frequently so out of touch with her feelings that she truly doesn't know what she feels—she prefers to seek help by talking about her physical symptoms. Physical illness is a more acceptable way of getting attention—from the doctor and from the family.

The coaddict's core beliefs are usually firmly in place by young adulthood, where they are likely to influence her choice of relationships. Diane, the 35-year-old school teacher, is married to a man who frequented pornographic bookstores and had anonymous sexual encounters with men. A big problem in their marriage has been that Diane's husband, Dick, is afraid to talk about his feelings. Communication between them has been consistently poor. Before her marriage, Diane had one other serious relationship.

I was unofficially engaged to Gerald in high school, and I went to bed with him a couple of times, feeling real guilty. At the end of my senior year he broke it off, saying that it wasn't fair to me. I don't know what he meant by that—he wouldn't go into it. He didn't express emotions at all. He was a real defensive kind of guy, and it was hard to get anything out of him.

This boyfriend sounds very much like the man Diane later married.

Jessica, the 45-year-old intensive care nurse, recalls:

When I first found out about my husband's affairs I felt like an innocent victim. I couldn't believe he'd done this to me; I was furious at him. I felt hurt, rejected, and betrayed. I was sure I'd never forgive him. I thought that he was sick and I was just fine. But when I got into a Twelve-Step recovery program, I realized I was as sick as he was. I did a First Step, which is when you write down your own relationship history. My first sexual relationship was with an exciting, very attractive man. When I took him home to meet my parents, they acted very strange. I could see they didn't like him, but they wouldn't tell me why. After we made love twice, he admitted to me that he was gay, and told me he really preferred his boyfriend. I was crushed. I was 21 at the time, and for the next 20 years every important man in my life was emotionally unavailable to me for one reason or another. My husband just happened to be the last one.

Although it is tempting for the coaddict to feel like a victim and to cast all the blame at her straying spouse, the fact is that her choice of partner is no accident. The coaddict's core beliefs do not begin when she marries an addict, and the men she selects tend to follow a pattern.

Before you read the next chapter, I would urge you to write down a history of your important relationships, from childhood to the present time. Were they satisfactory? Were you nurtured? You may be surprised to find a pattern, as Jessica did, of emotional unavailability. If so, then look closely again at your childhood. The seeds of the future coaddict can be found in her family of origin.

CHAPTER THREE

The Family Connection

I grew up in a normal family. My mother was 33 when she had me; my father was 39. He was a very loving husband and father. My parents had a good, closely knit relationship. My father was in the liquor business, but my mom and dad had only one drink a day. My father never ran around, and neither did my mother. I was an only child, and both of them doted on me. They were good parents. My mom never worked and was always home for me. So there was no dysfunction in my family.

I was very independent outside the home, but at home I was very dependent on my mother. She picked out my clothing. I felt I could never please her; very few people ever pleased her. She was one of those people who couldn't be pleased, and I certainly always came up short. When I met Lawrence, I just transferred my dependence from my mother onto Lawrence, who was very willing to accept it. He would pick out my clothes, tell me what to wear, what jobs to take, and how I should run my life.

—Linda

Linda is an elegantly dressed, 45-year-old wife of a computer programmer and mother of four children. Slender and athletic, she exercises daily and eats only nutritious foods. For years her husband had multiple affairs with both men and women. In addition, Lawrence wanted sex with Linda several times a day, every day. Afraid of abandonment, she never refused Lawrence sex and pretended ignorance about his affairs. Now both are in recovery programs for sexual addiction and coaddiction. According to Linda, her codependency was a result of her unhealthy relationship with her husband; she believes her childhood was normal.

Mary Ellen, a 45-year-old social worker divorced from a philandering husband who is a recovering alcoholic and sex addict, also believes she had a normal childhood.

My childhood was happy. I lived on a farm, had many responsibilities, was with a family which was very busy and traveled a lot. My mother became totally deaf when I was 10. From then on she became insecure and I did too. I felt that I couldn't talk to her, that what I had to say wasn't validated, particularly when she wouldn't put on her hearing aid or wear her glasses to read lips. So I began to have a negative self-image, as did my brother.

My mother would never allow my father to be with us without her. She was very demanding of his time. As children we never felt we knew him. It was like being raised in a single-parent family. My mother was so insecure that she needed my father all the time. We did things together as a family, but there was never a chance to talk with either of them separately. I was the one with the broad shoulders in the family, so my mother used me as her confidante. She really had no friends—she was extremely jealous of women. She was not a forgiving person, very ritualistic—everything had to be a certain way. I was brought up with a lot of "shoulds" and "oughts."

My mother drank—only one martini before dinner, but she was out of it. There was no way we could have discussions at dinner; it was a monologue. I remember realizing that feelings were not appropriate; crying and being emotional were not appropriate. Tears were punished. I stuffed everything by overeating and overexercising. My mother was an impeccable dresser. If I was ten pounds overweight, she made me feel I weighed 300. If I came in wearing something that was dowdy, she sent me back to change. She didn't want to be seen with me because I was such a country rube.

My father enabled her, he worshipped her. We had a dominant mother who was unreachable by anybody. She commanded—we called her the queen. We never lived up to her expectations.

Codependency

In the last chapter we saw that coaddicts share a common belief system that keeps them in a vicious circle in their relationship with the man who has affairs. How did they acquire those beliefs? Research in the alcoholism field has recently yielded important information on the family background of people who later become alcoholics or codependents. Although the specifics differ, the families seem to have certain characteristics in common. These characteristics have been studied most fully in alcoholic families, but it is now recognized that other kinds of families also fit the pattern. The most common types of families that produce emotionally disordered children are:

- Families where there is alcoholism, chemical addiction, or other addiction. In this category we might include workaholism.
- Families where there is chronic mental or physical illness.
- Physically, sexually, or psychologically abusive families.
- Familes that practice religious fundamentalism.

These families, which have been termed dysfunctional families, can raise children who show codependent behavior; this behavior can lead to both addiction and coaddiction. Both addicts and coaddicts may start out as codependents, although they may have different ways to cope with painful experiences.

An early description of codependency came from Bill W., the co-founder of Alcoholics Anonymous, who after many years of sobriety continued to have bouts of depression. Bill wrote in a letter more than 30 years ago:

> Suddenly I realized what the matter was. My basic flaw had always been dependence—almost absolute dependence—on people or circumstances to supply me with prestige, security, and the like. Failing to get these things according to my perfectionist dreams and specifications, I had fought for them. And when defeat came, so did my depression. . . . My dependency meant demand—a demand for the possession and control of the people and the conditions surrounding me.[1]

Bill recognized that beneath his alcoholism lay personality traits we now term codependency.

Robert Subby defines codependency as

> an emotional, psychological, and behavioral condition that develops as a result of an individual's prolonged exposure to, and practice of, a set of oppressive rules—rules which prevent the open expression of feeling as well as the direct discussion of personal and interpersonal problems.[2]

In other words, it is the rigid family rules which produce codependency. Subby also states:

> Co-dependency is a condition which *precedes* the (addictive) experience. In essence, it is the practice of oppressive rules within the family which support

compulsive-obsessive behavior patterns such as alcoholism, overeating, overworking, and perfectionism.[3]

The most fundamental characteristic of codependency is looking outward for one's self-worth. In a dysfunctional family the child may not be allowed to develop. Let's think of a young boy who lives by rules dictating which feelings are okay and which feelings aren't. As a result, he only changes in ways he believes will please the adults, and he suppresses his individuality. The child loses touch with his feelings because he is not allowed to express them. When he grows up suppressing his private self and perfecting his public self, eventually there is no private self, but just a reaction to others. By the time he reaches adulthood, he doesn't know what his valid thoughts or feelings are.

Codependents constantly worry about what others will think. Their main goal in life is to try to figure out what other people want, and then give it to them. Their self-esteem comes from their success as people-pleasers. To assure success at pleasing, they become extremely sensitive to the momentary mood of their parents and other important adults. In their home, they "walk on eggshells" so as not to make a mistake. This characteristic behavior is called *hypervigilance*, which is an extreme sensitivity to signs of approval or disapproval from others that continues into adulthood. The slightest evidence of disapproval from another person is enough to make them steer a different course.

The Dysfunctional Family

The young child in the dysfunctional family can develop a core feeling of shame. How does this happen? A young child is egocentric—she feels the world revolves around her and that she is the cause of whatever happens. Thus, if her parents do not treat her with love, she believes that it is because *she* is not lovable. If she is not lovable, it must be because she is not a worthwhile person. She not only feels guilty about specific things she may have done or not done, but she also develops a deep feeling of shame about her very existence. If adults criticize her repeatedly (as is common) and if she feels that she can never measure up to their expectations, her feeling of shame is validated and reinforced. Because of her egocentricity, she blames herself for the bad things that happen around her. She feels responsible for the worsening situation at home, and feels guilty over her inability to make things better. Although feeling responsible causes her guilt and shame, it enables her to believe that she has some control over her environment. This is safer than feeling that things are out of her control.

If we hypothesize that the dysfunctional family can be the origin of codependency, then how do we explain the many addicts and coaddicts who say that their childhood was normal? Did Mary Ellen and Linda have normal childhoods, as they believe? What is "normal"? Is it the same as "average"? Is it the same as "healthy"? One approach to answering these questions is to describe the features of life in a dysfunctional family, and then to see if these key elements were present in the childhood lives of some coaddicts.

The oppressive family rules that often lead to codependency have been summarized by Claudia Black as "don't talk, don't feel, don't trust."[4] This means, don't talk to anyone about what is happening at home and about your feelings; don't express your feelings because feelings are painful and they make other people uncomfortable, and don't trust anyone but yourself. The child who comes to believe these rules feels isolated, unworthy, and even emotionally numb.

A common rule in dysfunctional families is it's not okay to express feelings or to talk about problems. Mom and Dad often do not discuss the real problems. The children are often urged not to tell their teachers or the neighbors there is anything wrong at home. Sexually abused children may be threatened with dire consequences if they admit to anyone what is happening.

Helene, the 38-year-old recovering alcoholic whose former husband had several affairs, was the daughter of alcoholic parents. "When I was ten years old, my father began molesting me. He started touching me right in front of my mother. I didn't feel comfortable with this, but my mother's silence told me to be silent." She submitted to the abuse, which eventually included years of sexual intercourse.

What are the consequences of a rule against discussing problems? Robert Subby states:

> Since we aren't supposed to talk about problems, we begin to believe that if we admit having problems, then there will be something horribly wrong with us that is not wrong with most people. If we admit to having a problem, then we fear that we will also be judged by others as weak and unhealthy. Ultimately, this results in a deep sense of shame about a very real part of everyday life, i.e., that we *all* have problems.[5]

In the family of Alice, the 42-year-old scientist, she frequently heard her father say, "Children should be seen and not heard." No one was interested in the children's feelings. Alice's father was a self-made man who thought that talking about feelings was a waste of time; only actions counted. Alice's little brother was told, "Big boys don't cry," and he learned not to.

The result of not expressing feelings is that, eventually, the child learns to deny having feelings. She no longer knows what she feels; everything is blocked out. Helene relates:

When I was 21 my father visited me at college. He invited me to stay with him at his motel. I knew what was

*going to happen but I went anyway. I remember going into
the room and kissing my father but I don't remember anything else until after the weekend was over. I know we had
sex but I don't remember it. Later, when I got married,
my husband and I never talked about feelings. After I was
divorced from my husband, a sex addict, I had a lot of
men in my life. We had sex, but I didn't love them. I had
no feelings.*

Gillian, the 44-year-old lawyer who divorced her husband because of his affairs, characterizes her family as
"very loving and perfect. My father never showed his anger. If it got too bad he would just leave."

Mary learned not to show her feelings. She did not confront her husband about his affairs, and in fact "didn't
feel anything until I caught him in his office in flagrante
delicto [while the crime is blazing]."

Cynthia Koestler gained notoriety when she killed herself at age 55 in a double suicide with her terminally ill,
77-year-old husband, a well-known writer and acknowledged philanderer. Her suicide note said, "I cannot live
without him." In her autobiography, Cynthia said she
learned to control her feelings early in life.

I was always rather proud of the way I could keep my
feelings under control. During my school days we had
been taken to see a film called *Mrs. Miniver* and while
the whole school sobbed during the performance, I had
not shed a tear.[6]

There are many times when it is inappropriate to cry,
but a pattern of suppressing emotions can be an unhealthy
precursor to psychological and emotional problems, such
as chronic depression.

Another rule common in dysfunctional families is "be
strong, be perfect, make us proud, don't be selfish." This
rule consists of unrealistic expectations. Children who live

with this rule find they can never measure up. They grow up feeling they can never please their parents, no matter how hard they try. Despite their accomplishments, they feel like failures inside.

When Alice brought home a 95 percent grade on a math test, her workaholic father took a look at it and asked, "What happened to the other 5 percent?" Alice and her brother eventually got Ph.D. degrees and prestigious jobs, but Alice still fights feeling she should always be doing more. She also tends to have unrealistic expectations of other people.

In Marilyn's family of origin, nothing she accomplished was ever good enough for her parents. No matter how hard she tried, she always failed to please them. Eventually she gave up trying. After graduating Phi Beta Kappa from a prestigious college, she drifted from job to job, finding ways to sabotage any possible success. For a while she experimented with mood-altering drugs. Her marriage to an abusive alcoholic lasted fifteen years; she divorced him after he had a series of affairs. Now 43 and active in Al-Anon, Marilyn has just finished a master's degree in counseling and finally has a job she enjoys.

Children who experience unrealistic expectations in their families often take either the path Alice chose (and become very successful workaholics) or they may give up early, as Marilyn did. In both situations they tend to feel guilty and inadequate.

A common unrealistic expectation is the "don't be selfish" rule. This rule teaches that it is selfish to attend to one's own needs. As Subby writes:

> If we believe that our own needs are wrong, we will never be able to get those needs met. What often happens in codependency is that we try to feel good about ourselves by taking care of others and eventually our self-esteem becomes dependent on caretaking. Without someone to take care of, the codependent is left with

no purpose or worth. The more we take care of someone, the more we fail to take care of our own needs. In time we start to feel resentful toward those whom we care for because they fail to recognize what we are doing for them. The result of these angry feelings is that we experience even more shame, and so even more caretaking. As the pain builds in each of us, we begin to blame and point out the failings of others.[7]

Since everyone has needs, the "don't be selfish" rule is guaranteed to produce shame and guilt.

Another consequence of this rule is that many codependents find it difficult to have fun. In a dysfunctional family, there are always jobs to be done that are more important than having fun. The child learns that he doesn't deserve to enjoy himself. In adulthood, he has difficulty relaxing and playing.

A third important rule in dysfunctional families is "do as I say, not as I do." When Jack, Irene's womanizing husband, was a boy, he used to accompany his father on the rodeo circuit during the summer. He recalls:

I witnessed a lot, and I was expected to keep my mouth shut. I didn't understand some of what was going on. I just knew that you don't tell your mother these things you see, the drinking, the women, and about being left alone in a motel room while your father and his buddies were out drinking and womanizing.

Jack's father used to talk to him about honesty, responsibility, and commitment, but Jack learned from what his father *did*, not what he said—he learned how to lie, cheat, and manipulate. He also learned not to trust people. Jack's father told him to treat his mother with respect, but reality was very different:

I witnessed beatings just like you'd see if two men were in a fistfight. I recall one night when he actually dragged her across the front yard by her hair.

From his father's behavior Jack learned to pay lip service to one code of behavior while actually engaging in another. He learned he could not trust what people said; what they may have felt on the inside was very different from what they presented to others. Jack held responsible jobs, juggled a wife and girlfriends, but inside he felt like a worthless person.

A fourth rule the child learns is not to rock the boat, to maintain the status quo at all costs. This rule teaches a child *enabling*, that is, protecting the addict from experiencing the consequences of his behavior. The child watches as Mother stands at the window for hours waiting for Dad to come home, crying as she wonders who he's with. The next day, life goes on as though nothing happened. The child sees that Mother does not confront Dad, and he learns that it's more important to keep peace at home than to risk an unpredictable reaction by bringing it up.

According to Robin Norwood, author of *Women Who Love Too Much*, a key element in every dysfunctional family is keeping secrets. In the case of a family where the mother is chronically ill, the oldest daughter assumes many of the responsibilities of the mother. She cares for her mother and is praised for her role. Her feelings, however, are mixed. At times she feels that it's too much for her, she can't handle it, she's tired of feeling that she's holding up the world. She feels resentful and angry at her mother because of the burden the illness has laid on her shoulders. But it's not acceptable to express those feelings—after all, it isn't the mother's fault that she is ill. So the daughter not only covers up her feelings, which are natural under the circumstances, but comes to believe that she is a selfish, bad person for even having those feelings. *If I were a better person*, she thinks, *I wouldn't feel angry and re-*

sentful of Mother. She feels guilty, ashamed, and unworthy. When she gets praise for her devotion, she tells herself, *If they only knew what I was really like inside, they wouldn't praise me and wouldn't like me*. To atone for her sins, she tries even harder. She is firmly caught in the cycle of codependency.

The dysfunctional element in this home is not the mother's illness but the child's reinforced belief that she cannot express her feelings. The rule here is that Mother's illness takes precedence over the child's needs, and the child is accused of being selfish if she expresses those needs. In the dysfunctional family, children are not considered to have needs of their own.

An excellent television docudrama on the "Hallmark Hall of Fame" told the story of the hearing daughter of deaf parents. As is true of most such families, from early childhood on the daughter served as her parents' interpreter, their ear to the world. A poignant scene found her, at age eight or so, talking with an undertaker, making funeral arrangements for her brother who had just been killed by a fall from a balcony. Rather than react to her brother's death like a little girl would, she immediately had to assume the role of an adult and negotiate the financial arrangements for the funeral. Her parents expected her to always be the responsible one, and she was. They did not acknowledge the feelings of a child her age and essentially did not permit her to be a child.

In young adulthood she had difficulty establishing intimate relationships. It was only when she was finally able to accept and work through her resentment and anger over her lost childhood, and learned how to have fun, that she was able to feel emotionally healthy.

The dysfunctional elements in the daughter's home were her parents' unrealistic expectations of her and the family rules that prevented her from talking about her feelings. The family rules told her she was being selfish if she wanted to attend to her own needs or to have some fun. These rules denied that the problems of a little girl could have as much validity as those of her deaf parents.

The emotional consequences of living in a home with deafness were recently described by Lou Ann Walker in *A Loss for Words*, an account of her experience growing up as a hearing child with deaf parents. Her parents were loving and caring, yet she grew up feeling guilty, ashamed, isolated, and wanting to please others. How did this happen? Walker states:

> I acted as interpreter and guide for my parents the entire time I was growing up. I was an adult before I was a child. I was quiet and obedient around people because I didn't know what was expected of me. Outside our house speaking and hearing seemed to be valued more than anything. And that's what we had nothing of at home. I was the child who did all my parents' business transactions, nearly from the time I was a toddler. I was usually the one to relay to Mom and Dad that a friend had died when we received a call. I was the one who had to call up other friends or relatives to give them bad news. A child doesn't know that his childhood is sad; it's just his life.[8]

Lou Ann learned to cover up her feelings and to behave like a responsible adult instead of like the little girl she was.

She also learned early to feel guilty.

> In a family where there is deafness, guilt is a constant undercurrent, tainting relationships, sometimes even shattering that family. My own grandparents constantly exhorted me to *be good*, themselves feeling guilty for not doing more for their children, hoping somehow I would make up for things.[9]

Lou Ann's pervasive feeling of guilt came about because she had come to believe that her feelings were wrong. For example, she was tempted by an offer her uncle and aunt made to spend some time with them, to live in a normal family. She let herself fantasize about life with them.

What an ache, what a longing, what a maze! At that very moment I was deeply ashamed of myself. I loved my parents fiercely. I would jump to their defense at any time. And yet I had these horrible, treacherous desires. And after the two weeks, when I got back home, I was terrified Mom and Dad would figure out the secret.[10]

Because there was a significant gap between Lou Ann's inner repressed feelings and what she believed she should express, she felt more worthless and more guilty.

My greatest fear had always been: The more you get to know me, the less there is to know. I was a black void. On the outside I was bright and shining and cheerful. Inside I was hollow. I was a caretaker and I felt deep down inside I could never do enough for others because I could never make my mother and my father whole. On the outside I was trying to remain the good girl my aunts and uncles had warned me to be. The difference between the facade and the interior kept growing. I felt guilty. And never once had I ever been able to indulge myself in feeling bad. 'You shouldn't feel sorry for yourself. Think of your mother and father. It wasn't their fault,' I'd been told. In a bizarre psychological turn of events, I couldn't even feel sorry for myself without feeling the guilt. I had no right to feel bad, to feel lonely or out of touch or anything else. I had been boxed in on every side and that was what was struggling to get out. Just the right to feel.[11]

Lou Ann subsequently talked with her sister about their childhood. For the first time they shared their feelings of guilt and inadequacy. "Both of us began to cry. She and I had been so close all the time we were growing up. We'd talked about everything—except this."[12]

Despite the closeness and love in the family, Lou Ann learned that only certain feelings were acceptable, and that she was responsible for other people's happiness. She grew up with a pervasive feeling of shame and guilt. Only an emotional crisis years later forced her to face her feelings, share them with others, and begin healing.

In this chapter we have seen examples of homes characterized as normal and as loving, but in fact dysfunctional enough to produce codependency in the children. What, then, is a normal family? First, let's define *normal* as healthy rather than as statistically average. I would say that a healthy family is one in which it is acceptable to discuss problems and to express feelings, in which expectations of the children are realistic, in which the values the parents teach the children are actually lived by the parents, and in which unacceptable behaviors are confronted and dealt with rather than covered up.

Furthermore, a healthy family nurtures the children and values them for who they are so they grow up believing they are worthwhile people, regardless of what college or trade school they attend or what career they choose.

A normal family is *not* the same as the stereotypical American family, with two parents, two children, a dog and a cat, a family in which Mom spends all day at home while Dad goes to the office. A normal family can be a single-parent family, or one in which both parents work, or one in which there is physical disability.

Now let's look again at Mary Ellen and Linda, the two women quoted at the beginning of the chapter, who believed they had healthy childhoods but somehow ended up married to sex addicts. Linda's mother had unrealistic expectations; not only was she very controlling, but she seemed to want to make Linda into an extension of herself. Not surprisingly, Linda could never please her critical mother, no matter how hard she tried. Giving up any attempt at autonomy, she let her mother make all the decisions for her; in that way, Linda could avoid taking responsibility for the consequences of those decisions. Later, Linda transferred her dependence to her husband. Today, at age 45 and in a recovery program for spouses of sex addicts, she is learning that she doesn't have to please her mother. Despite her stable childhood home, she lived with unrealistic expectations and rules against expressing feelings.

Like Linda, Mary Ellen also grew up in a stable home. But her mother's reaction to becoming deaf when Ellen was ten created significant dysfunctional elements in the family. Ellen no longer was permitted to have a one-on-one relationship with her father. She was cast in an adult role as her mother's confidante. At the same time, she was not permitted to express her feelings or discuss problems. She was not able to live up to her mother's expectations.

Research on adult children of alcoholics has shown a tendency of these children to minimize the problems of their childhood. "It wasn't really that bad," they will say. "There were a lot of good things in my family. It's true that my father yelled and hit me when he was drunk, but when he was sober he was wonderful to me. He was always trying to make it up to me. It's true he forgot his promises to take me to the ball game, but when he sobered up he was really sorry about it."

From my interviews of wives of men who have affairs, I found a similar tendency on the part of some women to remember only the good. They attribute their problems to the marriage rather than to the family of origin, especially if there was no alcoholism or violence in the childhood home. But just as with Linda and Mary Ellen, when one asks for details of the person's family of origin, it becomes evident that enough of the unhealthy family rules were present to explain the person's codependency.

The belief that *it wasn't that bad* is an aspect of the codependent's lack of knowledge of what is healthy and normal family interaction and her consequent high tolerance for inappropriate behavior. Because she lacks confidence in her judgment, she is likely to accept someone else's word that a given behavior is acceptable even if she suspects it is not. When her husband tells her it is her possessiveness and insecurity that make her want monogamy in their relationship, she believes him and tries to change her views for him. If he asks her to sleep with another man while he watches and assures her that lots of people do it, she tries to suppress her discomfort and assumes that her husband knows best. She tolerates inappropriate behavior from herself and her partner because she's not really sure what is appropriate.

It is unusual to find a woman who has grown up in a healthy family stuck in an addictive relationship with a sex addict or other addict. When a woman tolerates years of emotional abuse, alcoholism, or other active addiction in her partner and seems unable to do anything about her situation, the appropriate question to ask is, "Why?" Often the answer lies in the dysfunctional family life in which she was raised. She is a codependent who is addicted to her man. A woman who struggles for years with the unpredictability of living with a sex addict or alcoholic and says she is unhappy and yet is unable to make any changes in her life, is likely to be a codependent who grew up to marry an addict and is now playing the coaddict role in the relationship.

Many women would like to leave a bad marriage, but economic considerations keep them bound in unsatisfactory relationships. A woman with no wage-earning skills and small children often has no immediate options besides staying in the marriage.

On the other hand, many single women are managing

alone, with or without children. Many are in underpaid jobs and have a low standard of living, but they are coping. A two-parent family is no longer the norm in this country. In 1984, 23 percent of families were headed by single women, and approximately 50 percent of marriages were second or third marriages. There is no way to determine what proportion of formerly married women were left by their husbands, but clearly, many women are choosing to leave their marriages.

Clearly, financial and emotional dependency cannot be changed overnight, and a woman shouldn't be blamed for not leaving a bad marriage until she is ready. Nevertheless, it is often true that relationship addiction, rather than lack of funds, is the primary reason that keeps a woman in an unhappy or even abusive marriage with an addict.

Family Background of Coaddicts

I have often heard the question, "Is it a matter of chance that one woman marries an alcoholic, another a workaholic, and another a sex addict? Or is it something in her childhood?" The answer is far from clear, especially since the husband frequently has several coexisting addictions, such as alcoholism and sex addiction. Many sex addicts were sexually abused in childhood; so were many women who married sex addicts—but many were not. It is impossible to find a common element in their childhoods.

Nonetheless, factors in one's family of origin and early experiences do influence the nature of one's compulsive behavior. One way or another coaddicts eventually learn that sex is the best way to get love. Some learned this by being sexually molested; others, hungry for love in junior and senior high school, found that giving sex guaranteed many boyfriends. Some girls grew up in families where affairs were happening, although they may not have realized it at the time. Although they may have only learned about them in adulthood, the affairs influenced their childhood home environment.

Diane, a school teacher who is very active in her church, grew up with a workaholic, emotionally distant father and a domineering, controlling mother. After a stormy relationship, her parents divorced at the time she graduated from high school. Diane does not remember receiving much physical affection from her parents; she does remember trying hard to get her parents' approval. Diane doesn't recall any family problems when she was growing up. "I either wasn't aware of problems, or I didn't want to know about them." Nevertheless, when she told her father about the problems she and her husband were having with the husband's sex addiction, she learned some surprising facts about her childhood years.

I've recently found out from my dad that he was involved with other women in the course of the marriage. One of them was my mom's best friend, and they did some things like spouse-swapping. He didn't tell me anything about my mom's activities, only that he thought that since we were having some problems in our marriage it might be helpful for us to know that he'd had some problems in that area too. But the implication I got was that maybe my mom had done a lot of that too, playing around with other men. . . . I wonder if they weren't both having sex with a lot of other people and I had some indication of it on some level, that something was wrong which I didn't want to look at too closely, and maybe that's why I don't remember much about my childhood.

One woman who clearly remembers an intensely sexual atmosphere in her childhood is Nancy, a 40-year-old mother of five. Nancy and her husband, Monte, had a stormy marriage marked by several separations and reconciliations because of his affairs.

My father never physically molested me, but he was verbally sexual with me. He would make dirty jokes about my body. At times I'd be in the bathroom putting on makeup and he'd come in and urinate and walk around naked. I was disgusted by him. I had one aunt who was very pretty and very well endowed, and at one party I saw him feeling her. I can still remember the disgust I felt. I felt very sorry for my mother, and angry with her at the same time. My father used to keep Playboy *magazines in the house, so I grew up looking at pornography, reading all the books that he had.*

I think my father also had affairs. One day when I was in the house and my father was outside washing the car, the phone rang. It was a woman on the phone and she wanted my dad. I asked, "Who is this?" She answered, "It's Baby." So I went out the back door and I called, "Dad, there's a woman on the phone and she says her name is Baby." My dad turned white and proceeded to have a heart attack. I can still remember him walking into the house, having this heart attack, and the doctors coming. I thought it was my fault, and I went around for years feeling guilty of having caused his heart attack.

I felt so lonely all of my life, so I tried to find companionship by having boyfriends. As early as fifth grade I was going steady with boys, and by the following year I was kissing and petting because it gave me a feeling that they cared about me. If someone wasn't being sexual with me, they didn't care about me. All through high school I had boyfriend after boyfriend.

Not surprisingly, she married a man to whom sex was very important.

Alice, the 42-year-old research scientist whose parents were divorced when she was very young, was brought up by her father.

I always thought of my father as a very sexual person. He has been married five times, and each wife was in her

30s when they got married. His current wife is only a few years older than me. When I was in high school he was between marriages. He used to tell my brother and me that he would be gone until morning because he had a business meeting. We knew darn well that he was going to spend the night with a girlfriend, so we'd laugh and say, "Enjoy your business meeting!" He was a very formal person who rarely hugged or kissed us, and he used to be very embarrassed by our laughter.

Alice married a man who was also very sexual, and whose affairs caused major problems in their marriage.

Several women I interviewed were molested sexually in childhood. Patty, a petite 25-year-old blonde married to a much older dentist, was repeatedly molested by two teenage neighbors when she was six or seven. They would lie on top of her and rub against her. She didn't understand what was happening, but had a sense that it was wrong and that she should not tell anyone about it.

Another woman was fondled sexually by a male babysitter. Other women were victims of incest. Rita, whose husband formerly had affairs, had sexual relations with two of her three brothers. She grew up in a chaotic household with an alcoholic father whose behavior varied unpredictably from being loving to being physically abusive. Rita's husband was also the child of an alcoholic.

Helene, a recovering alcoholic who is divorced from an alcoholic sex addict, was in an incestuous relationship with her alcoholic father for many years, beginning at age ten. She learned to stuff her feelings and to exchange sex for love in her relationships.

Several women, hoping to obtain love, engaged in sex early in life and became pregnant. Marcy, the wife of a philanderer, dated her husband against her parents' wishes and finally married him at age 18 after getting pregnant. Sarah, a certified public accountant who is now divorced from an alcoholic sex addict, grew up in a stable but rigid home. A model student in school, she became pregnant at age fourteen. After giving the baby up for adoption, she returned to school and to an active sex life.

This brief survey of coaddicts does not definitively answer the question of why they married men who had affairs rather than other types of addicts, but it does suggest that there were certain risk factors in their early years. There was often a heightened awareness of sexuality in the family of origin. Early sexual experience, either with peers or through sexual abuse, was another frequent finding. One way or another, these women came to believe that sex is the most important sign of love.

Obviously, more research needs to be done in this area in order to understand how this belief—sex is the most important sign of love—originated. What seems clear, however, is that coaddicts learn in their formative years to be "comfortable with the uncomfortable"; for coaddicts married to sex addicts this includes the sexual arena.

Family Roles in the Dysfunctional Family

Now that we have explored the rules and circumstances in the family of origin that can predispose one to codependency and sexual coaddiction, let's turn to the roles that children play in the dysfunctional family. These roles, in alcoholic families, were first delineated by Sharon Wegscheider-Cruse.[13] It is now recognized that the family roles can occur in all types of dysfunctional families. The roles described by Wegscheider-Cruse are the Hero, Scapegoat, Lost Child, and Mascot. The child does not consciously choose these roles; rather, she finds an available niche in the family panorama and is supported by the family in her position because each role contributes to the stability of the dysfunctional family in some manner.

These roles are not fixed nor mutually exclusive. For example, when circumstances change such as when an older child leaves home, the roles may change. Moreover, a child may display elements of more than one role at a time. Nonetheless, it is particularly valuable to look at these patterns because each role tends to be carried over into adulthood where it can cause problems.

The role typically assumed by the oldest child is the Family Hero, also termed the Responsible Child by Claudia Black.[14] The Hero is the child who feeds and dresses her younger siblings when the parents are too involved with other things. If her father throws a few dishes around in a fit of anger, she will clean up in order to help out her mother. When her mother is so depressed about her father's behavior that she lies in bed all day immobilized, the Hero will take over the household responsibilities. Her goal is to maintain the status quo and prevent things from getting worse. Deep down she believes if she does a good enough job, things will improve and her parents will be as happy as they used to be. By helping out as successfully as she does, she unwittingly enables her parents' compulsive behavior—she helps prevent them from experiencing the consequences of their addiction and coaddiction.

Beverly, the attractive socialite and divorced mother of three small children, grew up in an alcoholic family.

My father always came home at six, but his drinking progressed to the point where he could barely make it in the back door. As he fell asleep at night in his room he would rant about those "goddam women," meaning his wife and daughters. I tried to be his son, to help him repair things around the house. I tried to be pretty and good to please him and to make him stop drinking, but he didn't. My efforts were just not good enough.

No matter how hard she tries, the Hero inevitably fails. She feels guilty and inadequate over her inability to make things right in the family. Her usual response is to try harder, and this becomes her usual behavioral style. She becomes an overachiever. She gains her self-worth from her accomplishments, and judges herself by her achievements. She may develop a compulsive drive to achieve.

Often admired at school, the Hero may excel at scholastic activities or at sports. Her parents support and promote her single-minded pursuit of excellence. She sets high goals for herself, and often expects too much of others as well. In adulthood she usually is good at whatever task she undertakes. Her career choice is likely to be a helping profession—teacher, counselor, nurse, physician, or minister. No matter what career she chooses, she is likely to take it very seriously and do well at it.

The Hero's primary emotions are guilt and inadequacy. As Wegscheider-Cruse tells us, "The Hero goes through life always feeling that no matter how good he is, he must be a little better before he has a right to take satisfaction in his achievements."[15]

The second child in a dysfunctional family often assumes the role of Scapegoat, who Claudia Black calls the Acting Out Child. Because there is already one Hero in the family, the next child seeks attention through negative behavior, which becomes her usual behavioral style. She covers her underlying hurt with anger. This is the child who is most likely to become addicted to alcohol and other drugs, to become pregnant, to drop out of school, or to get in trouble with the law. Because she is the identified problem child in the family, her presence makes the rest of the family members seem healthy by comparison. When whole families come into treatment, it is often because of the acting out of a Scapegoat Child.

Although approximately 20 percent of adult children of alcoholics identify with this role in their childhoods, adult Scapegoats are under-represented in the community and in treatment programs. This is because many have eliminated themselves in their youth—by committing suicide, or by dying of a drug overdose, car accident, in street violence, or having committed a crime and ending up in jail. A Scapegoat may change roles and become a Hero when an older sibling leaves home and her position becomes vacant. If the Scapegoat survives to adulthood, she is likely to carry her "it's not fair" attitude with her. Having learned in childhood that chemicals kill pain and provide pleasure, and that family life centers around the addict, she has greater than normal chances of becoming chemically dependent. Although she comes across to the world as a rebel, her primary emotion is hurt.

Another family role is that of the Lost Child or the Adjuster. Usually a younger sibling, this child has found the best way to avoid trouble is to adopt a behavioral style of invisibility. She lives in a fantasy world, playing elaborate games with her dolls, and may become an avid reader or television viewer. Her activities are mostly solitary. The Lost Child gives her parents a sense of relief. "At least we don't have to worry about *her*," they tell themselves. She avoids taking responsibility, and develops no particular opinions on any issues. Her primary emotion is loneliness. The Lost Child does not do well, but gets attention by developing illnesses such as asthma and allergies. The Lost Child feels ignored and forgotten. She may comfort herself with food and become obese.

In adulthood, the Lost Child becomes the student or office worker whose name you just can't seem to remember. Accustomed to living in chaos, she tends to marry a mate who causes uproar. She may become a collector of material goods.

The remaining role is one Wegscheider-Cruse terms the Mascot. Often the youngest child, she defuses explosive situations in the family by focusing attention on herself through humor. Tension and hyperactivity constitute her behavioral stye. As she grows older she may take tranquilizers and other drugs to calm herself down. In school, she is the class clown. In adulthood, she finds that people do not take her seriously. Her predominant emotion is fear, which she covers with her clowning behavior.

Although the Responsible Child is the one whose enabling activities are most clearly visible in the family, children in each of the other roles are also contributing to the stability of the dysfunctional family system. Thus, the escapades and problems of the Scapegoat can become the focus of concern of the entire family, so that they don't have to confront the addiction and coaddiction of the parents. The Lost Child, by not making waves, tries to minimize the need for change. And the Mascot, with her clowning and hyperactivity, defuses the crises which may be necessary for the parents to realize that they need help.

Thus, children who play any of the roles described—the Hero, Scapegoat, Lost Child, or Mascot—may simultaneously be enablers: they may feel responsible for the problems in the family and try, with whatever behavior they have adopted, to improve the situation at home. This was confirmed by most of the women I interviewed. They tried their best in childhood to please their parents and to make things better at home. Accustomed to being caretakers in their families of origin, they were attracted to men who needed fixing.

Why Learn About Our Childhood?

In a letter to a newspaper column dealing with alcoholism, a reader questioned the preoccupation adult children of alcoholics have with learning about their childhoods. The reader wrote:

"Once again we are blaming Mommy and Daddy for whatever the individual does, and that's just another cop-out. This is similar to blaming poor potty training for a murderer's crime. If our society would force people to take responsibility for themselves this would be a better world."[16]

Al, the recovering alcoholic who writes the column, replied, "Once I was led to understand who I was and why I acted the way I did, I was able to become a socially and personally responsible member of the human race *for the first time.*" An important step in the early stages of recovery is understanding the roots of one's codependency. If we can review our childhood in order to understand rather than to blame, then we can move forward. By defining the rules which govern our lives and the part they played many years ago, we can begin to change them for rules more appropriate to our present situation. It's also important to understand that our parents did the best they could under the circumstances. Often they were enmeshed in their alcoholism or other addiction or codependency and had very little left for their children.

In early recovery, many people experience a great deal of anger at their parents. One of the tasks of recovery is to forgive them, and a good way to do this is to ask our parents to tell us about their childhood. Addictions typically span several generations, so we are likely to find that our parents grew up in a family in which *their* needs were not met. Asking for this information can be very difficult for any addict or coaddict who grew up in a family where secrets were hidden.

Bill is a recovering addict of infidelity who felt he was never able to please his father; nothing he did quite measured up. Bill's father, a self-made man, was contemptuous of his son's failures. Bill eventually decided that if he didn't try, no one could blame him for not succeeding. He focused his energies on pursuing women rather than a career, and became very successful at his chosen occupation. His marriage to a career woman permitted him to live in comfort while devoting his energies to womanizing. At age 40, Bill was still preoccupied with winning his father's approval and felt worthless because he could not do so.

When Bill eventually entered a recovery program for sexual addiction and learned about the family dynamics that can produce codependency, he found himself feeling very angry at his father. Bill felt he could not share his feelings with his father, a prominent leader of his community who was very sure he was right about everything. During his next visit to his parents, Bill did ask his father about his own childhood.

Bill's father, outwardly self-assured and self-confident said:

My father had to work hard all his life. He never really had a childhood. He had to support his mother and brothers because his father was too busy running around with other women. My mother and I were very close; we have the same personality and were always on the same wavelength. My father was very fond of me, but he spent a lifetime putting down my mother. I was very resentful of him for doing this, and I kept defending her. I said to him, "If she's so terrible, why do you stay with her?" My father was always hugging and kissing me, but it took me many years to be able to stand up to him.

I've been very successful. Everywhere your mother and I have lived, we've always been respected. But in my heart of hearts I've always felt like an outsider. People say all these nice things about what we've done for the community, but I realize that deep down they think we're outsiders, we're those aggressive, rich carpetbaggers. If you realize that people don't really care, you don't get hurt. I always say, eternal vigilance is the best defense.

Bill learned from this discussion that his great-grandfather had been a sex addict. He also began to see his father in a very different light. Bill's father felt like an outsider who always had to have his defenses up to avoid being hurt. In childhood, Bill's father listened countless times as his father denigrated the mother with whom he so strongly identified. Undoubtedly Bill's father had felt he could not measure up to *his* father. When Bill began to see his father as a human being with weaknesses and a troubled childhood, instead of as an all-powerful judgmental figure, he was able to feel more sympathetic and less angry with him. He realized that his father was the product of *his* upbringing.

Seeing our parents as real people is the first step toward change. Understanding our origins does not negate the need to grieve for our lost childhood and to experience anger over our parents' role in our present difficulties. Other steps which are necessary for our recovery include understanding the family patterns, building an emotional support system, allowing our feelings to emerge in order to experience the grief and anger, and, finally, taking responsibility for changing our behavior.

When we look back to our childhood and identify the dysfunctional elements, we can use the information as a springboard to change. The goal here is to understand the family roots without blame. Accusing our parents of having caused our present problems will not accomplish anything. Just as our personality and behavior are in large part an outcome of our childhood experiences, so too was our parents' behavior an outcome of their childhood experiences. Our parents did the best they could given their limitations. Once we understand the origin of our codependency, we have an opportunity to deal with the challenges that improved well-being will require.

If we can make some changes, then the next generation—our children—will have an easier time of it than we did.

CHAPTER FOUR

The Thrill of the Chase

Characteristics of the Man Who Has Affairs

When Bruce was six years old, his mother became ill and died and his father began drinking heavily. Bruce and his older sister were pretty much left to themselves.

In the alcoholic family, I was the Lost Child. I spent a lot of time by myself. I didn't know how to make friends.

I was angry almost all the time. At night, when Dad drove me home, he would stop at a bar and leave me waiting in the truck. I'd sit in it until he got through drinking, which might be two or three hours. I spent a lot of time sitting and waiting. Finally, when I was eight or nine, I decided to walk home instead of waiting. It was scary walking home in the dark. That's when I began making plans to get away from Dad.

By age fifteen I had a job and was driving a car. I was very lonely, especially on Saturday nights. The filling station where I worked was in clear view of the baseball stadium and the lights and the crowd. I'd be over there pumping gas and listening to the crowd and wishing I could have been at the stadium with some friends.

Dad got a DWI (driving while intoxicated) citation

nearly every month and his name was often on the front page of the paper. He was the town drunk. I was embarrassed and ashamed, but I kind of repressed it. I learned not to feel. My friends didn't say anything to me—I can't remember anyone saying to me, "Your Dad's name was in the paper," or anything like that.

After college I became a hospital social worker. At a church dinner I met my wife, who was friendly and nice. She came from a stable family, and her folks were really good to me. Her home was my home, and I was there all the time. We got married and had a couple of kids. I didn't realize how difficult it was for a mother with two small children. I had a very responsible job at the hospital, helping a lot of people, and I was in my glory, getting all the strokes I'd never had. Meanwhile, she was at home with two kids, getting more and more angry. The angrier she got, the more I withdrew. I was unhappy with my marriage, but because I had my job and I was in my glory, I was able to make it.

After several years I realized I really wanted to be a minister, so I went to seminary. To work my way through, I got a job as a night watchman. I spent all day at the seminary, stopped by home for dinner, and then I'd be out until 2 A.M. walking the floors. I had no fellowship with the other seminarians; after class they'd meet and would go to one of the local pubs and drink some beer, but I had to leave for work. My life was strictly studying and working. I was an absentee father—Barbara had to handle everything at home. And she became angrier and angrier.

I was so happy to graduate from seminary! When I got to my first congregation, I didn't realize there were so many needy women; but there they were, both married and single. That's where I began my affairs. The church was a ready-made place because people were allowed to go there without suspicion; there were a lot of women there.

One day a woman came in for marriage counseling. I

tried to get her husband to come in but he refused. She kept coming back and one day when she cried, I hugged her, and that was my mistake. That was what she had wanted all along. Every woman I was involved with told me later on that she'd planned what was going to happen. So they sensed something in me, a loneliness. Their vibes picked up whatever was going on. I wasn't enough in touch with myself to know that I was putting out those vibes, but evidently I was.

After that there were others. With each one, when she first came I was serious about wanting to help her. When I saw it wasn't going to work, the husband wasn't going to come in, I think I just gave up. The women didn't come in with that in mind. I'd realize that when I did the holding and they responded. And I knew I was wrong. I don't know what was happening in terms of my own values and morals, but they took a backseat. My thinking went out the window and my emotions took over. When one woman would come in and we'd get something going, I would stay with her until something would happen and she'd decide or we'd mutually decide to stop seeing each other. We'd have sex right on the floor in my office. I think my wife suspected but she never said anything; she just wanted me home more.

I was very busy, very involved in community activities as well as the church, but I would get this longing. It would come over me almost like a hunger, and I'd call someone and ask, "Can you come over?" And they were always obliging. They were as codependent as I. And as lonely. I kept that up for ten years, until the woman I was then having an affair with told her best friend, who told her husband, who told the woman's husband who was on the church council.

I had to resign. After I left my job there was a hearing, and the result was that the church administrative body took my ordination from me. I can never go back into the ministry again. So all those years that I worked nights, all *that effort in school, all that has been taken away from me. It's down the drain.*

After that I went back to the hospital job. It was bad for me, because I met a lot of needy women there too, and although I managed to stay straight for a year, soon I was getting involved with women again. That's when I realized it was more than just loneliness. I met a woman—if I was ever in love with anyone, it was with her. And while I was going with her, I went out on her with someone else. This woman was at my beck and call, but I couldn't stay faithful to her. I realized that I just couldn't get enough love, it was almost like an addiction. The more people who loved me and stroked me, the more I wanted. It wasn't that I was oversexed; a lot of times we would just talk and hold each other. It wasn't just the sex. With all those women, we had a lot to talk about. We'd spend all evening talking, and would end by celebrating with sex. My relationship with every one of them was a very intimate one. They were very interested in what I was doing and what I had to say, so I felt important.

Bruce finds that he is still tempted by the many lonely women he meets professionally, but he is determined to remain faithful to his wife.

Barbara has told me if I have another affair she will leave me. I just don't want to hurt her and the children anymore. And I feel too much guilt for what I've done in the past. During those years, although I enjoyed the relationships with the other women, I went through inner turmoil and guilt. I knew what I was doing was wrong. Had I not been in the church it would still have been wrong, but in my position as a pastor, I can't think of anything worse than what I did. I was crazy to do that. I know the church will always remember the years I was there and how I left. Even though in every other area I was a straightforward, honest person, the black mark against me is what they remember.

Some people might say that Bruce was just a lonely guy in an unfulfilling marriage who was getting comfort where he could find it. What makes him different from the countless other men who have affairs? Addiction involves loss of control over a behavior with resultant negative consequences. Despite the guilt Bruce felt and the risk to his job and marriage, he continued to have affairs with his parishioners until inevitably he did lose his job and, even worse, was kicked out of the ministry. Bruce's life was unmanageable because of his sexual behavior.

Another example will illustrate this point. In a periodic police roundup, a prominent member of a university community was arrested for soliciting a prostitute. His name was on the front page of the newspaper, causing great embarrassment to him and his family. One month later the man was again arrested in the same neighborhood for soliciting a prostitute. He then resigned his university job and moved away. Many men have sex with prostitutes, so his first arrest might be considered as bad luck—he happened to be in the wrong place at the wrong time. But the second arrest strongly suggests that he could not control his compulsive behavior. He was unable to desist from the behavior even though an outsider could see it was clearly against his best interests. Despite the arrest, the pain to his family, and the risk of losing his job, he returned to the same location only to be arrested again. This is addictive behavior.

Bruce's story illustrates many of the typical elements of the sex addict. Bruce grew up in a dysfunctional family—his father was alcoholic and his mother was absent for most of his youth. In his family of origin, feelings were covered up and were not discussed; problems were not confronted. Bruce felt lonely and isolated. He compensated for his feelings of worthlessness by working very hard and suppressing his feelings. In his marriage, he continued the pattern of avoiding problems rather than dealing with them. When his wife became angry, Bruce withdrew further into his work.

In his ministerial work, he found a ready-made way of being valued and accepted—sexual involvement with the many needy women who came to him for help. It is to Bruce's credit that he recognizes that although the women came to him, *he* was sending out signals that encouraged them. Bruce became addicted to the affection he received from the women he was involved with, and as his addiction progressed he found himself unable to be faithful even to the girlfriend he thought he loved. That was the event that caused him to seek help.

Bruce's story is not uncommon. Members of the clergy are at high risk for extramarital affairs. In *Avoiding the Scarlet Letter*, Dr. Louis McBurney lists several reasons why.

Men in ministry are especially vulnerable to sexual temptation because they work in what is often a female subculture, the church. Simply their presence on the job exposes them to potential romantic or sexual relationships.

Another reason for the increased vulnerability is the similarity between spirituality and sexuality. In both, we lower personal barriers, encourage intimacy, become open and vulnerable, and experience profoundly moving emotions. Some individuals compare their deepest spiritual moments to sexual climax. Both provide an intense response, a loss of ego boundaries, a sense of oneness with those who share the experience.

Our personality also makes us more vulnerable. As sensitive, caring, giving persons, we resemble a warm living room for the lonely and dependent. Thousands of people, single and married alike, seek closeness. Most married women name as their primary marital problem their husband's insensitivity to their emotional needs. It makes them desperate for a companion who will talk with them and listen.

Enter the minister, the model husband. As long as they don't consult our wives, women may see us as ideal—strong and capable, yet gentle, warm, and loving. The church even encourages us to be that sensitive person to everyone in need, which includes many lonely women, whose activity in church masks a hunger for attention and affection. Both our personal warmth and our professional calling put us in jeopardy. . . .

It's also critical that we know our particular vulnerability. Only I am aware of my individual sexual thoughts and drives. I may have frustrations with marital sex or doubts about my potency. I may find certain female physical characteristics particularly tempting. Midlife transition may raise questions about what I've been missing or how long I can continue to function successfully. Any of these issues may contribute to my vulnerability to an affair.[1]

In other words, the clergy is a profession where there is often the combination of a need to help and to be needed, coupled with limitless opportunities. For a man addicted to affairs, the clergy is an ideal career. I do not mean to imply that a person would choose the ministry in order to have opportunities for sexual contact. On the contrary—most young people become ministers, physicians, or counselors out of a sincere desire to help people. But for the budding sex addict who finds himself in the ministry, the opportunities are plentiful for carrying out his compulsive behavior. The same is true for the physician, psychiatrist, counselor, or other members of the helping professions.

Sexual addiction does not affect only professional people. The six percent of Americans who are estimated to be sexually addicted come from all areas of society. Certain careers may appear to be overrepresented among men who have affairs because they provide endless opportunities for meeting women. One of these is the police, as Ted's story illustrates.

Ted was the oldest of three children. In his childhood he witnessed his alcoholic father beating up his mother. Ted was the responsible child at home, cooking and cleaning for his younger siblings. Even in adulthood, his sisters seek him out when they have family problems. Ted knew his father was cheating on his mother, and soon began to imitate him. In high school he went steady with six girls at the same time, until they all ended up at the same party, compared notes, and gave him back his rings.

I was going steady with all of them, and I was juggling schedules and making excuses and lying about where I was going and what I was doing.

Ted barely got through high school, and was frequently in trouble with the law for fighting, siphoning gas, and other minor offenses. A stint in the military straightened him out, and he became a policeman upon his discharge. He married a shy, pretty girl, who soon bore him a son. Then he was assigned a night shift.

I got teamed up with some other cops who were single and I started thinking like them. Whenever they wanted to go and do something, they'd say, "Oh, come on, you can't let your wife run your life for you." I let myself be persuaded to go to bed with a girl at a party. After that first time, it was like I just fell back into my old routine in high school. . . . I knew what I was doing was wrong. Today, whenever I get a chance to talk to a guy who's just gotten married, I tell him, "Don't do it." It's like taking dope. You take your first hit and like it, it gives you a high, and then you're hooked. You'll never be able to quit, no matter what you try to do.

Ted began having one casual sexual encounter after another, always being careful not to get involved emotionally. He became such an expert on cheating that once, when he had to give a lecture on a topic of his choice in a class on public speaking, he spoke on "How to Cheat on Your Wife and Get Away with It." After the class, several men came up to talk with him to ask him for specific tips.

The first crisis in Ted's marriage came when his wife found out about one particular affair.

It wasn't even a relationship, it was a bet. One Thursday there was a new young lady in the office. Her husband was out of town and was going to come back the following Monday. I already had a reputation by then, so the other guys bet me that I wouldn't be able to get her to bed by Monday. I took them up on it—I bet twenty bucks. It was really a rotten thing to do to her, but I did it. I found out where she lived—it was in the area I patrolled—and that evening I stopped by her house and asked her, "You got a cup of coffee for a cop out on the beat?" She said, "Sure," so we had some coffee and started talking. I told her when I would get off and asked her if she'd like to go out with me afterwards and unwind. But she had a baby and no babysitter. I said, "Could I come over here for a drink?" and she agreed.

So I went back there after work, we had a few drinks, and then we made love on the living room floor and I won my bet. Sure, I told the guys at the office, and they paid off. That was the kind of dumb, animal stuff I used to do.

Ted's current awareness that his prior behavior was "animal" most likely resulted from his exposure to counseling and to a self-help recovery program.

Ted's wife discovered the lipstick and makeup on his clothes and left him, but soon they reconciled. He continued to have casual affairs, but when his wife found out

about the latest, Jan, Ted decided he was really in love
with Jan. He felt so torn between the two women, so full
of guilt, that he considered suicide. Eventually he leveled
with his wife and broke up with the girlfriend. Currently
he is trying to become more involved with his wife and
children and thus avoiding temptation. However, he
doesn't give himself much hope of staying straight.

*Yes, you could say I'm addicted. Sometimes when I'm
driving home I get to feeling desperate, like I'm going to
explode, if I don't call Jan. I know I have to get home and
be around my wife and have her touch me and put her
arms around me so that I don't call Jan. You know, guys
get the bad rap for this but there are also a lot of women
who know how to innocently put across the message that
they're available, and the guy who's streetwise knows how
to pick up on them. Guys like me, we're streetwise. I grew
up with it, it was my basic training. And when I have my
low periods I say, "What the hell, I guess I'll pick up on
the messages that this girl or that one puts out. Why don't
I give her a call?"*

*You know, we're nice guys, we're easy to get along with.
And we're probably the world's greatest liars. We're probably the hardest on ourselves, being the liars that we are.
If I could have the ideal situation I would like people to
like me just for me. I would like to be able to talk to
women without getting those messages. But then I wonder
sometimes if I'm not sending them without knowing it. I
want to just have people like me. I'd like to tell them that
I'm married, and be treated as a married person, to clean
up those signals I'm sending. But it doesn't work that way.
I go to a party; there's always someone who has to hang
on just a little longer than necessary.*

*When it comes right down to the sexual act, I've never
believed the act was the high. I think it's everything that
goes with it. In fact, sometimes the sexual part of it can
be very disappointing. Sometimes it's been so disappoint-*

*ing that I've asked myself, Why? Why did I do this? I
didn't want to. You make these little promises to yourself
like, I'd never mess with a friend's wife. But if a friend's
wife comes on to you like any other woman, then you
rationalize by saying, "Hell, if I don't do it, someone else
will."*

Ted is uncertain about his future with his wife. He loves
her, he considers her his best friend, and he feels guilty
about the pain he has caused her. In frustration he ex-
claims, "I wish there was a pill to make me stop thinking
and feeling this way!" Ted used to drink heavily, but has
hardly touched a drop of alcohol in fifteen years. He com-
pares his sexual addiction with alcoholism.

*In time maybe I'll come around. It's like the alcoholic—
he never says he's cured or that he's not an alcoholic. He
may be dry and he's trying. I'm at that point now sexually;
I'm dry and I'm trying, but . . . I don't know.*

Bruce, the former minister, is attempting to steer clear
of affairs primarily because of guilt over his past behavior.
Ted, on the other hand, has a loving wife who doesn't
believe him when he says he is a sex addict, thinks his
affairs are always the other woman's fault, and keeps trying in every way to make him stay at home. Ted's pain
comes from his recognition that his control over his behavior is very tenuous. Neither man is an abuser of alcohol
or other drugs; both came from dysfunctional, alcoholic
families and have chosen affairs as the means of dealing
with the pain and the isolation of their youth. Both men
are addicted to affairs.

Defining Sex Addiction

An allergy to chocolate will provide a simple illustration of the concept of addiction. Suppose you found that you broke out in hives whenever you ate chocolate. You would probably then choose to avoid chocolate, no matter how much you liked the taste. But suppose instead you eat some chocolate, develop itchy hives all over your body, eat more chocolate, get more hives, tell yourself you're not going to eat anymore chocolate but soon find yourself consuming a chocolate bar and you break out in hives. You are unable to stop eating chocolate despite the painful consequences. This is addiction.

Addiction is also characterized as progressive, with diminishing returns. This means you need more of the chemical or more of the compulsive activity to get the same satisfaction. Thus, as time goes on, alcoholics typically require more and more alcohol in order to feel good. The chocolate addict will find himself craving two chocolate bars instead of one. The sex addict will find himself taking more and more risks in order to get the same level of excitement. If a behavior is continued despite negative consequences, and if more and more of it is required in order to get the same effect, then an addiction is present no matter what the specific behavior.

All addictions have two elements—a behavior disorder and a thinking disorder. Thus, both elements are present in the definition of alcoholism proposed by the Committee on Alcoholism and Drug Dependence of the American Medical Association: ''Alcoholism is an illness characterized by preoccupation with alcohol and loss of control over its consumption.'' The inability to stop drinking is the behavior disorder; the preoccupation with alcohol is the thought disorder that maintains the behavior problem. Alcoholics will deny they have a drinking problem and at the same time will rationalize their drinking as the logical consequence of other problems, such as marital discord or the stresses of their jobs.

Sex addiction was recognized over 30 years ago by Erich Fromm, author of *The Art of Loving*, who wrote:

> The deepest need of man is the need to overcome his separateness, to leave the prison of his loneliness. . . . One way of achieving this aim lies in all kinds of *orgiastic states*. These may have the form of an auto-induced trance, sometimes with the help of drugs. . . . Closely related to, and often blended with this orgiastic solution, is the sexual experience. The sexual orgasm can produce a state similar to the one produced by a trance, or to the effects of certain drugs. Rites of communal sexual orgies were a part of many primitive rituals. It seems that after the orgiastic experience, man can go on for a time without suffering too much from his separateness. Slowly the tension of anxiety mounts, and then is reduced again by the repeated performance of the ritual.
>
> As long as these orgiastic states are a matter of common practice in the tribe, they do not produce anxiety or guilt. . . . It is quite different when the same solution is chosen by an individual in a culture which has left behind these common practices. Alcoholism and drug addiction are the forms which an individual chooses in a non-orgiastic culture. In contrast to those participating in the socially patterned solution, such individuals suffer from guilt feelings and remorse. While they try to escape from separateness by taking refuge in alcohol or drugs, they feel all the more separate after the experience is over, and thus are driven to take recourse to it with increasing frequency and intensity. . . .
>
> . . . In many individuals in whom separateness is not relieved in other ways, the search for the sexual orgasm assumes a function which makes it not very different from alcoholism and drug addiction. It becomes a des-

perate attempt to escape the anxiety engendered by separateness, and it results in an ever-increasing sense of
separateness, since the sexual act without love never
bridges the gap between two human beings, except mo-
mentarily.[2]

In other words, Fromm reasons that alcoholism and
other drug addiction in our society are unsuccessful ways
of overcoming isolation, and that sexual activity can be
used, equally unsuccessfully, to provide exactly the same
temporary relief.

Other contemporary writers have also likened some
forms of sexual behavior to alcoholism and other drug addiction. For example, James C. Dobson, a Christian minister, in his book *Love Must be Tough*, urges women to
stop enabling the behavior of their philandering husbands:

> The lure of infidelity is an *addiction* to [a certain type
> of] individual. . . . While some people are chemically
> dependent on alcohol or heroin or cocaine, this kind of
> infidel is hooked on illicit sex. Psychologically, he needs
> the thrill of the chase, the clandestine meetings, the for-
> bidden fruit, the flattery, the sexual conquest, the proof
> of manhood or womanhood, and in some cases, the
> discovery. And like the drug abuser, he is constantly
> attempting to reform. He promises with sincerity never
> again to yield to his habit. But unless his entire social
> milieu acts to support that commitment, he is likely to
> forget it.[3]

All of these writers emphasize that the essential element
of addiction is the *experience*, not the particular drug or
behavior chosen. The important elements are the compulsive nature of the experience, the repetition of the behavior
despite its negative consequences, the need for more and
more to achieve the same effect, and the bad feelings that
the addiction engenders. For the man whose addiction is

to affairs, the mood-altering experience is not just the sexual act itself. It is a mistake to think of this type of man as being oversexed, or just needing lots of sex.

As Troy, a 30-year-old, formerly married, recovering cocaine addict explains:

I was preoccupied with women. They ranked a real close second to drugs. I would go to the cocaine connection before I'd go on a date, but I tried to do them both. I had several one-night stands, but mostly I spent a lot of time in pursuit, not in the actual catch. Occasionally I'd score, but it was mostly the pursuit, it wasn't the scoring, that was fulfilling. It was more the rush and the adrenaline of the pursuit and of living in the fantasy of the pursuit, the possibilities that existed in that. Afterwards there was the guilt of whether Sara, my wife, found out. I always thought it was honorable if I went to great lengths to make sure she didn't find out.

Fantasy is a consistently found element in sexual addiction. ''When I was feeling bad as a kid,'' says Alan, a 45-year-old married philanderer, ''I could always escape into my room and create the kind of world I wanted. It was a world where I had lots of power, where women found me exciting and wanted to be with me.''

Typically, fantasy and masturbation became interconnected. One man told me:

I remember the first time I saw Playboy. It was like my A.A. friends when they told about having their first drink. I remember the feeling I got when I looked at those soft, friendly girls. I knew they'd like me and would take care of me. After I married, I masturbated before having intercourse with my wife because I thought it would improve my performance; I could hold out longer. After we made love she would fall asleep and then I would go to my secret stash of pornography and masturbate as I created in my mind the kind of lovemaking I wanted.

Alan says:

Fantasy was my first drink. I would see an ad for scanty underwear in a magazine and I would drink in the image. Then, when I was alone and in need of comfort, I would replay in my mind, over and over, the image of that girl in the ad. Masturbation just fueled the flame, and next thing I'd be on the phone calling a girl to set up a lunch date. I would then fantasize about what we might say to each other and how we might end up in bed.

For many sex addicts, as for Alan, fantasy leads to a compulsion to follow through with actual behavior. It is difficult for them to separate fact and fantasy. This was brought home to Alice, Alan's wife, when she told him she had had a vivid erotic dream involving one of her business associates. Alan's response was, "What will you do next time you see him?" Alice was surprised. "Nothing—it was just a dream!" But for Alan, such a dream would make him believe that there was a real connection with the person he had dreamed about, and he would be inclined to follow through with action the next time he encountered that person.

The fantasizing, the anticipation, the planning, the risk-taking—these elements are at least as important as the sexual act itself in the addiction to affairs. For some addicts the risk aspect adds real excitement; they call it, "living on the edge." Troy says:

Sure I was worried about catching a disease! If I got herpes or crabs or any kind of disease and brought it home to Sara, then it would be certain I'd be caught. That element of risk just added to the excitement. I like taking risks. I was asked by my therapist, "If there were no more women on this earth for you to pursue, how would you carry on with life?" I answered, "I would do something thrilling like jump out of an airplane or race fast cars." Even today, in my work several stories up at the end of a man-lift, the adrenaline rush of the fear is a real high for me. It's one of the few things I get high on these days, besides sex, which is still a big addiction.

The sex addict has a set of core beliefs very similar to those of the coaddict. According to Patrick Carnes, author of *Out of the Shadows: Understanding Sexual Addiction*, these beliefs are: (1) I am basically a bad person; (2) No one would love me as I am; (3) My needs are never going to be met if I have to depend on others; and (4) Sex is my most important need.[4] The sex addict typically comes from a dysfunctional family. One or both parents may be alcoholic, workaholic, mentally ill, emotionally ill, physically ill, disabled, or abusive. No matter what the details, the child comes to feel unloved and unworthy. He feels isolated and different. He may take on the role of Family Hero, Scapegoat, Lost Child, or Mascot. He often learns to comfort himself sexually. If he is told that sex is wrong, as many children are, then he finds himself in the double-bind of knowing that what is so comforting to him is no good. This further lowers his self-esteem. As he grows older he feels different, that he doesn't belong. He feels like an outsider, as Bruce describes when he was pumping gas while others were attending baseball games, and when he was working nights while other seminarians were drinking beer and socializing. By the time he reaches adulthood he truly believes he is a worthless person whom no one would want if they really knew what he was like inside.

This belief leads the addict into a repetitive addictive cycle. In an attempt to cover up his painful feelings, he begins fantasizing. After being preoccupied with thoughts of sex or pursuing a woman, he takes action. He may call a married woman to arrange a clandestine meeting, cruise a bar until he meets someone, connect with a woman at a party, or visit a girlfriend or a porno shop. At this stage, every gathering is a roomful of possibilities. Alan, for example, reports that whenever he drove to a workshop or a meeting, his mind would be filled with fantasies about who he might meet there and connect with.

During the fantasizing and acting out stages, the addict feels no pain. But then immediately afterwards, the guilt and shame set in, and the addict feels at least as bad as before. His despair is relieved only by withdrawing into fantasy and preoccupation, and the cycle begins again.

Sex Addiction is Progressive

Sex addiction, like alcohol addiction, is progressive. In the early stages of alcoholism, the alcoholic establishes rules for himself that allow him to believe he has control over his drinking. Such rules are that he will drink only after 5 P.M. or only beer but no whiskey, or only on weekends, or never alone. With time, however, he finds himself breaking all his rules. The same sequence is found in the case of the man who is addicted to affairs.

An attractive older man who had had multiple affairs told me:

I never thought of myself as one of those "one night stand" kind of guys. I prided myself on getting to know the people I slept with. I conned myself that the latest affair was really the one. In reality, what I found was that once I had sex with her, she lost that mysterious quality and I began to get restless.

I had a set of rules regarding my playing around. At first I had affairs only on business trips out of town. I had vowed not to have an affair in my own city, certainly not with someone at work or in my own social circle. And I set myself a limit as to the age of the woman I would come on to. But I broke each of these rules as I began to take more and more risks. Soon being seen in public places with other women didn't seem so dangerous—I somehow thought that my wife would not find out. Then I began having girlfriends visit me at work even though my coworkers knew my wife. I finally realized how out of control I was when I made a play for the 18-year-old daughter of one of my friends. After being confronted by my friend, I decided I needed help.

For other people, the spiral of progressive involvement continues until their lives are so unmanageable that they lose their marriages and jobs. That's what happened to Virgil, a distinguished-looking, 50-year-old married university professor who had been having affairs with several of his students.

I was away from home at a conference and met someone from one of my classes. I hadn't been able to get a room at the hotel, so I asked if I could stay with her. We played around a little that evening but did not have intercourse. I thought if I didn't actually go all the way it wouldn't count. It was crazy thinking—just like the old days of the "technical virgins" when I was in college.

Later that night, she got angry about my holding out and we ended up making love. I got physically ill and told myself this was the last time I would cheat on my wife. I spent the next year "white knuckling" it. I was still using my radar, putting out signals like a bat and listening for what I got back. That's funny, thinking of myself as a bat. I remember dressing up as Count Dracula one Halloween in college. I liked that image—swooping down on defenseless women and making them my slaves as I drained their life force.

After several near-misses, I got involved with someone even though I had promised myself I wouldn't. It started innocently. Sybil, an attractive graduate student, stopped by my office a few times after class for some help with a problem. I began to look forward to these meetings and was concerned when she didn't arrive. Her perfume would fill my cluttered little cubbyhole and I would breathe it in for the rest of the day. I began to spend more time obsessing about her, even buying my wife that same perfume to maintain the connection at home and to decrease my risk of getting caught.

When Sybil called me about a missed assignment, I suggested we get together for coffee. I did this even though it broke one of my rules—not to be seen in public socializing with my students. In fact, my department head had warned me in a friendly way that it was common knowledge I had bedded several students and there was a big push on campus over the sexual harassment issue. Not only was I putting my marriage on the line, I was jeopardizing my career.

At the campus coffee shop where we met, I told her how bright she was and how much she added to my class. Somehow I managed to bring the conversation around to her personal life. She had been divorced about a year earlier from a man she said she'd outgrown. I told her that my own marriage was stagnant and that my wife was so busy with her own career she didn't have time for me. I was looking for someone to make me the center of her life. I wanted to recapture the high of first love.

She seemed interested and I felt I'd been given a new lease on life. I couldn't wait for my wife to leave in the morning so I could phone Sybil. Sometimes we'd talk for an hour. One morning I lost track of the time and missed my ten o'clock lecture.

I was conning myself that this relationship was different from the others. After all, we hadn't even held hands. Maybe I was really in love.

As we began to spend more time together I became more obsessed about making love with her. I arranged to go over to her apartment one Saturday afternoon when her children were with her ex-husband. I was like a nervous kid getting ready for his first date. I changed my shirt three times and doused myself with expensive cologne. I drove around the block twice and smoked a joint in the car.

When I finally got the courage to knock on her door, she opened it and we fell into each other's arms. I found myself being pulled into a whirlwind that eventually cost me my bid for tenure, my marriage, and my children.

I knew almost from the start I couldn't continue the relationship with Sybil. She began to make more and more demands on my time and her own course work suffered. She assumed she wouldn't have to do any more work for her class with me. When I suggested that I had to pull back from my involvement, she threatened to tell my wife and my department head. She eventually told a classmate who told my boss. It was at that point I realized my life was unmanageable.

The price the sex addict pays for his affairs is guilt and shame. Unlike a sociopath, who feels no remorse for his actions, the addict is at times aware of his dishonesty, ashamed of his lies, and feels guilty for the pain he is causing his spouse. Although he is unable or unwilling to stop the behavior, he judges himself at least as harshly as others do. In his guilt and shame, he promises himself to do things differently next time, and then feels twice as bad when he cannot keep his promises.

Shortly after Troy, the recovering cocaine addict, was divorced by his wife, he found Lisa, a new girlfriend to whom he felt very close. Nevertheless, he soon found himself sexually attracted to a nineteen-year-old girl and became involved with her.

My life is again unmanageable. I'm living in dishonesty and fear of getting caught. I tell one I'm somewhere else when I'm with the other, I tell the other I'm somewhere else when I'm with the first. There's fear and dis-

*honesty in both relationships. I love Lisa and I don't like
being dishonest with her; she deserves better than that.*

Despite his guilt feelings, Troy is still seeing both
women.

Ted, the policeman who is trying hard to remain monogamous, says:

*I think the reason I'm still with Theresa is that I could
never tell myself I don't love her. I could never walk away.
When the guilt caught up with me, when I realized how
much I was hurting her, that's when I got into crying spells
and thought of suicide. Theresa's been through some real
tough times. She stuck it out with me through thick and
thin. And I kept trying to lay a lot of blame on her. So
now I'm trying to concentrate on Theresa and the family.*

Ted describes Theresa in martyr-like terms, hoping this
picture of her will help him stay away from other women.
But he realizes it is unlikely he will succeed.

For Bruce, the former minister, his guilt over his many
affairs has so paralyzed him that he feels he will never be
able to leave his wife—he is hoping she will make the
decision to leave.

*She'll have to be the one to kick me out, I won't leave.
I'm hoping she'll meet some charming man at work who's
divorced and he'll say, "Let's you and I try to make it,"
and she'll come home and say, "Well, I've found someone
else, good-bye."*

Since in typical coaddict fashion his wife has buried her
head in the sand for so long, it is unlikely that she will
leave him. Bruce typifies the addict who is able to stop his
sexual acting out but whose progressive disease now takes
the form of depression.

Some are Reluctant to Marry

Sex addicts have difficulty integrating their sexual wants into the larger world of human relationships. Sexual activity is not perceived as part of a committed relationship, but rather as an end in itself. Not surprisingly, monogamy—and the intimacy it implies—is a fearful prospect.

The sex addict may agree to marriage only because his girlfriend gives him an ultimatum after waiting for what seems like forever. He may remember his wedding as a terrible occasion, something that he knew at the time was a big mistake.

Ted, the policeman who married at nineteen, remembers:

I don't even know how we got married. I know I asked her, and then I went overseas as a soldier. When I came back, all the arrangements had been made. I thought, wait a minute! Things are going too fast. I know I asked her to marry me but I wasn't quite ready yet. In fact, on the morning of our wedding I couldn't get out of bed. I couldn't wake up psychologically. But I went through with it.

Frank, a wealthy businessman with a younger mistress, recalls:

Our wedding was a terrible experience. I didn't want to marry her. I probably did it because the option of not having her was the immediate hurt that I could define; the other seemed too far away.

For Frank, however, marriage was not the end of other relationships.

Troy, the recovering cocaine addict, says:

Tina and I lived together for ten solid years. During that whole time there were other women in my life. She finally pressured me into getting married. I asked her what she wanted for Christmas and she said a ring. So I got her the ring. I don't know why I married her. I remember all the way to the wedding my dad was saying, "Okay, this is your last chance. You don't have to go up there." And I remember the feeling in my gut, even though I was totally wrecked. I'd been doing tons of cocaine the night before and all that day, and drinking. I remember my gut saying, don't do it. And I said to myself, if it doesn't work, I can always get a divorce.

John, an insurance salesman who had multiple affairs, went through two weddings reluctantly. Recalling the first one, when he was 24, he says:

I tried everything I knew to get her to call off the wedding. I became morose and deliberately picked arguments with her. I "forgot" to make reservations I had agreed to make. I objected to whatever arrangements she suggested. I told her I didn't want my parents at the wedding. I wanted her to take the responsibility of canceling the wedding. I repeated this pattern in my marriage. It was important to me not to be the one to end the marriage, to fail. She finally kicked me out after catching me with another woman in our house.

I didn't want to get married the second time either. Melissa and I had been living together for a few months, under ideal circumstances. Her kids were living with her ex, and we could just enjoy each other. I couldn't make up my mind to make a commitment to Melissa. Finally she said, "If you can't decide when there's just the two of us, how will you ever know once the kids are back with us?" She knew it would be even harder for me with the stresses of parenthood. She said, "If you can't decide by the end of this year, that will be the end of our relationship." I knew she meant it, and I couldn't stand the thought of losing her. So I agreed to get married. But I remember standing up there at the wedding, as the minister was reading the service, and thinking, my God, I don't know how this is going to work. But then I comforted myself with the thought that even if it only lasts a year, at least she'll know I tried.

The Role of Other Addictions

As we have seen, alcoholism plays a prominent role in the families of origin of many men who have affairs. In adulthood, alcohol is often an important factor in the lives of sex addicts. Alcohol addiction and sex addiction tend to reinforce each other. Approximately 60 percent of sex addicts who have been in an inpatient sex addiction treatment program are also addicted to alcohol.[5] Patrick Carnes notes that "one of the greatest unacknowledged contributors to recidivism [relapse] in alcoholism is the failure of treatment programs to treat multiple addictions."[6] It is becoming better understood in alcohol treatment programs that sobriety from alcohol is difficult to maintain unless all addictions are addressed. An example of the interaction of multiple addictions was seen in the case of a young lawyer who, after six years of sobriety from alcohol, was found drunk in his house. After going through treatment again for the alcoholism, he said:

The real problem isn't alcohol—it's my sex addiction. I felt so bad about what I was doing sexually that I started drinking again to feel better. If I could get that part of my life straightened out, I know I'd have no trouble staying away from alcohol.

When one addiction becomes very problematic in one's life, it is easier to switch to another than to learn nonaddictive ways of dealing with life's problems. It is much more difficult to make a fundamental change in one's coping strategies than it is to find a new way to avoid facing reality. Thus, at an Al-Anon meeting, a woman tearfully described how her husband had begun pursuing young women after he came out of a treatment program for alcoholism. He had no difficulty finding needy women at his A.A. meetings. Infidelity had not been a problem during his drinking days. Now sober, he had switched addictions from a mood-altering chemical to a mood-altering experience.

Not all sex addicts have abused alcohol or other drugs. For example, in Alan's family there is no history of alcohol dependency. Nor have chemicals ever had much appeal for him. "Women were always my drug of choice," he says. Nevertheless, he does find that alcohol lowers his resistance to interacting with women. In order to remain monogamous, he realizes he needs to have his brain functioning at full capacity when in potentially enticing situations, so he has decided to avoid alcohol altogether when at parties.

For other men, workaholism is the addiction which coexists with affairs. Both Frank, the wealthy businessman with a mistress in another city, and Bruce, the former minister, were nondrinking workaholics. Both are now working harder than ever and claim that this relieves their obsession with women. This, however, must be considered only a temporary solution. Should they experience problems on the job, it is very possible that they will once again turn to their drug of choice—other women.

In summary, addiction to affairs can be thought of as similar to addiction to alcohol. Fantasy is the first drink to the sex addict. The endless ruminating about the other woman, the pursuit, the risk taking—all these are important elements of the addictive mood-altering experience. To many sex addicts, these elements are at least as important as the sex act itself.

The sex addict often realizes he has a problem. He may be reluctant to get married because he anticipates difficulties in his marriage. He is aware of society's moral values but is unable to square them with his own needs, impulses, and desires. His own moral values become fuzzy and compromised as he attempts to justify his behavior to himself. His confusion and conflict result in guilt and shame, but the only way that he knows how to cope with these feelings is to do more of the same. He is thus caught in a vicious circle. Eventually, if his life becomes sufficiently unmanageable, he may seek help.

The sex addict does not live in a vacuum. As we have seen, he is adept at finding a codependent to marry, a needy woman who wants to care for him and who is often willing to join him in his addiction. Their life together becomes a vicious circle which is described in the next chapter.

CHAPTER FIVE

"All our friends thought we were the perfect couple"

Life on the Roller Coaster with the Addicted Couple

In her book, *Stranger in Two Worlds*, Jean Harris writes about the collection of gold cuff links, gold watches, gold tie pins, and needlepointed vests and slippers that Herman Tarnower told her were gifts from "grateful patients." It did not occur to her that "grateful patient" was a euphemism for the latest woman in his life. Some of those women pursued Tarnower by letters, phone calls, or in person even when he was on vacation with Jean in another continent. Even when he kept disappearing from their room on some flimsy excuse, "I didn't suspect a thing because I didn't want to and I didn't want others to."[1] Like many women whose partners are philanderers, Jean Harris ignored the evidence of cardiologist Tarnower's involvement with other women because she preferred not to know. Moreover, because they were not married, she felt she had few rights in the relationship and therefore could not confront her lover when she did find blatant evidence that he had other women in his life.

In the relationship between Harris and Tarnower there were elements which are typical of the interaction between a sex addict and his mate. He often treats her with disrespect and she responds with denial and excuses. She explains away the bad times and cherishes the good. She hangs on to his loving words and gestures, believing they represent the real him, and she makes excuses for his hurtful actions. Her core belief that she is not a worthwhile person prevents her from realizing she deserves better treatment. Although she does not realize it, his mood swings are what keep her hooked in the relationship; she is attracted to excitement and unpredictability. There is always hope, she believes, that *this time* he will show her some real evidence of his love.

A pursuit-withdrawal cycle is also an element of the relationship. When she attempts to win him over with love, attention, and gifts, he withdraws. But should she finally get fed up with his uncaring behavior and talk of leaving him—or worse yet, actually walk out—then he will redouble his efforts to win her back. He will be as charming, tender, and loving as when they first were dating and will promise to make whatever changes she desires. Once she is safely back in the fold, however, the cycle will begin again.

Because of the coaddict's fear of abandonment, she does not dare to tell her man how she really feels about his behavior. Instead, if she does not completely deny to herself that there are problems, she is likely to develop resentment and anger, which she keeps buried inside. Afraid of confronting her partner, she lives in fear of disaster striking in the form of another woman. In an effort to prevent him from straying, she is likely to give in to his sexual demands, no matter how uncomfortable they may be for her, and eventually may begin to wonder whether she is a sexual addict herself.

Women the Sex Addict Chooses

Just as the coaddict seems instinctively to find an addict to marry, so the sex addict usually manages to find a needy woman with whom to connect. Frank, a wealthy, 40-year-old businessman, muses:

I've always been attracted to women who have screwed up home lives. I don't know if it's conscious or unconscious, but I always have. They're so intense, especially the ones who have no father. I'm everything to them—the lover, the father, the whole nine yards. They're extremely dependent.

Frank's wife came from a single-parent family; her alcoholic father abandoned the family when she was very young. The father of Frank's current girlfriend left his wife for a younger woman. At age 25, Frank's mistress already has had three divorces.

Alan, the remarried businessman, was like a "kid in the candy store" during the years between his two marriages. He seemed to have a knack for picking out needy women in a crowd. I asked him how he did it.

I'm not sure exactly—it was just an intuitive thing, a kind of radar. People carry themselves a certain way, perhaps they're a little overweight or they sit hunched over. They have a certain insecure look. They're also the women who are really touchy-feely; they hold a glance too long, their eyes are also sweeping the room. It's just something I developed.

Alan had a long series of relationships with needy women. The one he married was very dependent on him and was devastated when she eventually learned of the affairs he had during their marriage.

The sex addict generally gives his wife clues about his

sex addiction long before their marriage. When Troy was still single, he made a pass at one of his future wife's girlfriends. "After that she never trusted me. She kept real close tabs on my activities. 'Where are you going?' 'What are you doing?' If I went somewhere, I'd usually get a call there." She knew that Troy was interested in other women, and kept checking up on him throughout their marriage because of this, yet she still chose to marry him.

Alan, who had several affairs during his first marriage, had a stormy three-year courtship with his second wife. Several times during those years he broke off the relationship, insisting that he needed more space to meet other women. Alan and Alice had many discussions about his reluctance to commit to monogamy. They talked about open marriage, swinging, and separate vacations. He even asked Alice to find another sex partner for him. Yet Alice still chose to marry him.

How They Meet

Many of us who are or were in relationships with sex addicts might believe it was a matter of chance that we ended up with these men. It is instructive for us to recall the circumstances in which we first met these men and what attracted us to them. Although we may not have known it then (and it would have been difficult to know), often clues to the future problems exist at the first meeting. Many sex addicts are great charmers; consequently, several women report an instant feeling of knowing the person well, of being able to communicate with him on a deep level as though they have a window to each other's soul. In our attempt to understand the basis of our apparent knowledge of a total stranger, we may tell ourselves that God destined us for each other, or that we knew each other in a previous incarnation. Again, because sex addicts have to be charming and persuasive to keep their addiction going, they can make us believe these things. It's only during recovery from codependency that instant recognition or love at first sight is a lot less romantic—it is merely the recognition of a fellow codependent (the sex addict).

Here's how Patty, a petite, blonde, 25-year-old medical assistant, describes her first meeting with her husband:

The first time I saw Peter was in church. He was a very nice-looking person, but the first time I saw him he had been in a fight, he'd been drinking too much and got mad at another guy. Peter had black eyes, his nose was broken, and his hand was bandaged. I remember when I walked by him at church I thought, How sad! and I kept walking. I don't know why, but I remember being attracted to him. When we went out on our first date I remember thinking, you're making a big mistake. This guy's twenty years older than you. But when we sat and talked, we knew each other so well, it was just unbelievable.

Patty learned soon thereafter that Peter's first wife had left him because of his many affairs. Peter and Patty's marriage eventually was threatened by both his alcoholism and his womanizing.

Another woman who married a future alcoholic and sex addict was Ellen, a strikingly attractive 40-year-old psychologist.

I first met Ed on the sidelines of debutante parties. He was always hanging over the bar, drinking and talking. He was surrounded by people who loved his stories and his mind.

She realized he drank excessively, but somehow assumed he would take care of it. And for the first few years of their marriage, while he was in professional school, he didn't drink at all, but in later years his alcohol consumption escalated until he finally went to A.A. for help. His affairs kept pace with his drinking, but when the drinking stopped the affairs continued.

Some may ask, "Isn't it possible that a young, inexperienced, naive girl can unknowingly marry an addict, or even someone whose alcoholism or sex addiction only becomes apparent years later? Isn't it blaming an innocent girl unfairly to suggest that she must take some responsibility for choosing a partner who later made her so unhappy?" It's true, what we know today from past experiences would have been difficult for us to perceive back then. Interviews with women who met their husbands when they were teenagers show that in each case, clear clues to their future spouse's sex addiction were present early on. These women recognize this now, but at the time they met their future spouse the clues were much more difficult to interpret.

Beverly, the daughter of an alcoholic, married a man who had multiple affairs over many years; they are now divorced.

When I met my husband in college at age nineteen, I had been dating a man who worshipped me and I couldn't stand the sight of him. After the first date I had with Brian I told myself I wanted to marry him. We had spent the night talking about his family. His mother had just died, his father—an alcoholic—had died when he was a teenager, and his sister worked at a bar. I felt he needed me. Our romance was filled with his arriving late or not at all and my making special trips to bring him donuts at night or give him rides home from his job. When he would date someone else for a few weeks and not call, I walked around in a dark fog, hoping to get another chance. I told myself, I would be better this time. He would want to stay with me.

I was sure he was not going to become an alcoholic like my father because he had come from an alcoholic family himself and had felt the same pain that I had from that experience. I felt so comfortable with him even though our relationship was a series of fights and reconciliations. I felt like he was someone who would keep me in control and not let me get out of line.

All the patterns were there from day one; they didn't change in sixteen years. I guess you could say I was young and didn't know better, but I think I just replaced my dysfunctional family with an addictive marriage.

Rita first met her husband, Ralph, when she was sixteen. Having grown up in a chaotic household and having had incestuous relationships with her two brothers, Rita was looking for a knight in shining armor to save her.

When I saw Ralph across the room, he was like my karma, my destiny. I immediately latched on to him. He kept breaking up with me and I'd be shattered, and then we'd get back together. He told me he couldn't see me because his parents disapproved, but the real reason was that he thought maybe he could score with someone else. And if he did, then he'd stay away for a while and then return to the person who gave him some balance—me. Of course, I had no idea; I believed what he said about his parents.

The pattern of unpredictability that was established before their marriage continued for many years afterwards—until they both sought help, Rita for her codependency, and Ralph for his many affairs. Rita recognizes now that many of the problems that have plagued their relationship were evident very early on.

And Diane, a schoolteacher and mother of a young child, had such low self-esteem that what primarily attracted her to Dick was simply that he was interested in her. Once they began dating they got to know each other very quickly, and within a month they were considering marriage. Now married to Dick, Diane recalls they had a lot in common and could talk easily:

We just seemed to be able to communicate beyond words. There were a lot of times in those early days, when we just knew things that we didn't have any way of knowing about each other.

Yet a major problem in their marriage, according to Diane, is Dick's inability to talk about his feelings and his fear that any conflict could be fatal to the relationship. The most likely explanation for this discrepancy is that the closeness and ease they initially experienced was caused by their common codependency. Their very real incompatabilities did not emerge until later.

Dick began spending money for pornography out of their meager savings. This later escalated to random sexual encounters. Diane was aware before their marriage that Dick had a problem with pornography, but "it didn't seem like any big deal to me. I don't know if I thought that when we were married it would be better. It certainly didn't seem to me as big a problem as he made it out to be. He acted like it was a big problem and maybe I just chose not to believe him. I remember thinking it was kind of cute that he was so embarrassed about telling me. I didn't ask him for details, so maybe I didn't want to know." In her view, her sense of sharing deep communication with Dick more than made up for any potential little problems.

Alice first met her husband, Alan, at a singles party.

What first attracted me to Alan was his good looks; he was by far the best looking man I'd ever dated. He also came across as very sincere, very caring. He really seemed interested in what I was saying. He wasn't aggressive sexually, which I liked; I had the feeling that he wanted only what I wanted. But I was so attracted to him sexually that we made love on our third date. He was gentle, consid-

*erate, experienced, and interested in my reactions. He
asked me what I wanted and if what he was doing was
pleasing to me. I'd been to bed with a few men before, but
it was nothing like this. The next morning he called me up
at work and his first words to me were, "Do you still
respect me?" It was such a charming reversal of the usual
roles that I was totally won over; I knew right then this
was the man I was going to marry.*

*Our next three years together, before we got married,
were very stormy. At times he was the gentle, considerate
lover I had fallen in love with. But at other times he was
inexplicably distant. Whenever we got too close he would
ask for distance. Whenever, in response to his dating other
women, I would get close to another man, he would suddenly become the ardent wooer again and I would once
again be won over. I knew by then that he'd had affairs
during his first marriage and that he was having trouble
staying in a monogamous relationship with me, but I assumed that somehow he would work this all out as soon
as we got married. I really shouldn't have been surprised
that after our marriage he wasn't faithful.*

In Alice's mind she hung on to the good times they had
and assumed that the bad times would vanish after their
marriage. But the very traits that appealed to Alice about
Alan—his unpredictability and his excitement—made it
likely that there would be difficult times ahead. After marriage, she ended up with exactly the same type of relationship she had endured before marriage.

Problems after the Marriage

When the sex addict and his girlfriend get married, there
are often misgivings on both sides. As I pointed out in
Chapter Four, because the man realizes that monogamy is
a problem for him, he may be reluctant to get married.
He anticipates that there will be problems, but he marries

because he believes the alternative is to lose the woman. The woman, too, may have misgivings. My interviews indicate that she was aware before marriage that there were problems in the areas of sex, alcohol, or relationships, or all of these areas, but denial, being charmed and won over by the sex addict, and a reluctance to trust in her own feelings combined to make her believe that somehow everything would turn out fine.

For some couples the honeymoon period is truly that, but for others the problems begin quickly. Nancy, a 40-year-old mother of seven children, had the following recollections:

We got married about three months after we met. And right from the beginning it was bad. We had bad fights on our honeymoon. About a week after we got back we went on a hayride with the church, and he paid all sorts of attention to these little teenaged girls. I just couldn't believe it. I thought that when we got married he wasn't supposed to even look at anybody ever again! One day I went to his college with him to sit in on a couple of his classes and a girl came up to him and said, "Oh, man, are you married?" and he said, "Yeah" and she said, "Well, you don't act married!"

We had several separations and reconciliations in the following years. I left him when I was pregnant with my second baby, but I returned following the baby's birth. Nick was so supportive that I was sure everything would be wonderful. But within a couple of months he was treating me like dirt, so I left again and went back to my parents' house.

Nick wooed me back again, and the cycle continued. We had seven children over a dozen years.

Our life was pretty bad. I never knew what he was doing. There were times that I had an uneasy feeling, a feeling of disquiet, that something was wrong. But these times were interspersed with times when he was getting himself right again. He might go on for three or four months and be a really nice guy, and I'd think, he's changed; whatever the problem was, it's different now. And then he'd start going out again and being mean to me.

I tried to change myself for him. I dyed my hair different colors. I gained weight, then I'd lose it. I did anything sexually that he wanted me to, and I'd do anything to get him to make love with me. For me, when he was having sex with me, somehow that validated me. It was okay as long as he was having sex with me. That was how I was all my life—if someone was having sex with me, then they really loved me.

Nancy's story illustrates early difficulties following marriage to a sex addict, the wife's denial, her attempts to please her husband, and her core belief that sex is the most important sign of love.

Another woman, who suspected but had no definite evidence that her husband was having affairs, became afraid to deny him sex, believing that this would be inviting him to get it somewhere else. She also believed she could control her husband's sexual behavior by making sure he had good sex at home. To this end, she always arranged a romantic, sensual encounter the night before he left on a trip. Because she believed that her husband's sexual interest in her was the most important sign of his love, she would wait to see how anxious he was to make love to her upon his return from the trip. She also used his desire for her as a clue to whether or not he'd had sex while away. She ignored her own sexual needs; all that mattered to her was pleasing her husband.

Whether the problems are present initially or begin after some years, the situation worsens with time. The coaddict reacts by intensifying her efforts to understand her husband, to please him, and to control him. She looks for reasons for his behavior, and when she thinks she has found one, she will eliminate it and hope that this will make him change. Because her partner can find a new excuse as fast as she can rectify the previous one, she becomes involved in endless, fruitless attempts to please him. Unaware of her mistaken assumptions about the cause of his behavior, she increases her efforts to please him—and increases her resentment and anger at her lack of success.

Financial and Job Problems

Chronic job dissatisfaction often accompanies sex addiction and causes financial problems that add an additional burden to the marriage. Some men crave excitement and novelty on the job as well as in their sexual relationships, and quit a job when it is no longer new. Others are so preoccupied with their sexual activities that they perform poorly at work and keep getting fired. Some men have an affair with a woman at work and then change jobs to get away from her. Still others hope for a geographic cure for their problems and repeatedly move their families to new cities.

One woman, whose husband had multiple affairs, reported the following:

My husband hasn't worked steadily in years. He can never seem to get along with his boss, and keeps quitting his job. We have three small children, so I haven't been able to work. We've been on the verge of bankruptcy several times. Each time my husband has asked me to talk to my parents. Each time, even though I felt humiliated, I swallowed my pride and asked my parents to bail us out. We now owe them thousands of dollars; I don't know how we'll ever pay it back.

Another woman told me that, because her husband kept getting new jobs, they had moved cross-country ten times in the previous ten years. Each time she would get a job too, but because of the frequent moves she was never able to build up seniority in any one job. The family was chronically short of money.

Often, the fiscally irresponsible man marries a responsible, caretaking rescuer who lands a good job and becomes the financial support of the family. Because she seeks his approval and is terrified of abandonment, she is likely to turn over control of the funds to her husband. Many codependents have difficulty spending money on themselves. *I'm just not worth it*, she believes. Resentment may build up inside the self-denying family breadwinner as she sees the money passing quickly through her husband's hands.

The wife who does the family accounting may find certain sums of money unaccounted for, or she may notice charges for long-distance telephone calls or hotels in other cities. One young wife found a $100 credit card charge for "ABC Services" after her husband returned from an out-of-town business trip. His explanation to her seemed contrived, so she phoned ABC Services, which turned out to be a massage parlor where one could get "full service" for exactly $100.

Even when family income is adequate, money can become a pawn in the game of control that a couple plays. For example, she may spend money for revenge for his affairs, or to make up for his lack of attention to her. One woman described buying a very expensive pair of shoes to punish her husband for his latest affair.

Sexual Activities

Beverly, the child of an alcoholic, married a dashing, exciting man whose alcohol consumption gradually increased.

About a year and a half before my second child was born, Brian's job began to get routine. Because he started to turn down clients who didn't interest him, he had more free time. So he began to drink heavily and look for any excuse to go out. He was very nervous and antsy. He couldn't sit in one position for very long, and when he was at home he always wanted to be somewhere else, but when he went somewhere else he wanted to be in yet a different place.

After a couple of unpleasant episodes he realized that his drinking had become a real problem and he stopped, but the sex in our life never changed. He said he wanted to try new things so I bought new underwear, then lotions, then he bought a dildo, then we went to porn shops together to see porn movies, then we went to a motel that featured closed-circuit pornographic movies, then we went to the hot tubs, then he started to tie me up, then he wanted me to tie him up, then he wanted blindfolds and gags, then he purchased a box of props—leather belts, whips, and chains. This took place over a period of about two and a half years, and in the meantime we had two more children which meant my attentions were now turned to taking care of babies, being exhausted, and feeling angry at being asked to do all this.

I know what it's like to be sucked in by the seduction of a sexual fantasy because in my attempt to please him I joined him as a sexual coaddict. I let him call me "cunt" and "whore" as we made love, and for a short time I found it exciting and then crushingly degrading.

By this time he had also started to have affairs. Right after the birth of one baby, and when I was pregnant with the next, he stopped coming home at night. I felt very vulnerable. I felt I couldn't compete with someone else who must be more beautiful, intelligent, and was certainly new and available.

At the end of two and a half years he got to the point where he was having sex with me very early in the morning, then I would iron a clean shirt for him, and he would put on after-shave lotion for his luncheon date. He would

*call me about 4:30 to tell me he was going out for a beer,
and he would return about 7 P.M. (to a dinner I had kept
warm for him), smelling like perfume. At night he would
get up about 11 P.M. to "go back and finish some work at
the office." It was a nightmare come true.*

*Although during this time I had many arguments with
him and often made threats and gave him ultimatums, I
never followed through or took any action. As I look back
on it now, I was more comfortable coping with the chaos
in my life than taking the risk of my changing and his
changing. I knew I was good at being the "wronged
woman." I knew I was good at taking care of him, but
without these roles I had to be myself, and I had lived my
life so much for him that there wasn't anything left of me.*

Beverly's story illustrates denial, attempts to please her
husband, comfort with the martyr role, participation in the
husband's sexual activities, and unwillingness to risk
change.

At times, involvement in sexual activities goes beyond
monogamous sex. As the stories in Chapter Two show, in
an attempt to hold on to her husband, the coaddict may
agree to swinging, group sex, or sex with strangers. Ellen,
the 40-year-old psychologist who for years had only infre-
quent sexual relations with her husband, was glad to have
an opportunity to please him when he finally told her what
he liked.

*We did a whole thing of sadomasochism. I tried all kinds
of things to satisfy him. We did the whips and chains, the
leather, anything and everything. Then he asked, "May I
watch you with another man?" So I'd have sex with
younger men in front of the fireplace while he watched
through the window.*

Not surprisingly, women who have participated in unusual sexual activities at their husbands' requests—and en-

joyed it—sometimes wonder whether they are sex addicts. Some women who have come to self-help recovery groups for spouses of sex addicts have wondered whether they belong there or with the addicts. The key is to determine the *goal* of the behavior.

The coaddict is addicted to her spouse, and will do practically anything she believes will keep him from abandoning her. The spouse of an alcoholic will sometimes drink with him to keep him at home. Similarly, the spouse of the sex addict will join him in his behavior, which is sexual. She may enjoy it—after all, sex is supposed to be fun, but the point is her goal to satisfy the needs of another person.

In contrast, the goal of the sex addict who engages in the same behavior is the sexual gratification of the self: the fix, the connection, the chase, the conquest, and the new experience. The goal is not to please another person.

The Coaddict Attempts to Control Her Spouse

In her excellent book, *The Booze Battle*, Ruth Maxwell describes the misguided thinking and actions of the wife of the alcoholic. Exactly the same can be said of the wife of the man who has affairs.

Virtually every wife who is responding to the disease of alcoholism by herself is guided by two specific principles that set the tone for all her actions and that ultimately guide her toward her own destruction. First, she attempts to control her husband's drinking, and second, she concentrates on his reasons for drinking and attempts to eliminate them.

With every attempt at controlling her husband's drinking, the wife creates new sources of anger for her husband to use against her and as reasons for further drinking. . . . By attempting to control her husband she is setting herself up as a target for his frustrations and is granting him the very justifications for drinking that he is looking for.

Wives of alcoholics spend an inordinate amount of time and energy trying to discover the reasons, past and present, for their husbands' drinking. They become preoccupied with events, circumstances, people, places, and things in their husbands' lives. They believe it is forces in this outside world that are somehow causing it all, and, sadly, they often assign themselves first place among these causes. They do not see the addiction that has to be fed at *any* cost, no matter what is or was taking place in the life of the alcoholic.[2]

The partner of the man who has affairs suffers from the same thought disorder as does the partner of the alcoholic. She mistakenly believes that external factors are responsible for her husband's behavior and that through her own efforts she can control his behavior. She believes if she can keep a close eye on him she can prevent him from interacting with other women and getting into trouble.

One woman who believed she was ideally situated to keep track of her husband's activities was Patty, a beautiful, blonde, and very insecure woman who for a while worked as a dental assistant for her dentist husband.

I loved working in Peter's office, because I thought I could monitor every woman. If I was in the reception room and saw the best-looking patient that came in that day, or a woman of the type that he was usually attracted to, I'd go to her chart and I'd look up how old she was and whether she was married. Then I would start up a conversation with her. I was very good at getting people to reveal things about themselves. I'd get them to talk and tell me about their lives. I'd never let them know I was his wife; I kept my maiden name. I had a terrific personality and came across great with people. I would try to stay in the room while he was treating her so I could see what the interaction was and if it was a threat or not. If I couldn't be there, I'd find out from the other dental assistant how he acted around the patient.

I did much the same thing at parties. I'd look around the room and find the woman that he'd be most attracted to and I'd watch them carefully. I'd look at his eyes to see if he met hers. It was like a prison. I was so consumed with his behavior.

Despite Patty's vigilance, her husband managed to arrange meetings with other women. All of Patty's efforts to scout out the competition did not prevent her husband from doing exactly what he wanted to do.

Attempting to control the partner and the environment is the coaddict's way of trying to cope with the unmanageability of her life. The less control she has over her life, the harder she tries.

It is very common for the wife of a man who has affairs to attempt to control her husband through sex. Nancy, the mother of seven, recalls:

If there was going to be a problem, I knew I could smooth it over by having sex with him. If I had to tell him the checkbook was all out of whack or I'd overspent our budget, then I could ease into it with sex. I'd get him into a good mood. If one of the kids did something wrong, which he always thought was my fault, I would always try and not tell him about that until after we had sex.

Interestingly, the addict who recognizes his partner's need to control him can turn this behavior around to his own benefit. For instance, he may ask his partner to help him by policing his behavior. He probably does feel a genuine sense of the compulsivity of his behavior and a desire to stop it, but part of the reason he's involving his wife in being the policeman is to reassure her that he won't do it again. In other words, it's a con and she's buying it.

She thinks he must really be sincere, because he's so re-morseful. With his wife now believing that it won't happen again, the addict is free to pursue new relationships.

The Cost: Resentment

A feeling commonly shared by both members of the cou-ple is resentment. The woman who suspects or has evidence of her husband's affairs resents him for having fun while she is at home picking up the pieces—caring for the children, doing her best to make her husband happy, and getting very little in return. Her overt reaction may be to assume a martyr role. From this role she can obtain the sympathy of her friends and can hope to make her husband feel guilty.

The husband, meanwhile, is probably feeling guilty about his actions, and he is finding that the same sexual activities no longer make him feel as good as they used to. He is likely to resent his wife for her martyr role, her attempts to control his behavior, and her assumption that she is the only one who is suffering. They each are likely to deal with their resentment by doing more of the same: she will try even harder to make things right, and he will devote himself even more to his addiction in order to es-cape the bad feelings.

The Cost: Emotional and Physical Illness

One of the costs of living in an addictive relationship is the pain endured by the woman who suspects that her part-ner is having affairs.

Long before a woman learns for sure about her hus-band's affairs (most women never know for sure) there is often the nagging suspicion. Enormous energy is ex-pended in proving to her husband that she is the only per-son he needs. Additional energy is spent in denial. She tells herself that she must be wrong, since there is no definite proof of his infidelity. Unable to explain her feelings of pain and her forebodings of doom, she concludes there must be something wrong with her.

Her husband usually agrees it is her problem, and may suggest she obtain a psychiatric evaluation. Since the partner is more likely to believe her husband than her own feelings, she may well concur that she must be crazy.

Whereas some women develop emotional or psychiatric problems in response to life in a chaotic family, others may develop physical symptoms. Many physical ailments are known to be greatly influenced by the emotions: headaches, muscle spasms in the neck and shoulders, backaches, stomachaches, asthma, irritable bowel syndrome, hypertension, colitis (inflammation of the mucous membranes of the colon), chest pains, and menstrual cramps. In addition, depression, fatigue, and insomnia are related to one's emotions. Obesity can result from emotional problems, and can cause an array of physical problems including diabetes, hypertension, and knee pain. Smoking, which is often increased by stress, can result in lung cancer, emphysema, and bronchitis. People who are very stressed are more susceptible to viral illnesses and to heart attacks. Autoimmune disorders such as rheumatoid arthritis and systemic lupus erythematosus may flare up at a time of stress. In brief, a chaotic home life predisposes a person to illness.

Nancy, who had to cope with an unpredictable husband as well as seven children, experienced physical and emotional illness throughout much of her marriage. When one week after their honeymoon Nancy's new husband used the occasion of a hayride to pay attention to some teenage girls, Nancy reacted by developing sharp chest pains and hot flashes. Her symptoms immediately brought Nick's attention back to her. But Nancy's primary method of controlling her husband was through depression.

The main thing I did was to be really depressed. I did that even before I met him. My father did it to my mother.

He was always depressed, he was always going to psychiatrists, and I hated that in him, but I did the same thing. If I needed something or if my parents weren't treating me right, I would get depressed and sick and go to bed. And then the pattern was that they would come and bring me a present or something and I'd be better. Anytime I ever got into a situation that stressed me, I would get sick and depressed and go to bed. So I did it in the marriage. I spent an awful lot of time being depressed, and of course that would make Nick feel guilty because he was always going out and doing something to feel guilty about anyway. So he would come home and see me there, probably nine months pregnant, in bed, and depressed. I got satisfaction out of that. It was my way of relieving my tension, and it would get him back to treating me right again. He would treat me badly for several weeks, and then I'd get real depressed and then he'd shape up a little bit and treat me better. That way I tried to control him.

Nancy's depression resulted in several psychiatric hospitalizations.

The Cost: The Emotional Roller Coaster

Depression, anger, resentment, guilt, confusion, physical symptoms, a feeling of craziness—these are all common features of life in an addictive relationship. At a time when she was separated from her husband but still involved with him emotionally and sexually, Beverly tried to make sense of her life by figuring out the pattern of her interaction with Brian. She divorced Brian because of his many affairs, but realized that she was still addicted to him. She told me:

Brian's cycle is about three weeks long. It has six stages, and the sixth leads back to the first. I call stage one ''on

*the make." Brian has an intensity of purpose in his walk.
He takes pride in his clothes and acts aloof and distant.
This stage corresponds to Patrick Carnes' "preoccupation" stage. I find Brian very attractive in this stage. I try
to get him to go to bed with me, especially if he has an
appointment to be somewhere else. If he does so, I feel
validated—he loves me; he puts the rest of his life on hold
so he can be with me.*

*In stage two, Brian is on top of the world. He used to
bring me flowers; now he phones and sounds as if we're
best friends and still married. He's in Carnes' "retreat
from reality" phase. I have a gut feeling at such times that
he has just connected with someone else, but if I confront
him with that he is explosively angry so I am afraid, confused, and angry.*

*When we were married, stage three consisted of Brian
arriving late smelling of perfume. He made sure I knew
he had just slept with someone. Then almost immediately
he would become morose and would begin lying. My response was anger. I hated him and felt very bad about
myself.*

*In stage four, "the hook," Brian would give me a look
of love and need and tell me of his genuine feelings for
me. Now in Carnes' phase of "sincere delusion," he would
promise not to do it again, and said that he would change.
I felt very confused—my gut reaction was that he was sincere, but I also knew that he would soon be acting out
again.*

*Next, in stage five, Brian would be mildly depressed.
He'd be critical of me, trying to get me to feel down too. My
reaction was to feel strong. I was glad he felt down, and
I hoped that he would now change and not do it again. I
wanted to get him into a program so that he could change.*

*Stage six was the stage of "terminal loneliness." Brian
was obviously experiencing low self-esteem. Wherever he
was, he wanted to be somewhere else. I tried to hook him
in, to make plans so he would be busy with something he*

liked. I tried to make him happy and I never succeeded. Brian would finally snap out of this by going on the make, and the cycle would begin again.

Since Beverly and Brian share three children with whom he is actively involved, interactions between the couple continue. Beverly found her analysis of Brian's cycle and her responses to be helpful in changing her own behavior. Recognizing that some particularly attractive behavior on his part is but a phase in his cycle has helped her avoid being hooked in. She and Brian repeated the same cycle dozens of times over the many years of their marriage; currently, by identifying his actions as a predictable part of the cycle, it is easier for Beverly to detach emotionally from him.

The Cost: Tolerating Emotional Abuse

Because her life is so focused on her husband that existence without him is intolerable, the coaddict is willing to put up with abusive behavior a person with more self-esteem would not tolerate. Cynthia Koestler, the healthy 55-year-old woman who committed suicide together with her very ill, elderly husband, described their relationship in her autobiography. Her father had committed suicide when she was ten years old, and at age nineteen she was still complaining of "a paralyzing lack of self-assurance."[3] When Cynthia first met Arthur, she was an insecure, unassertive, self-effacing young woman of 22 who was thrilled to have obtained a job as secretary to a well-known writer. Arthur Koestler was then 44 years old, an arrogant man with violent moods, frequent depressions, and a thirst for new female conquests. All this was clearly apparent to Cynthia in their first few meetings. She notes that he appeared to be quite enraged at some minor transgression by the housekeeper. He drank a great deal, was arrested once for hitting a police officer while drunk, and had hangovers.

About a year after Cynthia first met him, he married another woman. On his wedding night he got drunk, argued with his bride, and drove away to spend the night alone.

Arthur was often depressed. His low self-esteem led a friend to comment, "We all have inferiority complexes of various sizes, but yours isn't a complex—it's a cathedral."[4] He apparently compensated for this with compulsive sexual activity; every new woman was a potential conquest. He recognized this in himself, reporting that he had "a persistent and well-nigh pathologic streak of promiscuity in my youth and early middle age." He collected women, referring to them as his harem. He complained in his diary that "my harem is wearing me out."

Entitling part of his notebook, "Chronology of an Obsession," he described his despair when a certain woman turned him down. He recovered from this terrible experience by seducing a different woman: "Whilst sitting at a table in a crowded bar he saw an Italian girl with her fiancé sitting at the far side of the room, and was unable to take his eyes off her. He carried her off for the night and was thrilled by this feat."[5] Undoubtedly what added to the thrill was that he won her over from another man. Later, when Cynthia, his lover, arrived in London for a brief stay, Arthur asked her to find a room for the Italian woman for the night. In her journal, Cynthia documented this and other episodes in an accepting and nonjudgmental way. In fact, she reacted to Arthur's story about stealing the woman away from her fiancé by asking for details because Cynthia was "thrilled by the exploit."

Despite the clues that Cynthia had about Arthur from their first meeting (or perhaps because of the clues) she found herself very attracted to him. After their very first meeting she wondered vaguely what he would be like in bed. His friends warned her against falling for him, but to no avail; she had already made him the center of her life and had given him the power to make her happy. "When Arthur left, I existed somehow. In the mornings I got up;

at night I went to bed and cared not whether I slept or did not sleep. I was conscious only of a pain in my heart which seemed to radiate to my lungs, stomach, and liver. Could a heartache be experienced not only figuratively but literally as well?''[6] When he didn't pay attention to her, she wrote, ''Worst of all, the brief illusion of being at times close to him faded, died, and was supplanted by a fathomless void.''

During this time, Arthur was married to another woman. When she decided to leave him, Cynthia was sorry: ''Life would never be the same again without her there. Like a devoted dog, I was happiest when I was together with both of them.'' Cynthia considered herself Arthur's slave; she signed her letters to him, ''your slavey.'' To be with him, she followed him from city to city, giving up jobs to return to him as soon as he asked for her. She attempted to do everything for him perfectly, and felt ''filled with guilt'' or ''black with guilt'' whenever she thought she had displeased him. Her moods swung from high to low depending on where she thought she stood with him.

Arthur Koestler knew very well how Cynthia felt about him. How did he treat her? ''Abominably,'' wrote George Mikes, a friend of Arthur's.[7] He humiliated her in front of other people and emphasized her mistakes. But ''Cynthia did not insist on being a person; she was content to be a function.'' Arthur's opinion of Cynthia's devotion was that it was boring. ''Cynthia—toujours là [always there],'' he wrote in his journal.

Cynthia never knew where she stood with him, which must have added to the attraction he had for her.

As always, he was unpredictably unpredictable and this side of him, fascinating though it was, had the effect of scattering my poor feelings in all directions, as if a whirlwind had been through them. I was constantly receiving some sort of jolt, of which Arthur of course was quite unaware. Sometimes I felt happy, at other times I went home with a sinking heart.[8]

She constantly sought his approval. "When he told me in a joking way that I was the favorite, I felt awestruck." But she knew how Arthur really felt about her. She wrote:

> I had often wondered whether he knew who was beside him at night, for sometimes an arm reached over to feel or he turned his head in the semi-darkness, as if he wasn't sure. I vaguely pondered the mystery. Perhaps I should have felt jealous, but I only felt lucky to be sharing his life.[9]

Although she coped with her pain primarily through refusing to recognize his ill-treatment of her, she did have episodes of depression and melancholia.

In 1965, sixteen years after they first met, Arthur and Cynthia were married. For the next eighteen years she continued her slavish devotion to him, and he continued treating her like a slave. Harold Harris writes in his introduction to the Koestlers' book, "It is hardly an exaggeration to say that his life became hers; that she *lived* his life. And when the time came for him to leave it, her life too was at an end."[10] This is a worthy epitaph for a relationship addict.

Like Cynthia Koestler, Jean Harris also gave up her life for the man who so often mistreated her. Currently in prison and likely to remain there for many years, she was living her life through Tarnower even before his death. This competent, intelligent woman was so distorted in her thinking that she believed this treatment was indicative of her lover's love for her. She constantly excused his behavior and tried to persuade herself that he was really there for her emotionally. She believed when she was with him she was safe, whereas away from him she was vulnerable.

Despite Tarnower's mistreatment of her, Jean viewed him through rose-colored glasses and attributed wonderful qualities to their relationship. She considered Tarnower her "sounding board, my oasis, my warm and reassuring friend. . . . Touching base with Hy gave me a feeling of safety and stability so I could cope with whatever traumas life tossed my way."[11]

Not surprisingly, the contrast between fantasy and reality threw Jean into periods of depression that Tarnower treated by giving her amphetamines. At one point she considered consulting a psychiatrist for her depression, and actually telephoned one. But her unwillingness to talk about her feelings overcame her intention to seek help. Instead, she bought a gun with the idea that she could kill herself if life became unbearable. Harris did eventually attempt to use the gun on herself, but killed Tarnower instead.

In thinking about why women choose to stay with emotionally abusive men, some skeptical readers may still feel that economic considerations predominate—that women stay primarily because they have no other financial options. If this were true for all women then one might expect a financially independent woman to leave the relationship if the going got bad. The fact is, however, that even some women who have their own income remain in the relationship far longer than any reasonable person would choose to do. Clearly, finances are not the deciding factor. Here again is Beverly, the wealthy society woman, talking about her relationship with her philandering husband, Brian.

I was lucky to have enough money to do all the things I wanted to and to feel financially independent, but the truth is I never used my money to be independent. Instead I gave all of my money to Brian so he could be in a business by himself and run it the way he wanted. I deluded myself into believing that he just needed time to establish himself

*and then he would support us and I wouldn't have to feel
guilty for the money I used to keep us going. Near the end
he invested "our" money to the point that we didn't have
enough left for groceries. He spent it on things like $50
campaign contributions to impress one of his girlfriends.*

*He never in fourteen years brought home enough money
to support us, but when he realized I was getting ready to
leave him he found a job that paid over $40,000 a year.
This was after bringing home no more than $2,000 in one
year previously. At tax time he'd have a fit because he had
to face that fact. We both always had the means to become
financially independent but chose to lean on each other
and we dragged each other down in a pit of low self-
esteem.*

In Brian and Beverly's addictive relationship, Brian never
had to use his skills to earn a living because Beverly was
always there to bail him out financially. Only when she
was ready to leave him was he forced into supporting himself.

For her part, Beverly saw her family's money as a means
of holding on to Brian and making his life more comfortable. As Brian's affairs became more obvious, Beverly
funneled more and more money into Brian's business in
the hope of showing him how much she cared. Although
she had the means at any time to leave the relationship,
she did not do so until things became intolerable, after
fourteen years of marriage.

Summary

The experiences of Jean Harris and Cynthia Koestler
and of women I interviewed reveal some common characteristics of life among addicted couples. Clues to sex
addiction (and, often, concurrent addiction to alcohol or
other chemicals) are probably present when they first meet
and are, in fact, part of his attraction for her. The woman

chooses to ignore the clues, or to believe that they are not relevant to the relationship, or that she can live with them. Their courtship is very exciting, unpredictable, and intense. These elements continue into the marriage, and keep her hooked even when the going gets rough. Their sexual relationship is often very good, at least for a while. If, in his search for the new and different, he asks her to perform sexual acts with which she is uncomfortable, she agrees because she fears abandonment. On the other hand, their sexual relationship may become more and more routine and thought of as a duty, as he focuses his attention on outside affairs.

In her marriage, she never quite feels secure; there is always the fear of an imminent disaster, most likely of his leaving her. Needing to see him in a positive light, she makes excuses for his hurtful behavior and tries to remember only the good times. For as long as possible, she denies any evidence of his affairs, and if confrontation can no longer be avoided, she believes his promises that he will change. Whenever what he says disagrees with the objective evidence, she prefers to believe what he says. She is always hopeful that things will be better in the future, and usually has an apparently plausible explanation for why they are not that good at the moment.

If she finally hurts enough to begin to pull away from him, he will suddenly find her very attractive and a new challenge. He will again become the ardent, sensitive, concerned lover she remembers from long ago and kept hoping would resurface all these years. Believing that her wish has finally been answered, she gives him another chance, only to find him returning to his usual behavior once she is securely back in the fold. Her friends cannot understand her changes of heart, and eventually stop believing her when she once again talks of leaving him.

He is usually just as dependent on her as she is on him, and the couple is likely to continue indefinitely in their unhealthy dance unless some treatment intervenes. Change will be particularly difficult for her, because her belief that he is everything to her and she cannot live without him is central to the traditional view of romantic love. Every day she cannot help but be exposed to support of this view—in songs, movies, novels, and in conversations with others. He, too, will find widespread societal support for his affairs. These concepts are expanded in the next chapter.

CHAPTER SIX

The Bigger Picture
How Society Supports Addictive Behavior

The essence of codependency is obtaining one's worth from the outside rather than from within. The codependent woman lacks a sense of identity. Her dependence on men for her identity is an essential characteristic of the traditional feminine role in Western society. The traditional wife's role is to support her husband in his career and to live vicariously through his accomplishments, to please him, to maintain a clean home, and, to raise well-behaved children who will make their father proud of them. Her husband is the center of her life. Lacking an independent self, she is dependent on him emotionally and financially. Her primary goal is to be the perfect wife and mother. Although she may decide what to serve for dinner, her husband decides where they should live and how to apportion the family budget.

The traditional woman, as pointed out by Betty Friedan 25 years ago in *The Feminine Mystique*, has no independent self; she exists only for and through her husband and children. She answers the question, "Who am I?" by saying "John's wife" or "Susie's mother," and is expected to be completely fulfilled in those roles. Friedan believed that the core of the problem for women at that time was their lack of identity as separate from men, marriage, and childrearing.

The view that women's main function is to attend to the needs and comforts of men was supported by Sigmund Freud, who believed women were inferior to men because they did not have a penis, and that they naturally envied men because of this lack. He concluded that women felt inferior because of their lack of a male organ and they could only feel whole when they acquired a penis, first by marriage and then by giving birth to a male child. What women were really envious of, according to Betty Friedan, were men's many economic and social advantages in Freud's Victorian society. Men had status, freedom, and pleasures women were denied. Freud erroneously concluded women were biologically inferior when in fact they were socially inferior in his culture.

The traditional role of women places a premium on sexuality, assigning it an unrealistic value in a woman's self-concept. Friedan says:

> For the woman who lives according to the feminine mystique [the belief that the highest value for a woman is the fulfillment of her feminine role as wife and mother], there is no road to achievement, or status, or identity, except the sexual one: the achievement of sexual conquest, status as a desirable sex object, and identity as a sexually successful wife and mother. And yet because sex does not really satisfy these needs, she seeks to buttress her nothingness with things, until often even sex itself, and the husband and children on whom the sexual identity rests, become possessions, things. A woman who is herself only a sexual object, lives finally in a world of objects, unable to touch in others the individual identity she lacks herself.[1]

Such a woman grows up to believe sex is the most important sign of love, and that sex can be exchanged for love and for material possessions.

The inner emptiness women feel in their traditional roles causes much unhappiness and dissatisfaction. Speaking of her mother's peers, Friedan laments:

> In my generation, many of us knew that we did not want to be like our mothers, even when we loved them. We could not help but see their disappointment. Did we understand, or only resent, the sadness, the emptiness, that made them hold too fast to us, try to live our lives, run our fathers' lives, spend their days shopping or yearning for things that never seemed to satisfy them, no matter how much money they cost? Strangely, many mothers who loved their daughters—and mine was one— did not want their daughters to grow up like them either. They knew we needed something more.[2]

The women Friedan wrote about were trying to fill their inner void with externals—with material possessions and by closely controlling the lives of their family members. But their efforts did not succeed in giving them a sense of themselves, an identity apart from their families. Rather, the traditional feminine role in American society succeeded in creating generations of codependents. Read this description of the traditional woman, written by Friedan almost twenty years after *The Feminine Mystique*, and you will recognize the typical traits of the codependent.

> Inauthenticity was bred into women by weakness. Lacking male power in society, she got her power in the family by manipulating and denying the feelings of men and children, and her own real feelings, behind the mask of superficial, sweet, steely rightness. . . . That *perfect* marriage, *perfect* house, *perfect* control of children, also hid some bitter negative feelings about that housewife-mother state of selfless service. Like all de-

pendent people, women couldn't express, even to themselves, the rage such self-denying virtue almost had to breed, and to mask. They took it out on themselves and covertly on husbands and children. The more powerless and envious her state, the more intense her buried rage, the more guilt over that rage, the more rigid the perfection and control over family and home required to mask those shameful feelings.[3]

Thanks to Friedan and other pioneers of feminism, significant progress has been made in the past 25 years in equality in the workplace, and in the availability of jobs that were formerly closed to women. Women who stay at home and fill the traditional housewife role are now barely in the majority. Women comprised over 40 percent of the civilian work force in 1984.

The problem for women now is different. In the second stage of women's liberation, according to Friedan, women lack a real choice; they cannot choose, for example, to have a child as well as to work unless there are viable options available for maternity leave and child care. Women cannot be expected to meet a standard of perfection in the workplace, set in the past by men who had wives to take care of all the details of living, and at the same time meet a standard of perfection in the home, set in the past by women whose entire sense of worth came from being perfect, all-controlling housewives and mothers.[4] Otherwise they are likely to continue to feel inadequate and unequal to the task. The solution is to involve men in the changes, to permit them to choose a lifestyle different from the rigid role which they too have had traditionally, and to enable them to find self-fulfillment in other activities in addition to their jobs.

Unfortunately, even in the 1990s there are many societal pressures that serve to keep women in their traditional codependent roles. In Western society today, romantic love is the accepted basis for marriage. To relinquish to another person the power to make you happy or unhappy is considered the norm in a romantic relationship, as is loyalty to the beloved no matter how bad his behavior. What is called romantic love can be addictive love, as discussed in the Introduction.

Songs, romantic novels, plays, operas, movies, and television stories, bombard us with the message that romance is the most important experience in life, worth any sacrifice—one's personhood or even one's life. Madame Butterfly, a young Japanese girl who is the heroine of the opera *Madame Butterfly*, is thrown out by her family when she marries an American naval officer. When his ship leaves Japan, she waits patiently for three years for his return, defending him against her friends who suggest he's unfaithful. When he finally returns, accompanied by a new American wife, she kills herself. The heroine of the opera *Aida* persuades her lover, Rhadames, to betray his country. Condemned to death for treason to the Egyptian cause, he is placed in a tomb to die from lack of air. She hides in the tomb before it is sealed, and they die together singing a romantic aria. Anna Karenina, heroine of Tolstoy's famous novel with the same name, throws herself under a train for love. In Henrik Ibsen's play, *Peer Gynt*, Solveig waits for Peer Gynt all her life while he fools around with other women.

Brought up in the tradition of the woman who finds life intolerable without her man, some women imitate art in life. Cynthia Koestler, her husband's "devoted dog," was one woman who chose to die with her husband because she couldn't imagine life without him. Jean Harris contemplated a similar solution to her problems when her lover Herman Tarnower rejected her, but in the struggle for her weapon, he died instead. Teenage suicide and suicide attempts are a major medical problem in the United States today. Suicide is the number three cause of death among teenagers, exceeded only by accidents and homicide. Many suicide attempts occur when a romantic relationship takes a bad turn. These young people are following a long romantic tradition that is typified by the story of Romeo and Juliet.

Many love songs are about addictive relationships. They extol suffering, possessiveness, and obstacles to happiness. Country songs frequently endorse the image of the woman who will do anything for her man, patiently waiting at home while he's out drinking or cheating on her. When faced with a decision between his wife and girlfriend, one singer proclaims that if he should have to choose, then everybody would lose. What he would like is "a good-hearted woman in love with a good-timin' man," a woman who would love him no matter how badly he treats her. The caretaker kind of woman who picks an addict because she believes she can fix him is praised in the song "She's the Rock That I Lean On." In this song, the singer acknowledges that no matter what the woman's faults, he will stick by her because she "rescued" him when he was down and out and made him the success he is today.

Men and women who grow up hearing these songs often believe dependency and self-sacrifice are desirable characteristics of romantic relationships. What they don't realize is that what is common in a relationship is not necessarily healthy. The romantic songs and novels don't usually talk about the resentment, anger, and loss of self-esteem that a woman feels whose husband is drinking or cheating and who is not there for her emotionally. They don't talk about her overeating, use of tranquilizers, her headaches or depression, as she tries to live up to her expected role while experiencing all these negative feelings.

Romance Novels

Romance novels, which are read by millions of women, consistently model codependency as the ideal in a romantic relationship. The typical relationship in these books is addictive. Romance novels are an important part of the fantasy life of many women. Approximately 22 million romance readers bought 200 million Harlequin novels in 1982 as well as millions of other romance novels. I believe that it's worth analyzing one in some detail to evaluate the concept of a romantic relationship that it models. To do this, I chose at random a Harlequin novel, *Afraid to Love* by Margaret Mayo,[5] from among the hundreds displayed on the shelves of a bookstore.

In this book the heroine, Ruth—who serves as a role model for many of her readers—falls in love with Matt, an arrogant, abusive, overconfident, violent, and jealous man. She spends her time obsessing about him, feeling responsible for his feelings and actions, feeling hurt and humiliated by him, and falling ever more in love with him.

Robin Norwood has pointed out that codependent women usually have all the clues about a man's character long before they marry him. Rarely does it happen that a healthy relationship suddenly becomes abusive or plagued with problems of drinking or affairs. Instead, the personality traits or behaviors that would turn away another person are what attract the codependent. Matt's arrogance and reputation for leaving women made him all the more appealing to Ruth.

When Ruth encounters Matt on a helicopter six years after he had walked out on her, she experiences humiliation, a feeling that returns again and again through the book. The humiliation and shame serve only to make him more attractive to her. Apparently she does not believe she should feel good around a man. Like the typical sexual coaddict, Ruth confuses sex with love. Whenever in the midst of an argument with Ruth, Matt grabs her and kisses her passionately. She is again convinced that he loves her and doesn't mean all the harsh words he just uttered.

When Ruth insists to Matt that she is no longer in love with him, he responds by violently kissing her, thereby proving to her again that she still cares for him. Ruth does not consciously realize that she wants Matt *because* she views him as despicable, not despite his behavior. She is attracted to him because of the feelings she has with him— the uncertainty, the excitement, the shame, the embarrassment, and the sense of incompetence. The contradiction between common sense and passion is a recurring theme in the novel.

Throughout the book, Ruth reacts rather than acts. Her decisions are based on what she imagines Matt will think of her actions, not on what she wants to do. Ruth's reactions reveal several codependent beliefs: (1) that any kind of attention, even brutal, is a sign of caring; (2) that sex equals love; 3) that her own doubts are to be discounted; and (4) that she doesn't deserve happiness, and therefore ought to take what few tidbits might come her way. At one point, Matt spanks Ruth until she cries out for mercy. An emotionally healthy person who has just been beaten by her boyfriend would probably end the relationship. Ruth, on the other hand, assumes that she deserves the spanking and continues to want Matt.

In summary, the heroine of this novel exhibits the following codependent personality traits: (1) She has low self-esteem. She does not think she deserves much and does not believe that someone would love her for herself. (2) She gives someone else the power to make her happy or unhappy. (3) She thinks she is not whole without a man. (4) She takes blame for another's feelings and behavior, even when the behavior is verbally or physically abusive. (5) She confuses sex and love. (6) She is constantly obsessed with her man. (7) She does not trust her own feelings and ignores the warning signs of problems in a relationship. (8) She is attracted to a man who gives her many clues that he is emotionally unavailable to her.

What can we predict for Ruth and Matt—will they live happily ever after? Hardly. Matt is likely to continue to be uncaring, changeable, and abusive. Ruth's self-esteem will drop further, and she will become more of a martyr, blaming herself for each of Matt's outbursts. She will obsess about him, endlessly trying to figure out how to change him. She will alternately love and hate him. She will probably end up in a shelter for abused women and will ultimately divorce him. As for Matt, he was probably already drinking heavily when they got married, and his drinking is likely to accelerate. He will probably have a few affairs before Ruth has the courage to leave him. He will have no trouble finding another partner to take Ruth's place.

Some may argue that readers of romance novels know they are reading fiction and do not apply the same rules to their own lives, that readers of such novels want an escape from their ordinary routine and understand these stories are not realistic. Many readers of romance novels consume 30 titles per month. Romance novels constitute approximately one out of every four paperback books sold in the United States. And for those who are more visually inclined, original romances are now available on videocassettes for TV viewing. I believe a steady diet of romance stories cannot help but influence the reader's perception of romantic love and is likely to spill over into the way she behaves in her own relationships. Romance novels affirm the codependent's belief system, support her lifestyle, and aid in her rationalizing, minimizing, justifying, and blaming.

Advice Books

Another influence on women's thinking is the nonfiction advice book. If today's marriage has problems, the wife is still likely to blame herself and to feel that she is the only one who needs to change to improve the relationship. This may explain the appeal of the best-seller *The Total Woman* by Marabel Morgan, whose underlying theme is that if you can accept your husband, admire him, adapt to him, appreciate him, and in general cater to all his needs while ignoring your own, you can "put sizzle back into your marriage."[6] The phenomenal success of this book indicates that its basic assumptions about the nature of the male-female relationship were in agreement with what its readers already believed.

Marabel Morgan was very much a traditional woman. She saw herself as a loving wife and mother, who coped beautifully with difficult situations and never raised her voice. She waited for her husband to come home at the end of the day so she could "love and care for him." Nevertheless, her husband considered her to be uptight and no fun to be with, so she undertook a program of change. Believing that she was solely to blame for the problems in her marriage, Morgan constructed a program that requires the woman to make many changes without asking anything of the man. Her program worked so well that her husband's behavior changed too—he bought her a new refrigerator-freezer, for which she had nagged him for years without result, and he gave her permission at long last to redecorate the family room.

Marabel Morgan's personal program was so successful that she began workshops to teach it to others. Her book includes several success stories.

> Another graduate appeared in a sheer, black lace gown. Her husband was speechless when he opened the front door. . . . She told me later that the evening was not only lots of fun, but he had also suggested a cruise to Nassau the following week![7]

Another woman "lost fifteen pounds in six weeks. Her husband loved her new body so much that he bought her a whole new wardrobe. You've never seen a happier woman.'' In this case, the woman earned her husband's love by becoming sexier, and he rewarded her with new clothes. The connection between love, sex, and material possessions is a recurrent theme in the book. This is stated explicitly:

> A woman expresses her love by words and expects words in return. A man expresses his love by actions— by sexual intercourse, bringing home the paycheck, or buying his wife a house.[8]

This passage illustrates a typical codependent core belief—that to a man, sex equals love. If the man is sexual with his wife, this means that he loves her.

Another of the core beliefs of the codependent that is shared by Morgan is that a woman must earn a man's love, she is not worthy of being loved for herself. Keeping the house in order is one recommended way of doing this.

> Every man appreciates order and he'll be especially glad to find it in his own home. He will be pleased with you, your accomplishments, and your sense of well-being. When you're organized and efficient, his flame of love will begin to flicker and burn.[9]

The tools for making your marriage come alive consist essentially of (1) organizing your time better so as to be a better cook and housekeeper; (2) making your man feel like a king by accepting him, admiring him, adapting to him, and appreciating him; (3) adding variety to your sex life; and (4) improving your communication with him. Your husband will be so grateful that he will treat you better.

All of these activities are very reasonable and are indeed likely to improve a marriage. A problem arises only when these activities are promoted as prerequisites for winning the husband's love.

Morgan recommends that the Total Woman make a list of her goals and work to accomplish them. "A salesman's wife told me that her short-term goals were to run a smooth home, cook good meals, be a listening mother, be more fun and less frumpy." These goals are all directed at pleasing other people; absent from the list were such items as pursuing her own interests, having fun (rather than being fun), or getting together with friends. Her own needs were not considered.

Part of the Total Woman's job is to admire her husband.

> You are the one person your husband needs to make him feel special. He married you because he thought you were the most enchanting girl of all. The world may bestow awards on him, but above all others, he needs your admiration. He needs it to live. Without it his motivation is gone. . . .[10]
>
> Put your husband's tattered ego back together again at the end of each day. That's not using feminine wiles; that is the very nature of love. If you fulfill his needs, he won't have to escape some other way.[11]

These paragraphs imply two codependent beliefs: (1) An addictive relationship is the norm—your husband needs you in order to feel whole. (2) You are responsible for your husband's feelings and behavior. If you don't fulfill his needs, you cannot blame him if he has affairs; you can only blame yourself.

The next step in making your marriage work is to adapt to your husband. Here is what Morgan advised one unhappy woman:

> She was tired of Norm's never-ending football schedule, his endless appearances and speaking engagements, and her having to bear sole responsibility

for disciplining her children. In fact, the heartbreaking question of her little boy, "Isn't Daddy ever coming home for dinner again?" prompted her to seek a solution.

Adapting was the only thing I knew that would work. "Bobbie," I told her, "adapt to his way of life wholeheartedly, even if he doesn't come home for weeks. When he is home, make life so attractive he won't want to leave. Don't make him feel guilty and don't complain. Instead, treat him like a king and cater to his needs."[12]

Morgan's advice to Bobbie was essentially to forget her own needs and those of her son.

Sex occupies an important place in the Total Woman's plan for improving her marriage. This is not surprising, since Morgan seems to equate sex with love.

This is all your husband asks from you. He wants the girl of his dreams to be feminine, soft, and touchable when he comes home. That's his need. If you are dumpy, stringy, or exhausted, he's sorry he came. That first look tells him your nerves are shot, his dinner is probably shot, and you'd both like to shoot the kids. It's a bad scene. Is it any wonder so many men come home late, if at all?[13]

The implication here is that if the husband stays out late or plays around, it's the woman's fault, because she didn't look attractive enough when he comes home. That she may have had a hard day is irrelevant.

Morgan understands that men get sexually bored with their wives. Her solution? Change your appearance.

You can be lots of different women to him. Costumes provide variety without him ever leaving home. I believe that every man needs excitement and high adventure at home. Never let him know what to expect when he opens the front door; make it like opening a surprise package.[14]

Regarding the woman who met her husband at the door dressed in a sheer black lace gown and was rewarded with an exciting evening and with a cruise to Nassau, Morgan concludes that when a man's need for an attractive and available wife is met, he'll be so grateful that he will begin to meet his wife's needs. This statement clearly implies the codependent core belief that no one would love me as I am. She implies that a man can be expected to begin to meet a woman's needs only after she has dressed and behaved seductively. Morgan amplifies the same theme a little later. Again referring to her husband's arrival home at the end of the day, she tells us, "His senses will be anticipating food and sex. If he wants to make love tonight, love him extravagantly and wastefully. If you pour out love unconditionally, he'll want to love you in return."[15] That is, the woman must love the man *unconditionally* so that he will love her *conditionally*!

The Total Woman does not let angry feelings show.

An angry outburst can scar your husband's emotions and create barriers between you. Stop and think before you blurt out what you might regret later on. Prepare to express your feelings without becoming emotional. . . . No matter what his reaction, your final step in dealing with anger is to forgive your husband and forget the incident.[16]

This advice suggests that men's emotions are fragile and therefore women are responsible for their husband's emotions. It also tells the woman that her feelings don't count and that feelings must be covered up, a classic rule in dysfunctional families. If she follows this advice, she is likely to become resentful and depressed and to feel like a failure.

In summary, the woman who reads *The Total Woman* and incorporates its principles into her life will accept (1) that her husband's love is conditional and that she must buy it by being a perfect housekeeper, a sexy lover, and an admirer and servant of her husband; (2) that her own needs and feelings don't count; (3) that her husband needs her in order to feel whole and that she is responsible for how he feels; (4) that her husband has all the power in the relationship; (5) that if her husband leaves her or is unfaithful, it is her fault; (6) that she can control her husband by what she does or does not do; and (7) that to a man, sex equals love. If she can get him to be sexual with her, then this will prove that he loves her. The Total Woman is thus a Total Codependent.

What is the effect on women of following Marabel Morgan's advice? Betty Friedan writes:

> Lecturing in Texas recently, several months after Marabel Morgan ran one of her "Total Woman" courses, I heard from some psychologists of the devastation to women, who had flogged themselves on to new depths of self-degradation and denial with these ostrich feathers and Saran Wrap maneuvers, when their husbands, in fact, did run off (maybe faster?) with the younger "chicks" from the office.[17]

Nevertheless, Morgan continues to promulgate the same tactics to get rewards and attention from husbands. In her latest advice book, *The Electric Woman*, she says:

> Your husband may be hoping that one night you'll meet him in an outrageously sexy outfit. If you do, he'll never forget it. And I guarantee, he'll never again bring anyone home for dinner without calling first. Dressing up in some sexy, outrageous outfit is guaranteed to pro-

duce results. You may not be able to predict what kind of results, but like the cross-eyed javelin thrower, you'll at least get his attention![18]

The implication here is that without such extreme measures, without casting yourself as an "outrageous" sex object, your husband will not pay attention to you. Moreover, the reward she describes—that your husband will call you in advance when he brings home a dinner guest—is not a sexual one; it consists of being treated with respect. In other words, to be treated as a human being the wife is advised to offer her husband sex. Thus, after a dozen years of lecturing and talking with women, Morgan still advises that a woman needs to *buy* her husband's attention and respect—and the currency is sex.

Social Institutions

A codependent belief system is promoted not only through books and the media, but, more pervasively, through the cultural institutions of school and church, which teach us to avoid feelings, strive for perfection, be dishonest, and control other people. This was addressed by Anne Wilson Schaef, a therapist who has taken a sociological approach to the study of codependency.

In *Co-dependence: Misunderstood-Mistreated*, Schaef points out that our educational institutions traditionally encourage us to express what we think, not what we feel.

In learning to respond to literature and art, for example, we are taught that it is not enough to "feel" something about a poem or piece of art. We must be able to analyze it and offer logical, rational reasons why it is good or bad. If we cannot justify, rationalize, and explain our response, it has no validity. It is not just that our schools do not educate us to know, explore, and express our feelings, they educate us *out* of them. They prepare us to fit into a society where "frozen feelings" are the norm.[19]

Traditional schools also teach that perfection is possible; the concept of grades assumes that perfection is attainable and should be sought, thereby setting individuals up to fail. In several areas, according to Schaef, schools teach the students dishonesty. In one example the principal advised a student who disagreed with a teacher to go along with the teacher's approach rather than to stand up for his beliefs. This type of advice teaches some students to try to beat the system rather than to behave with integrity. Finally, schools focus almost exclusively on logical, rational, analytic thinking, to the exclusion of intuitive thinking and feelings. They train us to focus on figuring things out, and persuade us that we have failed if we cannot figure out a problem. The belief that everything can be figured out if we can only analyze it thoroughly enough can lead to the type of obsessive thinking that is typical of codependency.

The other major cultural institution that promotes addictive thinking, according to Schaef, is the church. She writes:

> The perfect nun is always happy, always caring, always pious. In order to be this way, she must ignore, suppress, and freeze her normal human emotions. The same may be said of the "good Christian" woman, who is always sweet, caring, even-tempered, never angry, and always long-suffering. To try to fit this image is to deny our humanity and be basically dishonest. I have come to believe that "niceness" and dishonesty are inextricably bound together. . . ."[20]

In order to be what the church says we should be, it is frequently necessary to deny who we are. No one is always nice. No one is always even-tempered. No one is always willing to be at another's disposal. No one is always willing to sacrifice herself or himself for others. The co-dependent is, however, and co-dependence is considered a disease. In training us to be "nice," the church actively trains us to be co-dependents.[21]

Like the school, the church also expects its members, as well as its priests and ministers, to strive for perfection. Not only does the church set up an impossible goal, it also promises its members that it will help them achieve perfection, and in this way it tries to make itself indispensable to its members.

Finally, the church teaches its members that they can control their lives and destiny by doing the right thing and being the right kind of person. This, according to Schaef, is a fallacy; a person can influence his life, but cannot control it. "Thinking that is based on control leads straight to the addictive process and the disease of codependence."[22]

Thus, books, the visual media, cultural institutions, and the historical position of women in Western society all promote codependent behaviors and values. Western society as we know it can be viewed as an outgrowth of the male personality, since men dominate government, politics, economics, science, and even literature, art, and music. Is women's codependency a cultural phenomenon that affects all women and not specifically those who grow up in dysfunctional families? I believe that it is a question of degree. All women in Western society have some difficulty developing an identity and self-esteem, but those from dysfunctional families are even less able to do so and are even more dependent on others for their sense of value and self-worth.

Men Who Have Affairs

Women in Western society have traditionally been viewed as sexual objects, placed on earth for men's enjoyment. This view is still much in evidence today. Magazine advertisements and television commercials use sexy women to sell cars, after-shave lotion, television sets and other electronic equipment, and a multitude of other products likely to appeal to men. The implication is that if the man buys the product, he will get the woman as well.

Young men compare notes on their success with women: they talk about having "scored" the night before as they "screwed" or "nailed" someone. Even their language indicates that females are but pawns in a masculine competition. Given these ways of treating women as objects, it is not surprising that many men grow up believing that a casual affair is a minor matter; a one-night stand when away from home may, to some men, mean no more than eating an extra dessert. If a sex object becomes available, why should a man not enjoy?

Thus, just as societal factors support women in their failure to develop an identity, society also supports men who have affairs and deny that they have a problem. Society's traditional view is that not only is a man naturally polygamous, but it is manly for him to take advantage of opportunities for sexual involvement, even if he is married, as long as he is not found out.

A conspiracy of silence protects men who have affairs. Because sexual conquest is seen as admirable, most men do not hesitate to reveal to their colleagues the existence of an affair. They implicitly count on the cooperation of other men, who will not tell the man's wife no matter how well they know her. By protecting each other from experiencing the consequences of their behavior, men act as enablers for each others' affairs.

A man who refuses to drink at a party saying, "I don't

drink; I'm a recovering alcoholic,'' is often treated with respect. But a man who at a convention declines to accompany his colleagues in their pursuit of a one-night stand, is likely to be accused of being henpecked, or a prude, or afraid to enjoy the good things in life. A married, recovering sex addict who told his philandering business partner that he was in a self-help program designed to prevent him from having any more affairs, was greeted with laughing disbelief. ''I never let *my* marriage interfere with my social life!'' his partner told him. ''Your wife must be laying *some* guilt trip on you!'' Another of his partners, newly married, added, ''If your wife was emptying your balls every night, like my wife is, then you wouldn't have to look elsewhere,'' implying that the sex addict's only real problem was his wife's unwillingness to have sex with him often enough.

The absence of American society's recognition that affairs can be a compulsive, detrimental behavior pattern, coupled with daily evidence of married men who are having brief or lengthy affairs with no apparent adverse consequences, can severely strain a recovering sex addict's commitment to change.

In discussing the problems of recovery from addiction, psychologist Stephanie Brown, author of *Treating the Alcoholic*, gave an example of an alcoholic whose husband believed she should be able to drink the special wine they had stocked in their cellar. They had bought the wine on a special trip together and he was very hurt that she wouldn't drink just one glass.

This example illustrates what is perhaps the toughest problem of all: maintaining the identity as an alcoholic and the belief in loss of control in an environment that fails to comprehend the significance of those beliefs. It requires a strong support group and constant reminders about what it means to be alcoholic to counter environmental pressures to drink and control it.[23]

Exactly the same can be said for the man who recognizes that he is addicted to sex and that he cannot control it by willpower. The disbelief of his friends and their encouragement to continue the same behaviors will make it much more difficult for him to maintain his recognition that he is an addict and his commitment to his support group, psychotherapy, or whatever means he has been using to maintain his new, monogamous lifestyle.

CHAPTER SEVEN

"There's no reason to stop— I'm not going to die from too much sex"

I was pregnant and I knew he was having affairs with more than one woman. He came to tell me he had a sexually transmitted disease and his doctor had told him he had to tell everyone he had sex with to be checked. I was furious at first and then I was mortified. How was I going to face the family doctor I had known for years? I made the appointment and I went with mixed feelings: I was finally going to justifiably tell someone else what he had done. The other mixed feeling I had was I had to admit while I was carrying this man's child and it appeared on the outside I had an ideal marriage, I was unable to keep him sexually faithful to me.

I told the doctor the reason I had come and I cried. I was ashamed. This was not the image I had projected to my doctor in the past. He reassured me, "It happens all the time," but offered no advice. I needed to hear more. I returned to my husband and resumed sexual relations with him. I certainly knew now that I ran the risk of infecting the baby and of having to go back to the doctor, but the sex was more important to me at that time.

Beverly shudders when she remembers how oblivious she was to her own responsibility for her health and that of her unborn child. At times when she is tempted to lay all the blame on her former husband, recalling this period in her life helps remind her that she was just as troubled as he was. Her addiction to her husband was more important to her than her own health or the baby's. Knowing that she was risking contracting another sexually transmitted disease (STD), she nevertheless continued to have sex with him.

Beverly is not alone. Thousands of women who know or suspect that their husbands are having sex with others continue to sleep with them. They feel caught in a double bind. On the one hand, they are fearful of catching a STD; but on the other, they believe if they deny their husbands sex then they will surely drive their spouses into the arms of the other women or men. Given the choice between their own health and their addictive relationship, they are far more likely to give the addictive relationship a higher priority. The coaddict's lifelong pattern is to put her own needs last, and this goes for her physical health as well as her happiness. Moreover, since one of her basic irrational beliefs is that sex is the most important sign of love, she will risk acquiring a STD in order to obtain this sign of "love" from her husband.

This decision is easy to understand. Denying a husband sex is not an easy thing for any woman, whether codependent or not. It is natural to want the intimacy of a sexual relationship with one's husband and it is difficult for any woman to decide to withhold sex.

The irony in the coaddict's fear of depriving her husband of sex is that giving him sex is not likely to prevent him from seeking it outside the marriage. The fact is the wife cannot control her husband's addiction; it is part of her codependency to believe she can. Thus, by risking a STD she cannot accomplish her goal of preventing him from having affairs. It merely forces him to find some other excuse besides, "My wife won't make love with me." Meanwhile, the price she pays is constant worry about disease.

In my practice I have seen several middle-aged women who come in periodically to be checked for venereal disease. These are women who have made the choice to continue having sexual relations with their husbands who they know are having affairs. They have decided their current situation is preferable to getting a divorce and living alone. They are unwilling or unable to consider making a change.

In the past, when gonorrhea and syphilis were the most likely STDs that one could catch, a periodic check for STDs was reasonable, because both of these diseases are easily cured with antibiotics. Unfortunately, the STDs of the 1980s are viral diseases, not curable by antibiotics and often permanent or even fatal. Thus, a STD check is no longer a viable option for the woman who values her health. Avoiding sex with a potentially infected partner is the only reliable alternative.

For some STDs, visual inspection of a partner may decrease the risk of acquiring the disease. For others, use of a condom improves your odds. Avoiding certain sex practices may help prevent catching some diseases. It is my goal in this chapter to give you information about the most important STDs, thus enabling you to make an informed decision about continuing to have sex with your husband if he is also having sexual relations with others. I will cover (1) the traditional STDs—syphilis and gonorrhea, (2) chlamydia, an infection caused by a one-celled organism, now considered the most prevalent STD in the United States, and (3) the viral STDs—AIDS, herpes, hepatitis B, and venereal warts. I will also discuss the most common causes of vaginal discharge—Gardnerella, Trichomonas, and Candida (yeast).

Until recently, when most people heard the term *venereal disease* or VD (now termed sexually transmitted disease, or STD), they knew it meant syphilis and gonorrhea.

Before the days of antibiotics these diseases were justly feared. Gonorrhea can cause sterility and syphilis can be fatal. The chemist Paul Ehrlich spent years searching for the "magic bullet" to cure syphilis, and thought he had found it in 1909 when he synthesized Salvarsan, an arsenic preparation.

Isak Dinesen, author of *Out of Africa* and heroine of the film of the same name, spent most of her life combating syphilis, which she caught from her husband in 1914, shortly after they were married. She had traveled from Denmark to East Africa to marry Bror Blixen. Later she would tell a friend that she discovered, sometime after their first year of marriage, that he was having several affairs and lying to her about them.[1]

After several months of illness with high fevers, fatigue, joint pains, and depression, Dinesen returned to Europe to seek treatment. She was first seen by a doctor in France, who diagnosed syphilis. The doctor told her that she would need long and painful therapy if she were ever to be cured permanently, and there was no assurance that she could be. She then returned to Denmark, where for three months she received weekly injections of Salvarsan, a toxic compound with unpleasant side effects. At the end of this period, spinal fluid tests showed that the disease had been arrested, and she was no longer contagious. The following year she again made the long journey to East Africa.

Dinesen's syphilis infection was not cured, and several years later she began to experience new symptoms. She developed syphilis of the spine. For the rest of her life she had difficulty walking, an impaired sense of balance, severe abdominal pains, and episodes of severe vomiting. By the time penicillin became available in the 1940s, Dinesen had been battling syphilis for 30 years. Her body had sustained too much damage to be cured by antibiotics. She had several operations to try to relieve her pain, but by 1960, when she was 75 years old, the ravages of syphilis had made it too painful for her to walk or even to stand. She was grateful when death came two years later.

Syphilis in the pre-antibiotic era was a fearsome disease, a potential life sentence of pain and shame. Although to forgive a husband in those days must have been just as difficult as it is today, at least now a few injections of penicillin will cure the disease. In the antibiotic era, the worst aspect of acquiring a case of syphilis or gonorrhea is its implication for a marriage.

Gonorrhea

Gonorrhea is caused by a bacterium, *Neisseria gonorrhoeae*. Cases of gonorrhea are supposed to be reported to the Public Health Service. About a million cases are reported annually. In addition, it is estimated that another 1.5 million cases go unreported each year in the United States. More men are affected than women. In infected women, symptoms begin two to eight days after intercourse. Only about 25 percent of infected women have symptoms, but all infected women, whether they have symptoms or not, can transmit the disease to their sexual partner. Except for newborns, who can acquire gonorrhea infection in their eyes as they pass through the birth canal, sexual activity is the only way to acquire gonorrhea. It can't be caught from toilet seats or towels.

Gonorrhea is spread more easily from man to woman than from woman to man. A woman has a 50 percent chance of contracting gonorrhea after exposure to an infected man, whereas a man has only about a 20 percent chance of getting it after sex with an infected woman. About 30 to 40 percent of infected men have no symptoms, and will probably not realize they are infected. Men and women who have no symptoms but who give the disease to others is the major reason for the continuing spread of gonorrhea in the United States.

In women, gonorrhea can cause inflammation of the

uterine cervix which can result in a vaginal discharge. Infection of the fallopian tubes, the tubes through which the egg passes from the ovary on its way to the uterus, occurs in about 20 percent of cases and results in a disease called salpingitis or pelvic inflammatory disease (PID). Salpingitis can also be caused by other organisms, but about half of all cases are caused by gonorrhea. The symptoms of the disease are fever, lower abdominal pain, and a vaginal discharge.

Infection of the fallopian tubes can cause them to be blocked off, permanently, resulting in sterility. With each episode of salpingitis there is a 15 percent risk of sterility. Salpingitis also increases the risk of a pregnancy occurring within the fallopian tubes (ectopic pregnancy), a dangerous event that can lead to death from hemorrhage. Salpingitis is responsible for half of the ectopic pregnancies in the United States.

About 40 percent of women who have a gonorrhea infection of the cervix also have the gonococcus bacterium growing in their anus and rectum. This is usually because vaginal secretions have contaminated the rectal area. Most of the time there are no rectal symptoms. In male homosexuals, infection of the anorectal area is acquired through anal intercourse with an infected man. Occasionally there is rectal burning, pain, and discharge, but more often there are no symptoms. Infection without symptoms can persist for months in the rectum and is probably the major reservoir of the gonococcus bacterium in male homosexuals. An untreated man is thus potentially infectious for months.

Another complication of gonorrhea is arthritis of one or two joints. This occurs in 1 to 2 percent of people who have gonorrhea. One or two joints, often the wrist, knee, or ankle, become hot, painful, and swollen. A few days before the onset of the arthritis, there is often a fever and a skin rash. The rash and arthritis are completely cured by antibiotic treatment.

Another location for gonorrhea infection is the throat.

Infection most often results from oral-genital contact with an infected woman (cunnilingus), and not from kissing, so that people with gonorrhea throat infections are women and gay men. There are usually no symptoms; however, a person with a gonorrhea throat infection can transmit the disease to a man by fellatio.

Gonorrhea is diagnosed by inserting a swab into the vagina, rectum, penis, or throat and sending the swab to the microbiology laboratory which determines whether the organisms that grow out several days later are gonococci.

When a woman contracts gonorrhea during pregnancy, she risks giving birth to an infected baby. Passage of the baby through an infected birth canal can result in gonorrheal infection of the newborn's eyes (ophthalmia neonatorum). To prevent blindness from this disease, almost all babies in the U.S. have special eyedrops put into their eyes at birth. Pregnant women who have untreated gonorrhea have an increased risk of miscarriage.

Currently there is an increasing incidence of gonorrhea infections that are resistant to penicillin. Fortunately, new antibiotics have been developed that can cure the resistant strains of the disease.

The chief symptom of gonorrhea in men is a thick yellow discharge from the penis (''the drip''). The discharge is loaded with gonococci. A good precaution for both sexes is to have the man use a condom—this will protect him from acquiring the disease and will prevent him from transmitting it via infected secretions.

Syphilis

The second STD, syphilis, is forty times less common than gonorrhea. The cause is *Treponema pallidum*, a corkscrew-shaped bacterium called a spirochete. About 95 percent of infections are acquired by sexual intercourse. A moist kiss on the mouth of someone who has a syphilitic sore on the lips or tongue explains a small percentage of cases. Babies can contract the disease from the mother before birth.

About three weeks after intercourse with an infected person, a sore appears at the site of inoculation, usually the penis of the man or the labia (the vulva) of the woman. A sore may develop on the lip after oral sex with an infected partner. A hard, painless ulcer (chancre) then develops. The ulcer teems with spirochetes and is very contagious. If not treated, it heals itself in two to four weeks. The disease is not cured. About two to eight weeks after the primary ulcer heals, a flu-like illness, called secondary syphilis, develops that consists of fever, malaise, muscle aches, and a body rash. Lymph nodes in the neck, armpits, and groin enlarge and become hard lumps. In two to six weeks all the symptoms go away, even without treatment. About two-thirds of people have no further symptoms. In about one-third of cases, however, serious complications develop later, especially in the heart and nervous system. These can eventually cause death.

Syphilis in pregnancy can harm the baby. Treatment of the mother during the first sixteen weeks of pregnancy prevents infection of the fetus. Later infection of the mother can result in the birth of an infected child. The baby may have the usual symptoms of secondary syphilis. In addition, it might have some permanent abnormalities of the facial bones and teeth which are typical of congenital syphilis.

Syphilis is most contagious in the first year after infection, less so each following year, and is not at all contagious after four years. Syphilis is diagnosed by means of a blood test. However, the blood test is abnormal in only 25 percent of infected people in the first week, 50 percent in the second week, and 75 percent in the third week. Thus, the test is reliable only at about four weeks after initial infection. Before this, diagnosis is made by microscopic examination of material scraped from the painless ulcer.

In the United States today, as many as two-thirds of the cases of syphilis are in homosexual men. Married men who have affairs with other men are at a higher risk of developing this disease and so, therefore, are their wives.

Syphilis is easily treated with antibiotics. To minimize the risk of catching this disease, do not have sex with a partner who has a sore on his penis.

Chlamydia

The most common STD in the United States today is Chlamydia, a frequent cause of non-gonococcal urethritis (NGU) in men (also termed nonspecific urethritis or NSU). It is also the most common cause in young men of acute infection of the epididymis, an organ in the scrotum. *Chlamydia trachomatis* is an organism that is often acquired together with gonorrhea.

A common scenario is the man who is treated for gonorrhea with penicillin, improves, but one to two weeks later again develops a discharge from the penis. The reason is this: The incubation period for Chlamydia infection of the urethra (NGU) is one to two weeks. This means that symptoms of NGU do not begin until a week or so after the symptoms of gonorrhea. Chlamydia is resistant to penicillin and ampicillin, the drugs most frequently used to treat gonorrhea. Thus, just at the time that the gonorrhea infection resolves, the untreated Chlamydia infection appears. About 30 to 60 percent of men who are treated for gonorrhea are subsequently found to have Chlamydia as well. For this reason doctors now routinely treat gonorrhea with drugs that are also effective against Chlamydia.

Like gonorrhea, Chlamydia is sexually transmitted. The organism can be recovered from the cervix of about 60 to 80 percent of female sexual partners of infected men. Although they often have no symptoms, infected women can transmit the infection to their partners. If not treated, cervical infections in women can last over 20 months, all the while being spread to their sexual partners.

The primary symptom of Chlamydia infection in women is the so-called "urethral syndrome," which consists of frequent urination and burning when urinating. These are also the typical symptoms of urinary tract infection (cystitis), but analysis of the urine does not reveal the usual high concentration of bacteria. In addition to infecting the urethra, Chlamydia can infect the cervix and travel up to the fallopian tubes. Chlamydia is an increasingly frequent cause of pelvic inflammatory disease in women, a condition that can cause sterility.

The most accurate diagnosis of Chlamydia infection is made by obtaining a specimen of secretions from the cervix and growing out the organism using special tissue culture techniques. This is an expensive test, whereas treatment with antibiotics is effective and inexpensive. Therefore, many physicians will simply treat with antibiotics if they suspect a Chlamydia infection on the basis of the urethral syndrome or yellow pus on the cervix.

The chief symptom of Chlamydia infection in a man is the presence of a thin watery discharge from the urethra of the penis. To minimize your risk of acquiring this infection, do not have sexual relations with a man who has a urethral discharge. Wearing a condom will prevent transmission of the infection.

AIDS

The acquired immunodeficiency syndrome (AIDS) is the most fearsome of the new STDs. This disease was at first predominant among men but it is now affecting more and more women each year. At the end of 1986, women constituted approximately 7 percent of all adult AIDS patients in the United States.[2] Women need to worry about their risk of catching this disease.

The day after a television program on AIDS appeared

that featured interviews of several women AIDS victims, my office received dozens of telephone calls from women requesting a blood test for AIDS. The 26 January 1987 issue of *Newsweek* magazine, which has approximately three million subscribers, had a full-page ad showing the worried face of a young woman, who says, in large letters, "I'll do a lot for love, but I'm not ready to die for it." The ad, clearly directed at women, proceeds to inform them that "the proper use of a LifeStyles Brand Condom can greatly reduce the chances of you or your partner contracting AIDS." Furthermore, they "help prevent other sexually transmitted diseases like herpes and gonorrhea." This was the first time I had seen condoms advertised in a major news magazine—and it is particularly revealing of the climate of the times that the ad contained no mention of contraception, the traditional purpose of using a condom. The major concern of sexually active women in the AIDS era is no longer unwanted pregnancy—it is now fear of contracting a fatal disease.

AIDS was first diagnosed in homosexual men in 1981. These previously healthy young men developed diseases usually seen only in people whose immune systems were somehow damaged, for example, by disease, cancer chemotherapy, or radiation. Presently this disease is fatal. The cause is a virus, the human immunodeficiency virus (HIV, formerly called HLTV-III), which damages the body's immune system. The virus is transmitted through blood and body secretions, much like hepatitis B. Among male homosexuals, the virus is passed primarily through semen. In the other high-risk groups—intravenous drug abusers and hemophiliacs receiving blood products to halt their bleeding—the virus is transferred through the blood.

The symptoms of AIDS are varied. Often there is weight loss, fatigue, coughing, and a severe pneumonia. Purple or brown patches or nodules may appear on the skin. Widespread fungal or viral infections or tuberculosis may appear. One infection tends to follow another, and the victim eventually succumbs. In other cases, the virus directly infects the brain, causing early senility and neurologic abnormalities.

The incubation period of AIDS can be up to five years. A patient of mine was a happily married, monogamous, religious young man. Unfortunately, before he became a born-again Christian five years ago, he had been a drug addict. I first met him at an emergency room where he had gone because of progressive weight loss, fatigue, shortness of breath, and a severe pneumonia, symptoms which turned out to be AIDS.

AIDS is currently an epidemic in this country. More than 50,000 cases were reported by early 1988. Approximately one and a half million persons have been infected with the HIV; 20 to 30 percent of those who have the virus will develop AIDS in the first five years after being infected. Healthy but infected people (carriers) are the major reservoir of infection for others. Their blood, semen, and other secretions are infectious.

Infection with the HIV is diagnosed by a series of blood tests. The screening test is often falsely positive (the person does not really have the infection), so every positive screening test must be confirmed with a more specific blood test. There is currently no cure for AIDS, although a new drug, zidovudine, may prolong the periods between hospitalizations.

In heterosexual transmission of AIDS, the virus is passed primarily through semen. In a recent study of women who tried to get pregnant by means of artificial insemination, eight women received semen from a man later found to be an AIDS carrier.[3] Four of the eight women became AIDS carriers, indicating that they had been infected by the semen.

Heterosexual sex partners of persons with AIDS account for 2 percent of men with AIDS and 27 percent of women with AIDS.[4] In other words, it is about ten times easier for a woman to catch AIDS from a man than vice versa. During heterosexual intercourse, AIDS is much more easily transmitted from male to female than from female to male. This is because transmission of the HIV is most efficient when there is transfer of body fluids such as semen, to the mucous membranes of another person. A tear in the mucous membrane is necessary in order for the virus to gain access to the bloodstream of the recipient. During intercourse, semen contacts the lining of the vagina, which is a mucous membrane. Any abrasion in the vagina will promote absorption of the virus. On the other hand, when the female is the infected partner, her vaginal secretions will contact primarily the skin of the penis, which is not a mucous membrane and therefore thicker and less vulnerable to infection. To cause infection in the male, there would have to be a significant cut or tear in the skin of the penis.

Transmission of HIV is even more efficient during anal intercourse than during vaginal intercourse. This is because the lining of the rectum is damaged more easily than the lining of the vagina. Abrasions of the wall of the rectum are very likely during anal intercourse, providing easy access to the bloodstream for HIV particles. This is why the cardinal tenet of safe sex, as it is now being promoted in the homosexual community, is to avoid anal intercourse.

What do we know about transmission of AIDS from men to women? In a recent study, blood samples were taken from the wives of seven married men who had AIDS or AIDS-related complex (ARC), a pre-AIDS condition present in some people who are infected with the HIV. Five of the seven wives were found to be infected with the HIV, and three of the five had AIDS-related complex themselves.[5]

In another study, 97 female sexual partners of 93 men infected with HIV had their blood tested. All the women had sexual contact within the year before their partners were found to be HIV positive, and none had other risk factors for AIDS. One-quarter (23 percent) of the women were found to be infected with HIV. The more times they had sex with their partners, the higher was their likelihood of being infected.[6]

Thus, in both studies, the AIDS virus was transmitted by repeated sexual contact between infected men and their partners.

Of the more than 13,000 AIDS cases among adults reported to the Centers for Disease Control by September 1985, 133 were heterosexual men and women with no risk factors for infection other than their sexual contact.[7] Of these, 118 were women and 15 were men. The majority said they had sexual contact with intravenous drug abusers. The nearly eight-fold excess of women confirms the easier transmission of the virus from men to women. The numbers also show that AIDS *can* be transmitted from women to men. This is important to know in view of the increasing prevalence of AIDS-infected prostitutes. For example, 57 percent of the prostitutes tested in Newark, Jersey City, and Paterson, New Jersey were HIV positive. Also HIV positive were 19 percent of the prostitutes in Miami, 6 percent in San Francisco, and 4 percent in Los Angeles.[8] The prostitutes often had become infected themselves because of intravenous drug abuse.

A striking example of the passage of AIDS from a man to a woman and then to a different man was reported in 1986 when a 37-year-old married bisexual man died of AIDS.[9] At the time of his death, his 33-year-old wife was examined and found to be healthy. Blood was taken from her and stored for future studies. Two years later, when it was possible to detect the HIV in blood, the woman's blood was tested and was very positive, indicating that she had been infected by her husband. By then the young woman had become intimate with her 26-year-old neighbor. They had vaginal intercourse almost daily for a year. The woman subsequently developed AIDS and died; the neighbor also now has AIDS. Neither the woman nor her neighbor had any other risk factors for AIDS.

How likely is a bisexual man, such as the husband of the young woman who died, to be infected with the HIV? Recently, 1,034 unmarried men in San Francisco had their blood tested for the virus.[10] Whereas none of the 204 heterosexual men carried the virus, 49.2 percent of the bisexual men and 46.2 percent of the exclusively homosexual men were carriers and therefore potentially contagious. The risk of being a carrier was proportional to the number of male sexual partners in the previous two years. Of the 83 men who had no or only one male sexual partner in the preceding two years, 18 percent were AIDS carriers, compared with 32 percent of men who had two to nine partners, 54 percent of those who had had 10–49 male sexual partners, and 71 percent of those who had had 50 or more partners. Thus, a woman who has sexual intercourse with a bisexual man is at significant risk of contracting AIDS, even if he has had only a few male partners; her risk increases as the number of his male partners goes up.

Another recent study dramatically confirms that a woman who has sexual relations with an infected man has a significant risk of becoming infected herself with the AIDS virus.[11] In this study, the spouses or steady partners of 45 adults with AIDS had their blood tested for the virus when the AIDS was first diagnosed and again every four to six months afterward for one to three years; none of the partners had any other risk factors for AIDS (that is, none of them were drug abusers, homosexuals, or recipients of blood transfusions). Of 28 female spouses studied, four (14 percent) already had been infected at the time AIDS was diagnosed in their husbands, and ten out of the seventeen uninfected wives (59 percent) who continued to have sexual relations with their husbands became infected in the next one to three years. Interestingly, of the ten couples who used condoms after AIDS was diagnosed, only one initially uninfected spouse became infected, where as 86 percent of uninfected spouses contracted the AIDS virus when sexual relations were without condoms. This study clearly demonstrates that wives of men with AIDS are at high risk of becoming infected themselves. If condoms are not used, they are extremely likely to catch the disease.

The conclusion is inescapable. In a medical journal there is an editorial titled, "The Age of AIDS: A great time for defensive living." Dr. George Lundberg, the author of the editorial, outlines the current efforts to contain the AIDS epidemic. He concludes, "This is a great time to practice monogamy."[12] For wives who believe that their husbands are at risk of becoming infected with the HIV, especially wives whose husbands have multiple sexual encounters with male homosexuals or with female prostitutes, avoiding intercourse is the safest alternative. Use of condoms is the next best choice, as a recent study showed that, in most cases, the virus cannot pass through condoms.[13]

Viral Hepatitis

Viral hepatitis is an infection of the liver. Its chief symptoms are fever, jaundice, abdominal pain, and fatigue. Several different viruses cause the disease. The Hepatitis A virus is transmitted through stools, traditionally via contaminated food or water supplies. Sexual transmission is possible between partners who participate in anal-oral sex. Hepatitis B, formerly called serum hepatitis, is much more commonly transmitted sexually than is Hepatitis A. Although hepatitis damages only the liver, in an infected person, the Hepatitis B virus is found in most body secretions, including blood, saliva, vaginal secretions, and semen. Ordinary sexual intercourse can transmit this potentially serious infection. Body secretions are infectious only in the early stages of the disease.

Currently, more than half of adult cases of Hepatitis B

are transmitted by sexual contact, with 25 percent of all adult cases related to heterosexual intercourse. This is a dramatic change from only a dozen years ago, when a blood transfusion was the typical way of contracting Hepatitis B.

Hepatitis B is easy to catch sexually. For example, when the Vermont Department of Health investigated a cluster of Hepatitis B cases in three young heterosexual men who lived in the same neighborhood, they found that all had recent vaginal sexual intercourse with an apparently healthy young woman who was a carrier.[14] Three other young men with whom she recently had sexual relations did not catch the liver disease from her. She had intercourse from two to ten times with the men who remained uninfected, compared with from one time to steadily for six months with the men who became infected.

About ten percent of people who have had an acute Hepatitis B infection become chronic carriers. These persons often feel well and are sexually active, but continue to be contagious. Chronic carriers are the major source of the sexually transmitted Hepatitis B epidemic that is current in the homosexual community.

To decrease the risk of catching Hepatitis B, one must minimize the number of sexual partners and avoid sex with anyone who is a carrier of the infection. A very effective vaccine to prevent Hepatitis B is now available but it is recommended officially only for high-risk people such as homosexuals and medical personnel who handle blood. Use of condoms is also a helpful preventive technique.

Herpes

Before the AIDS epidemic, the disease that most frightened people away from casual sexual encounters was herpes. "Love is for now, but herpes is forever" is a popular saying. A current advertisement for a herpes medication in a medical journal shows a very sad young woman sitting alone on a park bench; the caption reads: "He never even mentioned a word about herpes. . . ." The media has reported the case of a woman who was granted a huge sum of money at her divorce hearing because her unfaithful husband had given her herpes. The number of people in the U.S. who are living with herpes continues to increase.

Herpes is a virus (*Herpes simplex*) which causes blisters and ulcers on the face and genitals. There are two *Herpes simplex* viruses: type one, which traditionally causes infections above the waist, such as fever blisters, and type two, the usual cause of genital herpes infections. However, with the increase in oral-genital contact, this distinction is becoming less important because type one is being increasingly transmitted to the genitals from the mouth. Each type can be transmitted both sexually and nonsexually. For example, dental hygienists whose fingers touch herpes-infected lips, risk contracting a herpes infection of the fingers. About 20 percent of adult Americans have antibodies to Herpesvirus type two in their bloodstream, indicating that they had a previous Herpesvirus two infection.

The reason a herpes infection is so feared is that there is no cure. Once people have an infection, they are likely to have it for life. After they recover from the initial infection, they are usually not cured. The virus travels up the nervous system and stays dormant for a while, perhaps forever. But then something triggers a recurrence, and another attack occurs. In some people emotional stress, physical trauma, or the menstrual period seems to trigger an attack.

The first attack is the worst. Two to seven days after infection, there is a prickly sensation or pain which, after several hours, is followed by the development of painful blisters. In the man the blisters are usually on the penis; in the women, the blisters are in the vagina and surrounding tissues. The infection is usually more painful for women than for men. In addition to blisters, there is often enlargement of the lymph nodes of the groin, which become tender lumps. The blisters open up and become ulcers, which then crust over and heal after two to three weeks.

Recurrent infections are milder than the primary infection. The duration is less—usually less than ten days, and the pain is less severe. After the first infection, more than 50 percent of people have recurrences within six months. With time, recurrences become less frequent.

Most doctors diagnose herpes infection primarily by the appearance of the lesions. The main causes of ulcers on the penis are syphilis and herpes, and an important distinction is that only those of herpes are painful. Herpes can also be diagnosed by scraping the base of the ulcer and then growing the organisms from the scrapings or else staining the scrapings and examining them directly under a microscope.

Having had a couple of recurrences, a person can usually tell when another recurrence is about to happen because of a sensation of itching, tingling, burning, or tenderness at the site of the eruption. The person is infectious at this stage and needs to avoid sexual contact. The blisters and ulcers are also infectious. Sexual relations should be avoided as long as there are *any* visible lesions. In one study, Herpesvirus particles were found in over 50 percent of women during the first four days of a recurrent herpes attack, 26 percent on day six, and none after day ten. In other words, none of the women in the study could transmit an infection after the tenth day of an attack, so sex would be safe at this time.

There is still disagreement about the likelihood of transmitting the disease between attacks. Some experts believe that the risk is very small. Other studies show that up to 15 percent of men and 2 percent of women may harbor Herpesvirus in the urethra or vagina without any visible lesions and may be infectious. Using a condom helps to lower the risk of transmitting and of catching herpes.

Why is there so much concern about herpes infections? There are three reasons.

First, because Herpesvirus particles lie dormant in the nerve fibers, there is no effective cure, although some treatments can shorten a particular attack. An antiviral drug called acyclovir lessens the pain and speeds healing of herpes ulcers. It can help to prevent recurrences for as long as the medication is taken. Currently, it can be prescribed from six to twelve months. Acyclovir is expensive and, most important of all, it does not cure herpes.

Second, a baby born to a mother who has active herpes at the time of delivery is at high risk of coming down with a serious and potentially fatal case of herpes. Because of this possibility, a pregnant woman with a history of herpes infections needs to be monitored closely, usually with repeated tests for the presence of the virus in her genital tract as her due date draws near. If she has an active case or is shedding the virus at the time of delivery, most obstetricians will perform a Caesarian section.

Third, certain data suggest an association between Herpesvirus infection and cancer of the cervix. In women with a history of herpes infections, there is about a five-fold increased risk of the precancerous condition of the cervix called cervical dysplasia and of cancer of the cervix. Such women definitely need to have a Pap smear done by their doctor every year to screen for cancer. This test is a scraping of surface cells from the cervix—a painless procedure.

If your husband has herpes and you do not, then it will take a joint effort to keep you from acquiring this disease. First, you should not have intercourse with him from the time that he first feels an attack coming on until the ulcers have totally healed. Also, because of the small but definite risk of a man shedding the virus in the absence of symptoms, he should routinely use a condom, even when there is no evidence of infection.

Genital Warts

Genital warts (Condyloma acuminata) are caused by the same virus, the human papillomavirus (HPV), that causes ordinary warts. But unlike ordinary warts, genital warts rarely disappear spontaneously. They are painless but very contagious. They can be found on the genitals, anus, fingers, tongue, and roof of the mouth. They can be treated by freezing with liquid nitrogen, burning with a carbon dioxide laser, or by application of a chemical called podophyllin. The treatments often need to be repeated several times.

Papillomavirus infection of the uterine cervix is very common; evidence of this is found in 1 to 2 percent of all Pap smears. The virus causes changes in the cervix that look precancerous. There is some evidence that, like the Herpesvirus, the papillomavirus may predispose to cancer of the cervix and vulva. A woman whose husband has genital warts should have a Pap smear every year; the Pap smear detects precancerous changes in the cervix early enough to permit easy treatment. If your husband has genital warts on his penis, use of a condom will help prevent transmission of this disease to you. You must avoid unprotected contact with any genital wart.

Vaginitis

Every day in my office I see several women who have a vaginal infection. This disorder is extremely common. One of the chief concerns of most women who have a vaginal infection is, is it sexually transmitted? Although the common vaginal infections are not considered true sexually transmitted diseases, I feel that it's worth describing them briefly.

There are three common causes of vaginal infection; all produce a similar symptom, a vaginal discharge. The specific symptoms are sufficiently different that it is often possible, tentatively, to diagnose which particular infection a woman has just by talking with her. The three infections are Candida (yeast), Trichomonas (Trich), and Gardner-ella (nonspecific vaginitis or bacterial vaginitis). All are diagnosed the same way: Using a cotton-tipped applicator, the physician obtains a sample of the vaginal secretion and examines it directly under a microscope. Each of the three organisms has a distinctive appearance.

The woman with a vaginal yeast infection complains most about itching. She has a scanty, white, cheesy vaginal discharge. She may have recently been treated with an antibiotic. Pregnancy, birth control pills, and diabetes also predispose to yeast infections. Yeast organisms are natu-rally found in the vagina and gastrointestinal tract of most women. When any of the predisposing conditions are present, the organisms can start multiplying rapidly and will cause symptoms.

Yeast infections are not usually sexually transmitted, al-though occasionally the husband of an infected woman will develop a mild yeast infection on the skin of his penis. Effective anti-yeast vaginal creams or suppositories will usually eradicate the vaginal infection within a few days.

Trichomonas vaginalis is a protozoan, a one-celled or-ganism with a wiggly tail. The woman who has a Trich infection complains of a yellow discharge with an offensive odor. The discharge is frothy and profuse. *Gardnerella vaginalis* (formerly called *Hemophilus vaginalis*) also causes profuse vaginal discharge, but it is thinner and less odorous than Trichomonas. Both infections are effectively treated with the same antibiotic, taken by mouth. Both infections can be sexually transmitted (Gardnerella less so than Trich), but both are also found in women who are not sexually active. Because of the possibility of sexual transmission, some doctors routinely treat the sexual part-ner of women who have either infection. Other doctors treat only the woman. If she has a recurrence of the infec-tion shortly after treatment, the doctor assumes that it's being passed back and forth between the two partners. Only then is the man treated as well. There are usually no symptoms in men who are carriers of Gardnerella or Trichomonas.

The monogamous man or woman who develops a case of syphilis or gonorrhea can justifiably assume that the spouse has had extramarital sexual relations. Such is not true, however, for the vaginal infections I have just described. Like Candida, the Gardnerella and Trichomonas organisms may be found in the normal vaginal tract, just waiting to cause trouble under the right circumstances.

Summary

Medical literature has recently addressed the issue of avoiding sexually transmitted diseases. An article titled "Primary Prevention of Sexually Transmitted Diseases" advises:

> Abstinence is the only foolproof preventive measure. For sexually active persons, stable monogamy carries no risk of acquiring a STD, provided neither partner is infected. Because many STDs are often asymptomatic (gonorrhea, Herpes, hepatitis B, and infections with HIV and Chlamydia), infected persons may be impossible to identify and avoid. Simply reducing the number of sexual partners and avoiding persons known to have many other sexual partners should reduce the likelihood of exposure to an infected person.
> . . . Sexually active persons may also benefit from carefully inspecting each potential partner for genital lesions, a rash, or a discharge, and asking direct questions about possible infection.[15]

Women whose partners have affairs are justifiably concerned about their risk of acquiring a sexually transmitted disease. Becoming more informed about these diseases and about the possibility of protecting themselves from each disease is one useful step. When I advised a young single woman that she ask her new sexual partner, whom she hardly knew, to use a condom, she replied, ''I couldn't do that—he might be offended!'' As long as a woman is more concerned about offending a man than about protecting herself, she is unlikely to take precautions that would decrease her risk of contracting a STD. As long as a wife is unwilling to avoid sexual relations with her philandering husband for fear of alienating him or even losing him, she remains at risk of catching from him a potentially serious disease.

In order to be able to protect ourselves, we must first have sufficient self-esteem to realize that we have some real choices about our actions. Then we can make decisions based on our own best interest rather than out of fear.

The second half of the book examines the process of recovery from codependency and development of an improved self-esteem. The result can be an enhanced ability to take care of ourselves, both physically and emotionally.

Section Two:

The
Road to Recovery

CHAPTER EIGHT

"Where will I go for help? Who will understand?"

The Elements of Recovery

A survey of 123 Al-Anon wives in the Washington, D.C. area showed that the women delayed an average of more than seven years after the first episode of their husband's problem drinking before finally seeking help.[1] The husband's arrest for drunken driving was often the first episode. Acts of physical violence began an average of five years before a woman sought help. She typically waited two years after her feelings for her husband changed from love to hate.

Why did she wait so long? Some reasons may be her shame at revealing to outsiders the family problems; her feeling that she may be to blame for her husband's excessive drinking; and her hope that the problem is only temporary and will somehow improve. Unsure as codependents typically are about what is normal behavior, we often experience a long accumulation of problems and painful episodes before we finally break through our own denial and are ready to seek help. This is as true of the wife of the sex addict as it is of the wife of the alcoholic.

Some of us decide to get help in the aftermath of a marriage crisis precipitated by our husband's admitting to having an affair. Others who are aware of their husband's philandering come to therapy because of chronic depression or following a suicide attempt. Some may begin attending a self-help group only because their husbands have found help for themselves and urge their wives to go as well. And others, after a string of failed relationships, may eventually decide they need to find out why they always seem to choose the wrong man.

Whatever the reason, those of us who have spent years in an addictive relationship may finally be ready to get help and improve our lives. I have described women who succeeded in making changes as being *in recovery*. What does this mean? First, to be recovering implies to be recovering from something, a disease. The idea of recovery is therefore linked to the disease concept of addiction and codependency. To be an addict or a coaddict is to have a disease; recovery from the disease requires learning new ways of living which do not depend on a drug or an addictive relationship to solve all of life's problems. Recovery is learning to have a healthy relationship with ourselves and with other people.

Models of Addictive Behaviors

Are addiction and codependency diseases? One of the major contributions of the founders of Alcoholics Anonymous was to put forward the disease concept of alcoholism, which was first proposed by a physician treating alcoholics in the 1930s. The early A.A. literature stated that alcoholics were allergic to alcohol, that their bodies reacted to alcohol differently than did the bodies of nonalcoholic drinkers. This point is still being debated in the 1980s, with some research suggesting that alcohol is metabolized somewhat differently in alcoholics. There is no evidence, however, that alcoholics are physically allergic to alcohol. The primary value of the disease concept to alcoholics in the early days, when alcoholism was considered a sign of weak character, was that it gave legitimacy to the alcoholics' problem and allowed them to seek help without further lowering their self-esteem. It allowed them to say, "I'm sick; I need treatment," and helped their families to understand that once they had taken a first drink they couldn't stop from taking another.

Acceptance of the disease concept of alcoholism was long in coming, and even today is not universal. It makes more sense to look at addiction as an emotional or psychiatric disease rather than a physical illness. This is consistent with the Twelve Steps of Alcoholics Anonymous. Step Two states that we "came to believe that a Power greater than ourselves could restore us to sanity."* In other words, the Twelve Steps imply that the practicing addict is insane. Recovering addicts subscribe to this concept, often speaking of "the craziness of my thinking" or "my insane behavior." According to the disease model, addiction can be better described as a loss of control over a behavior, accompanied by a thinking disorder which attempts to justify and deny the loss of control.

What other models for addictions exist, and what therapies do they imply?

The moral model is probably the most widely accepted alternative. This model assumes that people have a free choice in their behaviors, so those who abuse alcohol, overeat to obesity, gamble away their savings, or frequent prostitutes are either immoral or have no willpower. According to this model, if people are shown the error of their ways they might be persuaded to reform. The threat of punishment is supposed to be another effective tool. Thus, fundamentalist preachers can be heard weekly on the airwaves urging their listeners to mend their evil ways—

---

*The Twelve Steps are taken from *Alcoholics Anonymous*, published by A.A. World Services, Inc., New York, N.Y., pp. 59–60. Reprinted with permission. The Twelve Steps are printed at the back of this book.

to stop drinking or lusting after their neighbors' wives—
or else risk eternal hellfire and damnation.

Imprisonment for drunkenness or for soliciting a prostitute is a secular therapy based on the moral model of
addiction. This approach assumes that transgressors have
a free choice in their behavior and therefore the embarrassment or inconvenience of a jail sentence will deter
them from repeating the offense. The singular lack of success of religious or secular threats of punishment suggests
that the behaviors being addressed are not based on rational choices.

Punishment as a solution to addictive problems further
assumes that the culprit is solely responsible for the offense. However, according to Dr. Patrick Carnes, most
sex addicts were sexually abused as children. Should they
be the only ones punished?

That many people subscribe to the moral model is
readily understandable; alcoholics sometimes *can* limit
their drinking, and can even stop completely for a period
of time. They can choose their time and place for drinking. The problem is, alcoholics cannot reliably regulate
their drinking, just as compulsive overeaters cannot reliably and for long regulate their eating. The moral model
assumes that because people at times are able to control
their addictions, they should be able to do so consistently.
If they can't, it is because they are bad people.

A second alternative to the disease concept is the socioeconomic model. This model defines the factors in people's environment that are responsible for their addictions.
Thus, people drink alcohol to excess because their peers
do, or because their jobs and home life are so dull they
need an escape. The man who has multiple affairs is
merely following the norm of American society; the
woman whose identity is totally submerged in her husband's is merely living out the traditional role of the mother
and wife. According to this model, women who stay in
abusive relationships do so primarily because they are eco-

nomically dependent on their husbands and have no other choice.

I have already described ways in which society condones men's affairs and women's codependency. I believe that the socioeconomic model definitely plays a role in explaining addiction and coaddiction. It seems too easy, however, to use these socioeconomic factors as excuses, and they are not the most important explanation for addictive behaviors.

A third model for addictive behaviors, somewhat related to the socioeconomic model, states that drinking, overeating, or having multiple affairs are symptoms of other problems in the person's life. For example, a man drinks because he is depressed; he has affairs because his wife is sexually unavailable or has gained so much weight that no one would want to sleep with her. This is the model that is most commonly accepted by the addict and by his family. Its therapy implication is vastly different from that for a model which treats the addiction as a primary disease. The therapy when alcoholism is a symptom is to treat the underlying problem—the addict's depression or the couple's sexual problems. It is assumed that if the psychotherapy or the sexual counseling is successful, the need to drink or have affairs will disappear and the behavior will stop. Unfortunately, this is rarely the case; psychotherapy that does not address the addiction as the primary problem is notoriously unsuccessful in bringing about behavior changes. Although the addict repeatedly rationalizes his behavior by pointing to external causes, the failure of traditional therapy to deal with addiction as a symptom suggests that this model is incorrect.

A fourth model for addictive behaviors is the genetic model, which states that the propensity for addiction is inherited. There is certainly evidence for genetic factors in alcoholism. If you have one parent who is alcoholic, you have approximately a 25 percent chance of becoming alcoholic; if both parents are alcoholic, your risk is closer to 50 percent. Studies of children of alcoholics who were adopted and raised by nonalcoholic families confirm that there is a definite genetic contribution to these dismal statistics. Biochemical studies of the brains of alcoholics and nonalcoholics are an active area of current research. The hope is to isolate chemical differences between the two types of brains and ultimately develop a chemical cure for alcoholism.

Unfortunately, the genetic model for alcoholism is not directly applicable to other addictions. How can a molecule that interacts with alcohol account for addictive behaviors not involving the use of chemicals, such as gambling or sexual relations? And how can this model explain the propensity to switch addictions when one addiction is stopped? The genetic model of alcoholism seems inadequate to explain other addictions.

The old disease concept of alcoholism shared the same drawback: it could not be applied directly to other addictive behaviors. A new disease concept, however, is gaining acceptance: Codependency, the common element of all the addictive and coaddictive behaviors, is indeed a disease entity, a type of Mixed Personality Disorder as defined by the third edition of the *Diagnostic and Statistical Manual of Mental Disorders* (DSM-III) of the American Psychiatric Association. This book defines psychiatric and emotional illnesses as they are currently understood by psychiatrists, and has been revised several times as understanding of psychiatric diseases has changed.

In his recent book, *Diagnosing and Treating Co-dependence*, Timmen L. Cermak, M.D., asks for the inclusion of the disease concept of codependency in the next edition of the *Diagnostic and Statistical Manual of Mental Disorders*.

For the purposes of clinical assessment of individual clients, co-dependence can best be seen as a disease entity. CD [Chemical Dependency] therapists speak of family members as being affected by co-dependence, or as being actively co-dependent. Such assessments imply that a consistent pattern of traits and behaviors is recognizable across individuals, and that these traits and behaviors can create significant dysfunction. In other words, co-dependence is used to describe a "disease entity," just as phobia, narcissistic personality disorder, and Post-Traumatic Stress Disorder (PTSD) are diagnostic entities.[2]

Cermak then proceeds to develop diagnostic criteria for the codependent personality disorder. He first addresses the difficulty of making this diagnosis.

A major roadblock to including co-dependence in any diagnostic nomenclature has been its apparent ubiquity. Described by some as "a condition of the 20th Century," co-dependence is often dismissed as social commentary. If nearly everyone appears to be co-dependent, the argument goes, then how can it be considered a disease? The answer lies in DSM-III's distinction between personality *traits* and personality *disorders*, a distinction which is directly applicable to codependence. According to DSM-III, personality traits are "enduring patterns of perceiving, relating to, and thinking about the environment and oneself . . . exhibited in a wide range of important social and personal contexts." Personality traits only become disorders when they are "inflexible and maladaptive and cause either significant impairment in social or occupational functioning or significant subjective distress."[3]

In other words, codependent *traits* may be nearly universal in American society, but codependent personality *disorders* are not so ever-present and are amenable to diagnosis and treatment. Cermak says:

. . . the critical point for our purposes is that while codependent traits may be widespread, *the diagnosis of Co-Dependent Personality Disorder can only be made in the face of identifiable dysfunction resulting from excessive rigidity or intensity associated with these traits.* Similarly, narcissism is a nearly universal human trait, but Narcissistic Personality Disorder only exists in the face of objective dysfunction. There seems to be no reason why the same line of reasoning cannot be applied to co-dependence.[4]

Getting Help

Suppose we believe our husband's affairs are a result of sex addiction and we are behaving like a coaddict in our relationship. How do we go about getting help? Although we'd like things to be different, we're afraid of making any changes in ourselves that will jeopardize our relationship. Holding on to our husband is probably still our number one goal. Making changes is not easy; we have to be sufficiently uncomfortable or dissatisfied with our life to be willing to take the risks that making changes involves. If we are at a point in our life when we know that change is essential, then a helpful first step is to begin attending Al-Anon or another Twelve Step meeting.

Recovery from codependency consists of three basic elements. The first is to identify our irrational belief system and behaviors that make us uncomfortable or are against our best interests. The second is to change these behaviors. Finally, since codependency is caused by a lack of self-nurturing and not having our emotional needs met when we were growing up, we must learn how to nurture ourselves and to be good to ourselves so that we come to believe we are worthwhile people.

All children have enormous dependency needs; they are totally dependent on adults for their physical and emotional well-being. If we grow up in dysfunctional families where those needs are not adequately met, we may later develop dependency problems. The unmet dependency needs are often replaced with addictions—to chemicals, addictive behaviors, or other people. Unfortunately, as co-dependency counselor Terry Kellogg explained in a lecture in Tucson, Arizona in February 1987, if we try to have our insatiable childhood dependency needs met in adulthood, we will act so needy that we will drive other people away. We can never get our childhood dependency needs met in adulthood. What we can do about this problem is first to grieve for our unmet childhood needs and then recognize our adult dependency needs. The difference is that although a child's needs are insatiable, an adult allows what is given to be enough. We can take what others are willing to give us, and let it be enough. The rest of the parenting that we need will have to come from ourselves. The process of giving ourselves emotionally what our parents did not is called reparenting and is an important element in the recovery process.

Recovery is best accomplished through a combination of counseling and attendance at peer group support meetings. Some may ask, why not counseling alone? Why the necessity for the self-help groups? Robin Norwood, an experienced codependency counselor, responded to this question as follows:

> Therapy alone does not offer an adequately supportive alternative to the alcoholic's dependency on the drug or the relationally addictive woman's dependency on her man. [Relationally addictive means being a relationship addict.] When anyone who has been practicing an addiction tries to stop, an enormous vacuum is created in that person's life—too great a vacuum for an hour-long session with a therapist once or twice a week to fill. Because of the tremendous anxiety generated when the dependence on the substance or the person is interrupted, access to support, reassurance, and understand-

ing must be constantly available. This is best provided
by peers who have been through the same painful withdrawal process themselves.[5]

Counseling can serve as a helpful adjunct to the support
provided by the self-help groups based on A.A. These
groups have several tools for recovery, which include

- attendance at meetings;
- telephone contact with other group members;
- having a more experienced group member as one's men-
  tor or sponsor;
- reading helpful literature; and
- meditation.

The Twelve Steps

The self-help groups that are best suited to promoting
recovery from codependency are those that teach the
Twelve Step program. These groups (free of cost to join)
meet weekly in thousands of locations across the country.
Based on the Twelve Steps of A.A., there are now also
groups that address narcotic abuse, compulsive overeating, compulsive spending, compulsive gambling, and
compulsive sexual behaviors. For most of these compulsions there are also support groups for spouses and significant others that function similarly to Al-Anon, the
Twelve Step group for family and friends of alcoholics.
None of these groups provides professional counseling;
they are gatherings of people who have experienced the
same problem and who have come together to share their
experience, strength, and hope with each other. Experience has shown that hearing what has worked for someone
who has been in the same situation is a strong stimulus
for change.

The Twelve Steps are a deceptively simple program for
recovery originated fifty years ago by the founders of Al-

coholics Anonymous. The program consists of three elements essential to making changes. The first is recognizing that our life is intolerable as is, and that change is necessary. The second element is deciding to do whatever it takes to implement the change, and the third element is acting to bring about the change.

The Steps are the basic tools of the program. The first three are belief Steps, and the last nine are action Steps. In brief, the program consists of recognizing we cannot solve our problems alone; believing that an outside force (a Higher Power) can help us; admitting our problems and character defects to ourselves and confessing them to another person; making restitution for our wrongdoing wherever possible; monitoring our thoughts and behavior on an ongoing basis; continuing to seek spiritual assistance in dealing with our problems; and letting other people who need the same kind of help know about the program.

Step One, as applied to sexual addiction, states, ''We admitted we were powerless over compulsive sexual behavior and that our lives had become unmanageable.'' For the coaddict this means we are powerless over someone else's sexual behavior. One woman described what Step One meant to her when she first encountered it.

When my husband first joined a self-help group for sexual addiction, he suggested that I go to Al-Anon for my own recovery. I didn't think there was any reason for me to go—after all, he was the one with the problem! But like the good coaddict that I was, I went in order to please him. What I heard at the first meeting made so much sense that I can still remember the impact it had on me. The topic was powerlessness over the addict. Until then, I hadn't realized I was powerless over my husband. On the contrary, I had been running my life for years on the principle that I had a great deal of power over him, although of course I hadn't realized I believed this. I continually tried to keep my children on their best behavior because I thought it would keep him from getting angry. I tried to stay slim and dressed becomingly so he wouldn't want to look at other women. I didn't confront him with my suspicions and fears. And when, despite my best efforts, his moods would swing like a pendulum, I analyzed what I might have done to cause this and what I could have done differently to prevent it. I would review what he had said to me and what I had said to him, and would plan what I might say to him next time the same situation arose. I devoted an enormous amount of emotional energy to try to please him, to understand him, and to prevent his recurrent unhappiness, resentment, and complaints of boredom with our marriage. And when my efforts did not succeed, I thought I just needed to try harder.

At Al-Anon, I realized how useless my efforts had been and how powerless I really was over his behavior. I learned that his craziness was not a response to me; it was a response to his addiction and to how he felt about himself. To my surprise, with the acceptance of powerlessness came a tremendous feeling of relief. I realized that I could relinquish the terrible sense of responsibility that I had felt until then for my husband's happiness and the blame that I had felt for his failures and his unhappiness. I believed I was responsible for his happiness; this was the core of my fruitless efforts and my obsession with him. To accept my powerlessness meant to give up that awesome responsibility. From now on I need to be responsible only for my own happiness. An enormous burden was lifted from my shoulders that first evening at Al-Anon, the burden of responsibility for another person's happiness. This is the powerful message of Step One, which to me was so freeing.

Other coaddicts have expressed the same feelings when they understood Step One. The wife of a cocaine addict who had multiple affairs said:

I just found out this week that I'm a real person. I had hooked onto him as though we were Siamese twins. Now I feel a tremendous relief because I'm responsible only for myself and not for him. It's up to him whether he wants to be in the program, and then I'll have to make my decision about staying with him.

A consequence of Step One is our ability to detach from a person or a problem. Detachment is a much misunderstood concept. It does not mean we do not care or we are washing our hands of the person. It means we recognize that we cannot solve another person's problems for him, and worrying about the situation will not bring about change. Learning to detach allows us to love without going crazy. It allows us to assess realistically what we can change and what we cannot change, and to make decisions accordingly.

Step Two—"Came to believe that a Power greater than ourselves could restore us to sanity"—and Step Three—"Made a decision to turn our will and our lives over to the care of God *as we understood Him*"—combat the isolation we feel and the belief that we alone have to solve our problems. In working these Steps, we come to understand that we have an external source of help. Being aware that we are not alone allows us to "let go and let God." This means stopping the controlling behaviors that have been inherent for so long in our relationships with others, and recognizing that we do not have the sole responsibility of solving everyone's problems. For the partner of a man who is addicted to affairs, letting go can include letting go of control, of anger, and possibly even of the man.

Coaddicts usually have a long history of trying to control the sex addict's behavior. We throw out the pornography. At parties we scrutinize his expressions as he looks at other women and watch him across the room to see who he's talking with. We don't dare leave town or even leave him alone for the evening. We phone him at work to check on whether he's really there, go through his pockets looking for strange ticket stubs, and inspect his shirts for lipstick stains.

Even after we get into a Twelve Step program and realize we cannot control his behavior—that the addict will always find ways to elude our control—it is hard for us to change our patterns of behavior. First of all, we are used to the behaviors and we're comfortable with them—they're almost automatic. Second, they served a function in the past. Facing the unmanageability in our lives would have overwhelmed us; thus, our attempts at control helped keep that reality at bay. We had the illusion that we did have some power over his behavior. We had *something to do*, and action is a strong antidote to despair and hopelessness. If we could lose weight, get our hair done, look extra sexy, or buy a new dress, perhaps he would stop being interested in other women. To give up these attempts at control, to face our powerlessness head-on, is frightening, yet it is a necessary first step in the recovery process. The only way to deal with this fear is to replace it with something positive—a belief that our Higher Power is watching out for us so that it is safe to let go.

Steps Two and Three allow us to do Step One without feeling total despair. We can stop trying to do it on our own, because we are not alone. The program does not require acceptance of a traditional God; all it requires is the belief that there is a source of power greater than ourselves. If we are religious, our Higher Power may be God; if we are not, it may be the strength and support of a Twelve Step group, or else the inner resources we were unable to utilize until we found the program. No matter how we define our Higher Power, its presence in our lives means that we are not alone.

Many of us have a great deal of anger and resentment toward our spouse, often so much that there is little hope of saving the marriage. Those of us with a viable marriage have to learn to let go of our anger and resentment—a difficult undertaking. Certain dates, songs, places, people, comments, newspaper articles, and situations will bring back the pain of the past. Suppressing these feelings or saying nothing about them will not keep them away. It is healthier to let our spouse know we are reliving the pain and anger. With time, the intensity of these feelings diminishes and the intervals between episodes of pain and anger lengthen.

If we believe in a Higher Power, we do not take it upon ourselves to punish our spouse for his past misdeeds; we will gradually learn that things somehow work out for the best without our direct intervention, and we trust that we will be shown the way to deal with negative feelings.

An important antidote to anger is realizing how we got into the relationship in the first place. One woman said this about her relationship with a sex addict:

I was a volunteer, not a victim. It was no accident that I found myself in a situation which caused me so much pain. I was looking for this kind of person, and I found him. If it hadn't been this particular husband, it would have been another man doing similar things. Knowing this doesn't give me any less reason to be angry at the very real hurts I experienced, but it does remind me that I share in the responsibility of having been in that situation.

We can help ourselves by doing a written account of our past experiences with relationships.

- Were your previous romantic partners as loving and as nurturing as you thought you wanted?
- Were they similar to your spouse in their lack of concern for your feelings?
- Were *you* the one who was usually the giver, the accommodating one, the nurturing one?
- Did you feel you did not really deserve any better?
- Did you have any signs before you were married that

your husband would not be the ideal mate that you were hoping for?

Many coaddicts who have searched their souls discovered aspects of their own personalities that helped them view their role in the relationship in a different light. One young woman related:

I saw myself as a victim my whole life. Men were to fix me and heal me and validate my existence. When people didn't meet my expectations I got very angry. Now I realize that I'm responsible for myself.

Another young woman married to a promiscuous husband said:

I've gathered people around me who have problems to prove that I'm okay. My script has been that I'm a good person and that I'm a survivor—look at how I get through these terrible situations! I've always lived in crisis—that is the way I define myself. Everyone tells me how wonderful I am, how strong and how helpful. If I didn't have these crises, I wouldn't know who I am. I thought it was an accident that I kept experiencing crises, but now I see that I was using people; I've done it since childhood.

By looking at our past, we can acquire a new understanding of our own behavior; our insights are the first stage of making changes in our lives.

The "letting go" that accompanies Steps Two and Three may involve letting go of another person. As coaddicts, we have been willing to subordinate our own needs to those of the other person. Often, we might have agreed to sexual activities we were uncomfortable with in order to hold on to the other person. In doing this, we let ourselves be treated disrespectfully, perhaps because we did not believe we were really worthy of respect. As part of our recovery process, we learn to treat ourselves with increasing respect and to ask the same treatment from our spouse. We need to set boundaries of what behaviors are acceptable to us and what aren't. If our spouse is not in a Twelve Step program and does not believe that his behavior is problematic, we may need to choose between continuing to live with the unacceptable behaviors or letting go of the other person. Because a sexual relationship is so personal, it is difficult to continue living with someone who has affairs with other women or men. If as sexual coaddicts we subscribe to the belief that sex is the most important sign of love, we're likely to be devastated by his continuing involvement with others. Recovery for us may involve removing ourselves from the situation. Letting go of a person we have been addicted to is very difficult but may be necessary for our recovery.

Steps Four and Five direct us to look at our shortcomings and strengths and to admit them to ourselves, to our Higher Power, and to another human being. Step Four asks us to make a "searching and fearless moral inventory." This may be our first honest look at our strengths and weaknesses in many years. We may have avoided the truth and our feelings for so long that facing the truth and these feelings is frightening. Knowing oneself, however, is necessary in order to be able to make changes.

As we take Step Four we're likely to discover that we are angry and resentful. Up to now we may have been able to justify these feelings—after all, our husband's behavior was certainly deserving of anger and resentment! But when we take a searching look at ourselves, we will find that with time we have become angry and resentful people. Anyone can be angry or resentful at times, but when we are chronically angry and resentful we are unhappy and unhealthy people who are usually depressed, have physical symptoms, or may be engaged in various compulsive behaviors. Recognizing our chronic anger and resentfulness is one of the first steps to making changes.

Codependent people might believe that if other people knew what they were really like, these people would not respect them. According to Step Five, "We admitted to God, to ourselves, and to another person the exact nature of our wrongs." Finding a trustworthy person with whom to take Step Five may be the first time we have dared to let someone else know what we are really like. Getting acceptance from this other person no matter what character defects we have revealed (jealousy, insecurity, anger, resentment, emotional withdrawal, criticalness), will assist us in recognizing that we are worthwhile people.

In the following four Steps, we enlist God's help in removing our character defects and then take some concrete actions. In Step Six, we "Were entirely ready to have God remove all these defects of character," and then Step Seven, "Humbly asked Him to remove our shortcomings." In Step Eight, we "Made a list of all persons we had harmed, and became willing to make amends to them all." Finally Step Nine tells us to make "direct amends to such people wherever possible, except when to do so would injure them or others." Our list must include ourselves, for there is no way we can make peace with others unless we can also make peace with ourselves.

Making amends first requires facing the truth about the effects of our behavior on other people. Did our critical attitude cause those around us to feel defensive? Did our need to control cause resentment by those we tried to control? Did our irresponsibility make others have to do our work for us? Did we hurt another woman by our unjustified jealousy? Did we bore our friends with our endless complaints about our husbands and then anger them by our refusal to do anything about our situation after asking their advice?

"Making amends" to others is painful; it takes courage and humility. But the result is an increased sense of self-worth and peace of mind. The objective of making amends is to accept personal responsibility for our past behavior.

This contributes to our self-respect. Amends can consist of a direct apology or other sincere actions made directly to the people harmed, or it may be an indirect reparation such as volunteer work or a financial contribution to a worthy cause.

Steps Ten and Eleven are "maintenance" Steps, designed to help the recovering person live a healthy life. Step Ten states, "Continued to take personal inventory and when we were wrong promptly admitted it." This Step is crucial so the coaddict can monitor the process of her recovery. In addiction to alcohol, recovery and relapse are clear-cut—a recovering alcoholic is one who does not drink; a relapse is resumption of drinking. Recovery and relapse in sex addition can also be defined in terms of specific behaviors. But codependency consists of so many behaviors that defining recovery and relapse becomes more difficult. To make things even harder, the same behavior may be either healthy or evidence of a relapse or slip, depending on the goal of the behavior. For example, if our husband asks us to go with him to a party and we agree because we think we'll enjoy ourselves, that's healthy. But if we agree because we know that an old flame of his will be there and we believe that our presence will prevent him from spending a lot of time with her—this is an example of the old coaddict type of thinking. In recovery, we must be very honest with ourselves about the motives for our behavior. By monitoring our feelings and thoughts, we can then choose different behaviors.

Two years into recovery, Alice found it increasingly easier to monitor her internal monologue and correct its misconceptions. She told this story at a recovery group meeting.

One day as my husband and I were on our way to a movie, I mentioned something about our 25th wedding anniversary, which is 21 years away. He said, "Maybe we won't be together by then." Instantly my coaddict stomach flipped over, and I thought, he's planning to leave me! But in the next breath I said to myself, wait a minute! Maybe he's afraid that I'm going to leave him. So I answered him, casually—at least I hoped it sounded casual—"Why, are you afraid I'm going to leave you?" He answered, "Well, yes, I do worry about it sometimes; after all, I've treated you pretty badly at times." What a lesson to me! I had rethought my first reaction, and the revised version had turned out to be correct. Meanwhile, instead of acting like a dependent, fearful wife, I had behaved as though I were self-assured and concerned about his insecurity.

I am learning that although I cannot control my initial reaction, I can choose what to do subsequently. I can evaluate that first negative reaction and if it doesn't conform to reality, I can say something positive to myself instead. I can then behave as though I believed it. Each experience like this one decreases the gap between how I behave and what I believe about myself.

We keep our bad feelings going with a constant stream of negative self-talk. If he's late, we think, I wonder if he's stopped off at the bar or a woman friend's house. I'm sure it's my fault. What did I do or say this morning that got him angry? Maybe if I hadn't complained about what he did yesterday, he'd be home by now. Why can't I stop being such a nag? The negative internal monologue is part of our codependency. In recovery, we learn to become aware of the self-defeating talk, to substitute positive self-talk and to behave *as if*. The more we do it, the easier it gets.

Step Eleven, another maintenance Step, states, "Sought through prayer and meditation to improve our conscious contact with God *as we understood Him*, praying only for knowledge of His will for us and the power to carry that out." Daily meditation is a very helpful part of recovery from coaddiction. One way to do this is to each day read and think about a page from the book, *One Day at a Time in Al-Anon.* This little book contains brief, thoughtful comments on subjects of concern to recovering codependents such as acceptance, changing what we can, controlling, detachment, honesty with oneself, problem solving, resentment, self-deception, and serenity. Daily recitation of the Serenity Prayer reminds us how to live our lives according to the Twelve Steps: "God, grant me the serenity to accept the things I cannot change, courage to change the things I can, and wisdom to know the difference." This brief prayer essentially summarizes the philosophy of Twelve Step programs.

Finally, the last Step urges us to carry the message of recovery to other people in need, and to live our own lives according to the principles of the Steps. Long ago, the founders of A.A. learned that the best way to remain sober was to work with other alcoholics. Seeing the despair and degradation practicing alcoholics experience is a sober reminder to recovering people of what life used to be like and how it could be again if they relapse. Twelfth Step work—that is, talking with the practicing addict or codependent about our own experiences and how we got better, is an integral part of the program.

When, in my medical practice, I advise a patient to go to A.A. or Al-Anon meetings, I often hear, "But I've heard that those programs are religious—they're always talking about God. I don't believe in God and I know that I'd be very uncomfortable at those meetings." The belief that the Twelve Step program is religious is a misconception. It is not religious, but *spiritual*. It does not require a belief in God, but only a renunciation of our isolation and of the premise that we each are at the center of our own universe. The spiritual program requires an acceptance of the existence of strength and help from sources other than our own intellect. For the atheist or agnostic, the source may be the self-help group, with its support and collective strength. A belief in God is not a requirement for membership in the Twelve Step programs, nor is it necessary for recovery from addiction. But recovery is very difficult without a willingness to develop one's spirituality.

Spirituality

Some may ask, "Why the emphasis on spirituality in the Twelve Step programs? What has spirituality to do with recovery from addiction?" The answer is that what people seek in the addictive high can really only be found in the spiritual experience. In his book *WE: Understanding the Psychology of Romantic Love*, Robert Johnson explains the confusion between romance and spirituality.

> When we are "in love" we feel completed, as though a missing part of ourselves had been returned to us; we feel uplifted, as though we were suddenly raised above the level of the ordinary world. Life has an intensity, a glory, an ecstasy and transcendence.
>
> We seek in romantic love to be possessed by our love, to soar to the heights, to find ultimate meaning and fulfillment in our beloved. We seek the feeling of wholeness.
>
> If we ask where else we have looked for these things, there is a startling and troubling answer: *religious experience*. When we look for something greater than our egos, when we seek a vision of perfection, a sense of inner wholeness and unity, when we strive to rise above the smallness and partialness of personal life to something extraordinary and limitless, this is spiritual aspiration. . . .
>
> What we seek constantly in romantic love is not human love or human relationship alone; we also seek a religious experience, a vision of wholeness.[6]

In romantic love, the beloved is seen as an ideal being who can reveal the meaning of life to the lover. Johnson says, "When a human being becomes the object of this adoration, when the beloved has the power to 'give light to our lives' or extinguish that light, then we have adopted the beloved as the image and symbol of God."[7] According to Johnson, because spirituality is out of fashion in our modern culture, our spiritual instinct finds expression primarily in romantic love. This is why some people tend to feel that their lives are meaningless except when they are in love.

All of us hope to find a special person to share our lives with. Brought up on childhood stories in which the hero and heroine get married and live happily ever after, it is natural for us to hope that our passion for this special person will last forever. Yet as we acquire experience, most of us realize that this is not possible. In Shere Hite's recent survey of 2,500 women, 82 percent of married women said real love is not passionately being "in love," but rather learning to know and care for the other person over time. These women also felt that early feelings of being "in love" generally grow into a deeper love, defined as caring and understanding—if the relationship continues.[8] The majority of women (59 percent) said passionate love cannot last. Many married women (54 percent) gave stability as their reason for preferring loving, caring feelings over being passionately in love.[9]

Couples who understand and accept the transition from passion to a deeper caring can experience long-term happiness in their relationships. But people who continue to expect their relationship to fulfill all their romantic expectations will be inevitably disappointed and may find themselves looking elsewhere.

The old unconscious belief returns to haunt them, whispering that "true love" is somewhere else, that it can't be found within the ordinariness of marriage. . . . These are the terrible splits that we all carry around with us. On the one hand, we want stability and relationship with an ordinary human being; on the other hand, we unconsciously demand someone who will be the incarnation of soul, who will reveal the godhead and the Realm of Light, who will move us to a state of religious adoration and fill our lives with ecstasy.[10]

Romantic love, as described in the preceding paragraphs, is not concerned with the other person's well-being or happiness—it seeks only ecstasy, drama, and passion. It is therefore very self-centered. How, then, do we resolve the dilemma that results from the incompatibility of romantic love and commitment to another person? The answer, according to Johnson, is to stop looking for wholeness and fulfillment through another person and instead develop our own internal spiritual life. Relieving another person of the responsibility for our happiness allows us to see our partner as a real person instead of a symbol. Instead of seeking spiritual fulfillment through romance, Johnson advocates a return to spirituality, an affirmative soul-life lived day by day through prayer and meditation. Spiritual growth can be sought either through organized religion, by oneself, or participation in a Twelve Step group.

In summary, Robert Johnson acknowledges a universal need to feel the "high" that for some people comes only by falling in love (and for some, through mood-altering experiences produced by the use of chemicals). He points out that the self-centered nature of romantic love is incompatible with long-term commitment to another person and with genuine caring. The solution to this problem is to find the same type of "high" through a spiritual inner life instead of through another person. To do this frees a person to truly love someone else. Johnson describes the kind of love that allows commitment to another person and fosters a long-term relationship.

Loving another person is seeing that person truly, and appreciating him for what he actually is, his ordinariness, his failures, and his magnificence. If one can ever cut through that fog of projections in which one lives so much of his life, and can look truly at another person, that person, in his down-to-earth individuality is a magnificent creature.

Loving is seeing another person for the down-to-earth, practical, immediate experience which another human being is. Loving is not illusory. It is not seeing the other person in a particular role or image we have designed for him. Loving is valuing another for his personal uniqueness within the context of the ordinary world. That is durable. It stands up. It is real.[11]

Forgiving Your Partner

In order to be able to get on with our lives, we must first forgive those who have hurt us. Otherwise the resentments that we feel about the wrong done to us will continue to eat away at us and prevent us from achieving serenity. The chief purpose of forgiving is to bring peace to us, not to absolve the other person of his wrongdoing. Forgiving is healing for the forgiver.

In his excellent little book, *Forgive and Forget*, Lewis B. Smedes describes what forgiveness is *not*. First, forgiving is not forgetting. By forgiving someone, we do not forget the hurtful act. We need to forgive precisely because we have not forgotten what someone did; our memory keeps the pain alive long after the actual wrongdoing is past. Because forgiving is healing, it will make it easier to forget. But it is not necessary to forget the past in order to forgive. What forgiving will accomplish is to heal the pain of the past.

Second, forgiving is not excusing. Excusing is the opposite of forgiving. We excuse a person when we believe that he was not to blame for the wrong he did; we forgive him because we believe that he was to blame. This is why excusing is easy whereas forgiving is hard.

Finally, forgiving is not tolerating. We can forgive someone without tolerating what he did. We can forgive our husband for the pain his affairs caused us without being willing to tolerate affairs in the future. Forgiving does not imply acceptance of the behavior in the past or in the future.

What then is forgiveness? Forgiveness is healing ourselves of the painful memories of the past. This is a slow process that may take years. It involves several steps, the first of which is to recognize that a wrong has been done to us. As people accustomed to denying our own feelings, making excuses for our husband's hurtful actions, and taking responsibility when things go wrong, we may not find this easy. We need to acknowledge that our partner's behavior was inexcusable, that he behaved in ways that caused us a great deal of pain.

The next step is to recognize that we have strong feelings about the wrong that was done to us and to *feel* those feelings, which undoubtedly include anger and hate. It is natural to hate someone who has hurt us and to feel anger toward him. Some women are afraid to feel such strong emotions, much less to express them. Psychotherapy may be helpful if this is the case for us.

Sharing our strong feelings with others is the next step toward forgiveness. It would be ideal to confront the person who has hurt us and tell him directly how we feel about what he did, but often this is not possible—he may not be available or he may have made it clear he is not interested in our feelings. Or we may be too fearful of his reaction to risk direct confrontation. In either case, sharing with our support group or therapist will allow us to express our emotions about the situation rather than swallowing them or turning them into depression.

Understanding our partner's addiction is another step toward forgiveness. Like most coaddicts, we may have given our husband enormous power over our happiness, expecting him to use it for our benefit. We may tend to idealize our partner, to view him as larger than life, a person with many virtues and few faults—and at the same time as a needy person for whom we have done so much that out of gratitude, if not love, he should act in our best interest. We might find it hard to understand how he could have done just the opposite. It may help if we recognize that a person is not the romantic figure we thought we were living with; on the contrary, that person is needy, fearful, and compulsive and has an emotional disease.

We also need to recognize that we have not been entirely the innocent victim. It has already been mentioned that a woman rarely marries a sex addict by accident. She usually has clues before marriage of the problems to come, but does not dwell on them. She expects her husband to make her happy and then becomes resentful when he fails to live up to her expectations. Accepting our share of the responsibility for our hurt will help us to forgive our partner.

The next step is deciding what to do with our relationship with the person who has hurt us. If our partner has left and is unavailable, if he is dead, or if we have decided that as part of our recovery program we cannot afford any communication with him, then all we can do is heal our bitterness toward him and wish him well. We cannot change the facts of his past actions, but we can divorce the past from how we feel about this person in the present. If he is still causing pain to others, we can say a prayer for him and hope that a Higher Power will eventually show him the way toward recovery. Forgiving him will give us a sense of serenity and allow us to get on with our lives.

If we or our partner is interested in salvaging the relationship we have an opportunity for further healing. Forgiveness will be easiest if our partner is willing to take several steps: to see that his actions were hurtful and unfair; to feel the pain he caused us, and feel guilty about having done so; to tell us he realizes what he did was intolerable, he feels the pain, and he wants to be forgiven; and to really want not to hurt us again and promise this. In this way, partners might be able to start rebuilding their relationship.

A note of caution, however: Addicts frequently feel real remorse for the hurt they have caused us. They may sincerely ask forgiveness and promise to change—but then go on doing the same things. Some of us have believed our partner's promises and then felt angry and hurt when he was gone yet another night or again showed interest in another woman. In order for us to believe that he will not hurt us again, he must follow his words with actions. These may include stopping the hurtful behavior, going to counseling, or attending a self-help group.

What if our partner wants to continue the relationship but is unwilling to ask forgiveness or even to recognize that he has a role in our suffering? We still need to forgive him in order to allow serenity to enter our lives. We need to understand that he was suffering from an addiction. We also need to recognize that forgiveness does not imply giving our partner permission to continue his hurtful behaviors. As part of our own recovery, we will need to decide which behaviors we can accept in our marriage and which we cannot.

For example, some women decide to accept their husband's affairs and to obtain the nurturing they need by having affairs themselves (this approach may eventually lead to the breakup of the marriage). Others decide they can tolerate their husband's constant flirting with other women, but would leave if he had another affair. Some women decide to stay in the marriage, but not to have sex with their husband as long as he continues to have affairs.

Whether or not we are in an ongoing relationship, whether or not our partner seeks our forgiveness, we need to forgive him in order to be at peace with ourselves. The primary goal of forgiveness is to heal ourselves and obtain serenity in our lives.

Counseling

Let's say we have attended some Twelve Step meetings but feel we also need some one-on-one psychotherapy or marriage counseling. Or we might be like some codependents, reluctant to talk about ourselves, especially in a group, and would prefer to first see a counselor in privacy. How do we begin to select one? Jessica, an intensive care nurse, describes what happened to her husband, Joe, when he went for counseling.

Before my husband became involved in a Twelve Step program, he tried several kinds of counseling. He realized his life was out of control because of his affairs, but he didn't know how to stop. At one point he went to a psychiatrist and told him about his latest affair, but not that it was still going on. Naturally he didn't get much out of the therapy.

Later in our marriage, he found himself in a complicated affair. It had begun as a casual fling, but when he found himself obsessing about her much of the time and feeling increasingly guilty about his involvement, he went to Jim, a highly recommended psychotherapist, in order to get help ending the affair. They spent many hours probing Joe's childhood, our marriage, and his feelings about his affair. Joe admitted to a one-night stand with an acquaintance some months earlier, but there was no recognition that his affairs were a pattern in his life.

One day Joe asked me to go to a counseling session with him. He told me that Jim, the therapist, had thought it might be helpful to Joe's therapy to have me there for one session. Jim asked me several questions about my relationship with Joe. He wanted to know what I would do if I found out that Joe was having an affair. I, of course, had no idea that Joe was involved in an affair or that this was not the first one during our marriage. I gave Jim the answer I'd given Joe on several occasions when the subject of infidelity came up—that I would end the marriage. Jim probed further, asking if there were any circumstances in which I would forgive and stay in the relationship. I continued to give answers based on my assumption that these were all hypothetical questions. At the end of the session Jim complimented me in several areas, giving his opinion that I was well-adjusted, secure, and sure of my own values—none of which, as it turned out, was true of me.

A week later, when Joe's girlfriend threatened to commit suicide if he ended the affair, he told me about it. In addition to my anger toward Joe, I found myself feeling angry at Jim. Even now, years later, I believe that his behavior was unethical. He brought me into the counseling session under false pretenses—not because I had asked for help, but in order to find out whether Joe could risk telling me about the affairs. In order to do this, he formed a coalition with Joe in which the two were dishonest with me about the real purpose of the visit.

Later Joe learned about a self-help program for sex addicts, recognized the problem in himself, and became active in the program. He was able to turn his life around and improve his self-esteem so that he could function well without the need for validation from other women. Hoping to share his success, he called Jim to tell him about the program, and sent Jim some written material about it. Joe was hoping that the next addicted client who came to Jim would get new understanding. But Jim never acknowledged receiving the information; he obviously did not want to be confused with new facts.

Joe spent over $1,000 and many hours in counseling that was not helpful. His counselor persisted in trying to fit Joe's problem into the particular counseling framework that he was familiar with. Today Joe regrets the months he spent in therapy. His marriage became more chaotic and his life less manageable throughout that period. Had Joe's girlfriend not precipitated a crisis, he might still be seeing the same therapist, still involved in affairs, and still feeling guilty and worthless.

This story is, unfortunately, very common. It points out the importance of choosing the right therapist. The wrong counselor can waste our time and money, can delay us in getting real help, and can prolong the secrecy and dishonesty that is already a prominent element in marriages where there is infidelity.

Contrast Joe's experience with that of Beverly, whose husband had a long string of affairs. When they told their marriage counselor about the affairs, she suggested that Brian was "sexually compulsive." The counselor showed them a newspaper article about sex addiction and invited them both to join self-help recovery groups. Later she attended a workshop given by Patrick Carnes, author of *Out of the Shadows: Understanding Sexual Addiction*, to learn more about sex addiction. The counselor continued to work with Beverly and Brian individually, and to support their attendance at self-help meetings. As a result of this positive experience, Beverly feels very knowledgeable about her own coaddiction and is making progress in her recovery.

Choosing a therapist can feel like guesswork. Therapists come from many different backgrounds. There are psychiatrists, who are medical doctors with at least three additional years of psychiatric training. There are psychologists, some with Ph.D. degrees. There are clergy people, counselors with master's degrees, psychiatric social workers, regular social workers, sex therapists, certified alcohol counselors, registered nurses, and self-taught counselors with undergraduate or no degrees at all. Some states have minimum requirements in order to hang out a shingle. In California, for example, one needs to have had at least 2,000 hours of supervised counseling to be a li-

censed psychologist. In other states, any one may bill him-
or herself as a counselor.

To compound the difficulty, the results that counselors
get often have no relationship to their degrees. Some of
the best counselors I know have master's degrees, whereas
some psychiatrists, who traditionally are considered the
most prestigious of those groups who counsel, are much
better at dispensing drugs than advice.

Finally, different counselors, no matter what their degree, favor different approaches to the human psyche.
Among the well-known schools of counseling are traditional psychoanalysis, transactional analysis, rational-
emotive therapy, Adlerian psychology, reality therapy, and
behavior modification. There is also a choice to be made
between individual therapy and group therapy. Some therapists are wedded to one approach or another; others call
themselves "eclectic," which means they take a little from
this approach and a little from that, depending on the particular client they are counseling and the specific circumstances.

There are literally dozens of schools of thought. The
most important element is the rapport we have with our
counselor and his or her understanding of addictions. Is
this a person who truly cares about us? Is this a person
who is familiar with the concept of codependency? Will
this counselor resist a tendency to enable us in our coaddiction? Or is the counselor an untreated codependent?

Leaders in the codependency field are beginning to
realize that many people in the helping professions are
unrecovered codependents. Robin Norwood stated in a talk
to counselors in 1986, "I don't believe there are any accidents in relationships, and I also don't believe there are
any accidents in careers. If someone told me that I had
one day to come up with, say, 200 people who were relationship junkies or codependents in their personal lives,
I would go straight to the helping professions." This is
not surprising, since codependents, accustomed as they

are to rescuing people, gravitate toward medicine, nursing, the clergy, counseling, and the teaching professions. The problem is that the counselor's codependency can interfere with the effectiveness of the therapy. If the counselor is afraid to risk another person's anger or disapproval, he may hesitate to confront the client when confrontation is needed. If the counselor has trouble setting limits, he or she may allow manipulation by the client and will schedule extra sessions or allow the entire counseling session to go on too long. If the counselor has difficulty making decisions, it is unlikely that the client will be taught to make decisions. If the counselor has a high tolerance for inappropriate behaviors, it will be difficult to realize if the client also has the same problem. If counselors' helping roles are very important to them, they will help clients do things that the clients need to do for themselves; a simple example of this is the counselor who makes a telephone call that the client should have made.

Codependents usually have a need to be in control; codependent therapists may need to believe that *they*, rather than the client, know what is best for the client, that they are in charge and have all the answers. The therapist may be unwilling to let the client work out solutions for herself. Finally, if the client becomes dependent on the therapist who in turn enjoys the approval, the therapist may prolong the therapy when letting the client go would be appropriate. Howard Halpern explains:

> The proper aim of all these professionals is to enable the person who comes to them to become strong enough and proficient enough to leave them. At times the process of leaving the therapist is difficult, painful, and enlightening. . . . When the therapist is not sufficiently helpful in weaning his patient from dependence on him, the most frequent reason is his own unresolved emotional dependence on his patient. The patient's looking up to him for help and guidance may be too gratifying

to easily give up; the closeness he may feel with the patient may satisfy some of his own Attachment Hunger needs. . . . These motives are often unconscious and are rationalized with interpretations and injunctions such as: "You are trying to run away to avoid looking at feelings that are beginning to emerge"; "You are stopping prematurely so that you can go back to your old patterns"; and "There is much more work."[12]

Codependents judge their worth by what others think of them; therefore, they can be very vulnerable to criticism. By taking criticism personally rather than examining it objectively, codependent therapists may miss an opportunity to confront a client who criticizes them. One counselor told me that when she brought up a client's pattern of affairs with unavailable, married men, the client accused her of insensitivity and not caring. Rather than explore the client's reluctance to discuss her relationships, the counselor found herself feeling defensive and needing to apologize and explain her position. Later she realized that her vulnerability to criticism had gotten in the way of her counseling.

Another characteristic of the untreated codependent counselor is that his or her personal self-esteem is bound up with the outcome of the therapy. If the client does not improve as quickly as the counselor would like, or if the client does not appear to benefit at all from the counseling, the counselor feels like a failure. The fact is, not everyone who comes to see a particular counselor can be helped. The self-esteem of emotionally healthy counselors is supported primarily by the self-knowledge that they have done their best, not from the "cures" they have accomplished.

To peg one's self-esteem on the outcome is to invite professional burnout. Here is what a physician who is also a codependent in a recovery program learned about burnout.

I spend a lot of time advising people to stop smoking, stop drinking, lose weight, and exercise more. I probably talk to ten people a day about these health practices! I tell them how much better they will feel if they follow my advice, and I describe to them all the bad things that are likely to happen to them if they don't. I use every argument I know to persuade them, but only about one in twenty even begins to do what I suggest. I used to get very discouraged; I'd feel that I might as well talk to the wall. My nurse and I used to joke about tape recording my standard antismoking, antidrinking spiel, and have the patient listen to the tape so I wouldn't have to waste my breath since they weren't likely to listen anyway. I felt like a failure with all those patients.

But since getting into my Twelve Step program I feel differently about my role as a physician. I now see that my responsibility is to give my best advice to patients and then to let them make whatever decision they want. Many patients who smoke claim that their doctors never told them to quit or they would have. Well, I can feel good knowing that my patients can never say they never heard it from me. I'm feeling a lot less burned out now that my sense of success or failure doesn't depend on the outcome of my advice. And I've also found that I no longer feel angry at the patient who hasn't followed my advice. I'm sorry that some patients are missing an opportunity to improve their health, but I can still have a friendly relationship with them.

Like this physician, untreated codependent counselors are also vulnerable to burnout and to feelings of anger and frustration if the client doesn't do the "right" thing.

Another consideration in choosing a counselor is the counselor's sex. In most psychotherapy situations, a therapist of either sex can be equally effective. But in the area of sexual addiction and coaddiction, the effect of the counselor's own sex must be carefully considered. First, a man who sees every woman as a potential romantic partner is likely not to take a female therapist very seriously. Instead of focusing on the therapy issues at hand, he will most likely concentrate on winning her over and on proving to her how charming, sincere, and psychologically healthy he is. He may tell the therapist how special she is and how much better she is for him than the previous six counselors he saw. Even if the counselor does not permit herself to be manipulated in this way, much time is likely to be lost and the real issues may never be addressed.

Similarly, the female sexual coaddict who is accustomed to relating sexually to men may have difficulty with a male counselor. She may be so anxious to please him and appear attractive to him that she will not let him see her as she really is. Moreover, she is likely to be particularly vulnerable to his sexual advances should he approach her in this way. It is unfortunately true that sexual relations between therapist and client are fairly common, and are usually very detrimental to the client and to the therapeutic relationship. For example, a 1973 survey of a random sample of 460 male physicians found that 7.2 percent of them had engaged in sexual intercourse with at least one patient.[13] More recently, a nationwide survey of American psychiatrists found that 6.4 percent acknowledged having sexual contact with their own patients.[14] Of the 1,423 psychiatrists surveyed, 80.6 percent were married or in a committed relationship; 84 of the total, including 75 men, admitted having had sexual contact with 144 of their own patients. One-third of the offenders, all male, had been involved with more than one patient.

Sexual contact between psychiatrist and patient is prohibited by the Hippocratic Oath and by the American Psychiatric Association's code of ethics. Nonetheless, in only 24 of the 144 cases did the physician think that the sexual contact had been exploitative, harmful, or inappropriate. In all the other cases, the psychiatrist believed the patient had found the sexual contact "caring," "therapeutic," or "helpful." Only 9.5 percent thought their patients experienced any harm from the relationship. Most of the psychiatrists who regretted the sexual contact did so because of the adverse consequences they suffered rather than the harm done to their patients. One psychiatrist wrote that the experience "cost me my self-esteem, nearly cost me my marriage, and may yet cost me my job or career."

The survey researchers, on the other hand, concluded that sexual contact between psychiatrist and patient is always inappropriate. They stated:

> Patients enter therapy in need of help and care . . . and voluntarily submit themselves to an unequal relationship in which their therapists have superior knowledge and power. Transference feelings related to the universal childhood experience of dependency upon a parent are inevitably aroused. These feelings further exaggerate the power imbalance in the therapeutic relationship and render all patients vulnerable to exploitation. [15]

In other words, in a counseling situation, it is very likely that the patient or client will develop strong, positive feelings toward the therapist, and to take advantage of these feelings is exploitative. The attitude of the psychiatrists who were engaging in sexual contact with their patients can best be described as denial. At the risk of censure by the American Psychiatric Association, possible lawsuits, and even the possible loss of their medical license, some of these psychiatrists had engaged in sexual relations with their patients. Some of them were undoubtedly addicted to affairs.

Addiction is both a behavior disorder and a thinking disorder. The irrational belief system of addicts serves to justify their behavior and at the same time helps them to deny that they have a problem. That the small group of psychiatrists who had sexual relations with more than one patient had a thought disorder typical of addicts is suggested by the disparity between their attitudes and those of psychiatrists who had no sexual involvement with patients. Whereas only one percent of the latter group thought that sexual relations could be beneficial to patients, ten of the sixteen offenders (62 percent) who thought that such relations could benefit their patients were repeaters.[16] In other words, many of the psychiatrists who had a pattern of sexual relations with patients rationalized and justified their behavior by adopting beliefs that contradicted those of the majority of their colleagues. Their beliefs were also directly opposed to the requisites of their own licensing body, the American Psychiatric Association.

It is interesting that among the psychiatrists responding to the survey who reported they had been sexually involved with their own therapists, the majority felt that such contact had been exploitative and harmful.

In 1985, the American Psychiatric Association dropped coverage for sexual misconduct from its liability insurance plan. ''We shouldn't insure an unethical act,'' said the APA's director of public affairs. ''It's not like negligence, which sometimes occurs despite good intentions. With sexual conduct, the physician knows, before he gets into it, that it is unethical.''[17] The nation's second largest liability insurance plan for psychiatrists already did not cover psychiatrists for sexual misconduct. The APA in 1985 also voted to establish a work group to develop an educational program to reduce or eliminate sexual activities between psychiatrists and their patients.

Robin Norwood, counselor and author of *Women Who Love Too Much*, counsels only women. Having spent most of her life in addictive relationships with men, she told an audience she felt it would be difficult for her to remain objective with male clients. When the counselor is a relationship junkie, one of the things that often happens between a female counselor and a male client or a male

counselor and female client is an exaggerated need to rescue the other person. It is a lot safer working with people
whom the counselor doesn't have an overwhelming need
to rescue or a need to be the one who understands better
than anyone else. Since many counselors are codependents, recovering or untreated, Norwood's comments
probably apply to most counselors who counsel addicts
and codependents; it is probably wiser, therefore, for a
client to choose a same-sex therapist for individual counseling.

How does a layperson choose the right therapist? First,
do not be overly swayed by degrees. The exact approach
to counseling is not that important either. Good results
have been obtained with all of the various methods. What
you need to recognize first is that some therapists are better at some problems than at others. Begin by asking
around for names of therapists who are experienced in
working with your issues. These may include your dissatisfaction with your marriage, your self-esteem, or your
suspicion that your husband is having multiple affairs. Talk
with other women who have struggled with these same
issues and who have seen a counselor. Find out how they
felt about their treatment and what the outcome was. Ask
your doctor or your clergyperson for recommendations.
Consider whether you would work as well with a man as
with a woman. Discuss with your husband whether he is
interested in marriage counseling or whether you will be
going alone.

When you have the name of a counselor you'd like to
meet, make an appointment to get acquainted. That first
appointment does not commit you to continue seeing the
therapist. This meeting is your opportunity to ask questions in order to find out whether you are right for each
other. After all, you will be confiding your most intimate
thoughts to this person and you have the right to get to
know something about your counselor before making that
commitment.

If, after reading this book, you have identified yourself as a codependent and if there is the possibility that affairs will be an issue in your counseling, then I believe there are a few key questions you should ask the therapist before you decide to continue seeing him or her.

1. Unless you and your husband have already discussed his affairs openly, he may have an ongoing affair he is hiding from you. If your therapist will be counseling your husband as well as yourself, you need to know whether or not the therapist is willing to counsel a couple if one of the partners is concealing an affair from the other.

I asked this question of a dozen therapists who do marriage counseling, and the answers I got were remarkably diverse. One master's level counselor felt quite comfortable in such a situation; if her counseling could strengthen the marriage bond, she told me, then the affair may become less important. On the other hand, another master's level therapist who was also a Certified Alcoholism Counselor insisted that couples she counseled had to agree to have no other relationships during treatment. If one of them was having an affair, he had to bring it up within two sessions, either in the counseling setting or outside; otherwise, she would terminate the therapy. Her reasoning was that intimacy issues were causing the couple problems. If one of them was having an affair, then he was not focusing his energy on the marriage relationship. If he was not willing to participate fully in the therapy, then the counseling was an exercise in futility. Moreover, this counselor was not willing to be party to a secret. If the man was a sex addict, then secrecy was part of his disease and she was unwilling to "enable" him.

Several other therapists, like the alcoholism counselor, alluded to their own discomfort with the dishonesty of being party to a secret. One Ph.D.-level counselor, who refused to work with a couple where there was a concealed affair, wanted to avoid a scenario in which the wife stated she suspected an affair or complained that her husband was acting distant, the husband denied everything, and the therapist had to act ignorant. "If it ultimately comes out that I knew about the affair, it would destroy the trust that the ignorant partner [the wife] had in me," she explained. Another therapist said she would feel inhibited in the session because of her knowledge and her need to hold back. Yet another counselor would be unwilling to collude in deceiving one of her clients. A male counselor said he would not want to be an accomplice to the husband's deception.

A more middle-of-the road approach was expressed by other counselors. Working with the husband individually, they would explore his motive for being in counseling. If it's to make a graceful exit from the marriage, then counseling is futile. If the husband's goal is a sincere effort to improve the marriage relationship, then these counselors might work with the couple for a while, meanwhile encouraging the husband in individual sessions to end the affair, or tell the spouse about it, or both. If the husband's energy is being directed primarily toward the affair and not toward the marriage, then they would terminate the counseling. These counselors did not see a problem with their having information about the affairs that they could not reveal to the wife.

Most of the counselors who would not counsel a couple if there was a secret affair would gladly work individually with the husband or wife. They would attempt to clarify with the husband the extent of his commitment to the marriage and would help him to end the affair if that was his wish.

It is important to know in advance how your counselor feels about the issue of concealed affairs. As my brief survey shows, opinions are varied. It is also helpful to consider how much *you* want to know. Perhaps you are not ready to hear that there is another woman in your husband's life. Many women would really rather not know. If you are one of them, then you and your husband may be better off getting individual counseling, at least initially. Whatever your preference, you need a clear understanding of your therapist's attitude *before* committing yourself to therapy.

2. Because sex addiction is so often linked to substance abuse, find out your counselor's approach to chemical dependency. A recovering cocaine addict related that when he told a marriage counselor about his cocaine use, the counselor stated, "Before I can do anything about your marriage, you have to first get treatment for your cocaine addiction." If your husband is a problem drinker as well as involved in affairs, will your counselor assume that the drinking is a consequence of the marriage problems? Or will he or she refuse to do marriage counseling until your husband is sober? You need to know this before you commit yourself to this counselor. Therapists who are familiar with chemical dependency know that the drug of choice has priority over everything else, including the marriage. An alcoholic cannot work on his marriage until his mind is free of the effects of alcohol.

The same is true of affairs. To the sex addict, the chase, the conquest, the clandestine meetings, and the secret telephone conversations have first priority. He cannot give your marriage the attention it deserves while he is still focused on the affair. Marriage counseling is not likely to be successful at this stage.

3. Does your therapist have any familiarity with addictions and codependency? Has she ever attended an A.A. or an Al-Anon meeting? Is she familiar with the Twelve Steps? Has she ever heard of sex addiction or is she at least open to that possibility? A psychiatrist who does marriage counseling in my community told a reporter that he thinks calling affairs an addiction "could amount to kind of a whitewash." According to a newspaper account, the psychiatrist says:

Couples are often mismatched in terms of sexual appetite, causing stress in their relationship. Rather than sexual addiction, he [the psychiatrist] said it sounded to him as if the members of a sexual addiction recovery program have difficulty maintaining a close and satisfactory relationship, so they keep changing partners as a way of avoiding closeness. Maybe they are people of normal sexual appetite who are afraid of getting close personally.[18]

How this psychiatrist would counsel a couple that is dealing with multiple affairs is obviously different from the counseling of a therapist familiar with the concept of sex addiction.

Unfortunately, even well-known experts in the field of sexuality may be ignorant about sex addiction and may do injustice to those who are dealing with this issue by suggesting that the problem may not even exist. For example, Dr. Ruth Westheimer, a popular television sex therapist, wrote recently in her column, "Ask Dr. Ruth," "I don't know what sexual addiction is and I suspect that it is a phony issue." She added that she does not believe that an inborn natural desire for sex can be equated with an acquired need for a harmful substance. Although people at times can let sex make them miserable instead of joyous, she concluded, sexual desire itself cannot be an addiction.[19]

A couple consulting Dr. Ruth about the husband's multiple affairs would probably be instructed in how to improve their own sexual relationship; they would be unlikely to get help for their addiction and coaddiction.

If you can identify yourself as a codependent and are aware of a pattern of addictions in your family or your relationships or both, you may wish to choose a counselor who is familiar with addictions and with the self-help recovery groups. Chemical dependency treatment centers are an excellent resource for the names of such counselors. Members of Twelve Step programs are also often familiar with knowledgeable counselors in the community. To such a counselor the Twelve Steps are a valuable tool in recovery. The counselor considers her work as complementary to the Twelve Step meetings that a client should attend.

Knowledgeable addiction counselors believe that group work is the mainstay of recovery from codependency. Group therapy counteracts the secrecy and isolation that are such an important part of codependency. Individual counseling is very useful at various times, especially at the beginning when many people are reluctant to go to and are fearful of group therapy. Some of us who feel ashamed about particular things we have done as well as about our husband's behavior, and who have often been brought up with the belief that "we do not air our dirty laundry in public," may be uncomfortable talking in a group. Attendance at a group is desirable, and is a goal to be worked toward. Ask your counselor where group therapy fits into the treatment plan. Does she think it would be beneficial for you?

In *Treating the Alcoholic*, Stephanie Brown, a clinical psychologist who founded the Stanford Alcohol Clinic at Stanford University, discusses the role of the psychotherapist who is treating a recovering alcoholic. She believes that the most effective use of the psychotherapist is as the third member of a triad that also includes the client and A.A. "Psychotherapeutic help may be necessary for some and certainly is desirable for most," she writes, "but only if the therapist can appreciate the positive ongoing value of A.A. and the importance of an integrated triadic therapeutic approach."[20] In early recovery, she advises the therapist to leave the behavioral changes and education of the client to A.A. and to provide the client with clarification or suggestions and with a supportive environment. She believes that the individual who forms a positive and active tie with A.A. may need little active intervention from the therapist other than wholehearted support for strengthening the A.A. tie. Later on, the therapist can work with the client on the strong feelings which emerge during recovery, such as anxiety and fear. The therapist can review the past and help to explain past behaviors, and can support the development of autonomy and the establishment of healthy relationships. In this phase too the therapist is urged to work constructively with A.A.

I believe that the same suggestions apply to the therapist who counsels a recovering coaddict. Working along with your Twelve Step meetings, an experienced counselor can facilitate your recovery whether you are alone or still married. Having worked with other women who made the same journey as yourself, your therapist can pretty well predict how you will feel at each stage in your recovery. She can tell you, "Soon you will feel scared about what's happening." When you do, she can reassure you that this is an expected stage in the process and can discuss with you how to deal with it. She can also determine whether couple counseling or individual counseling is best for you at any particular time, and when entry into a group would be helpful.

The Marriage

Can we recover from our coaddiction and remain married to men who are still having affairs? Many Al-Anon members have found serenity while continuing to live with a practicing alcoholic. They do this by "detaching with love" and avoiding all expectations of the alcoholic. They plan a separate life. If the alcoholic happens to show up at the ten-year-old daughter's birthday party, or if he remembers the twentieth wedding anniversary, great; if not, they celebrate without him. By doing this, they avoid disappointment, resentment, and anger. But—and this to me is a crucial point—they also avoid having any nurturing or supportive relationship with their spouse. The essence of a relationship is expectations; without any commitment on the part of the addicted spouse there is no relationship. They are merely occupying the same household.

Erich Fromm, in his book, *The Art of Loving*, lists four basic elements common to all forms of love: (1) *care*—an active concern for the life and growth of the other person; (2) *responsibility*—the ability to respond to the needs of the other, generally to the psychic needs of the other; (3) *respect*—the ability to see the other person as a unique individual, not as an object of exploitation; and (4) *knowledge* of the other person.[21] The active addict cannot consistently show caring, responsibility, and respect to his partner and therefore cannot love her.

I don't believe that an emotionally healthy woman would choose to remain with a spouse with whom there is no relationship and who cannot love her. To remain with such a spouse is to continue to believe that one does not deserve to be nurtured by another person. It is to let one's guilt ("He needs me—I just can't leave him") take precedence over one's needs. It is my personal bias that to remain in such a situation is a sign of unhealthiness. A certified addiction and codependency counselor whom I interviewed agrees: "Detaching, yes; you're not supposed to get in there and try to change him. But, by God, if he's not changing and it's really unhealthy, then part of *your* health is to say, 'This is not for me, I don't have to stick around. I hope you get better. Good-bye.' "

Another problem with "detaching with love" is that it can be a form of *enabling* the sex addict. If there are no consequences to his behavior, then he will have no motivation to change. Allowing the addict to experience the negative consequences of his behavior, which is the opposite of enabling, might lead him to seek help more quickly. In the chemical dependency field, an accepted method of "helping the alcoholic who does not want help" is *intervention*, which is a carefully planned meeting between the alcoholic and the people who are important to him, such as parents, spouse, and employer. At this meeting each of these people firmly tell the alcoholic how he has hurt himself and them by his drinking and ask that he enter treatment. Because the alcoholic cares about the people who confront him, the overall effect of the meeting is to break through his denial of the significance of his drinking; he might agree to immediate treatment.

Similarly, the woman who has recovered sufficiently from her own coaddiction so that she no longer is willing to live with the pain of her husband's affairs can sometimes break through his denial that he has a problem by deciding to leave, thus precipitating a crisis. The fear of loss of the marriage partner has brought many alcoholics and other addicts to treatment. However, this is true only if the wife is serious about her intent to leave, and is not using the threat of leaving as a way of manipulating her husband.

A recovering woman married to a man who is still having affairs faces additional challenges in her own recovery. Accustomed to believing her husband's word rather than her own feelings, she may doubt that she really needs a program—after all, her husband doesn't seem to think there's a problem. Or else, in her enthusiasm for her new discoveries, she will want to share the good news with him and to help him into treatment. She must fight this tendency to continue controlling him and running his life. Conflict between the pair may initially increase—he may feel threatened as he notices her behavior changing, and he may try to prevent her from attending self-help meetings.

Probably the biggest obstacle to recovery for a woman who is involved with a practicing addict is her fear of living alone. From her discussions with other recovering women and with her counselor she will soon realize that as she gets healthier emotionally she will most likely be unwilling to stay in the relationship unless he changes too. Terrified of having to let him go, she may decide instead to forego changing herself and maintain the status quo.

This fear is probably the primary reason that women drop out of self-help programs for partners of sexual addicts.

I have not yet met a recovering coaddict who is still married to a practicing sex addict and plans to remain married. The women I have talked with either are divorced from a man who continues to have affairs, married to a man who is also in a recovery program, or else are so early in their own recovery that they acknowledge their inability to get out of a relationship they feel they will need to leave eventually. These latter women feel that their current situation is temporary. One woman I interviewed who feels she has had a spiritual awakening and is now quite healthy has chosen to remain with her sexually addicted husband until she finishes college and is better able to support herself.

For some recovering coaddicts, there is no urgency in leaving the relationship. We are not in the relationship by accident; unless we understand *why* we are in it, we are likely to have to learn the same lesson in our next relationship. We will need some time in our own recovery process before we are really ready to make a decision about staying in or leaving the relationship.

CHAPTER NINE

"As long as the good outweighs the bad"

Recovery as a Couple

At a support group meeting, a divorced woman struggling to make it as a single parent looked enviously at one who was still married and said, "You're so lucky—your husband saw the light, recognized that he has a problem with affairs, and is getting help. You're still together, and you can get a new start as a married couple. You don't have to be alone. My husband never thought he had a problem—and still doesn't. Now that we're divorced, he's enjoying dating lots of different women, while I'm sitting at home with the kids, feeling lonely, and trying to convince myself that I'm really okay without a man."

Recovery from coaddiction or relationship addiction surely differs in some respects when you are married compared with when you are single. Chapter Eight discussed the situation of a woman who tries to recover from her coaddiction while her husband is still acting out or does not recognize that his affairs are a problem. Chapter Ten will address the problems of the woman who is recovering alone. This chapter is aimed specifically at the woman whose husband is also attempting to change his behavior and where both are committed to the marriage relationship.

In some respects the recovering couple is indeed very lucky. The partners have an opportunity to restructure their marriage and to establish a new level of honesty and intimacy—and with the same partner. They avoid the anguish of a divorce, the disruption of establishing separate households, and the pain of learning to live alone. The children are spared the turmoil of the breakup of their family. One of the priorities of the divorced woman is learning to make a better choice in subsequent relationships; the married woman does not have to test herself on the dating scene.

But in other ways, the recovering couple has particular stresses and problems that the single woman does not. First and probably foremost, powerful negative feelings have built up over the years that may be impossible to forget. Resentments over our husband's affairs, hurtful behaviors, and emotional unavailability have accumulated for so long they cannot be erased merely because his behavior has changed. Recognizing through our own self-help program and counseling that we are not entirely blameless can help us to let go of the resentments, but this is a lengthy process and can take years. Sometimes we are unable to forgive totally, and a residue of bitterness remains. Bruce, the former minister who has been attending a recovery group for sex addicts for the past two years, told me:

Sometimes I think it would be so much easier to start all over again with a new person. I can understand Barbara's resentment—all those years that I was putting out a lot of energy toward the women I saw and none toward Barbara. She kept the family going while I was having fun and giving her nothing. But now I've been in the program for two years, without a single "slip," and we still don't have a good relationship. She sees how hard I'm trying and she tries too, but I guess twenty bad years are hard to erase; I don't know if we'll ever really be close. Now that I feel so differently about commitment to a relationship, I fantasize sometimes how it could be with someone if we didn't have the accumulated burden of our past always with us. But how can we give up now, when we're both finally trying to make some real changes in our marriage?

Having interviewed women who were married between two and twenty-eight years before they and their husbands entered recovery programs, I found that those who were married for the fewest years seem to have the easiest time letting go of their resentment and anger. This is not surprising, since couples with a short history together have a shorter negative history as well. When I asked Rita, who has been through addiction treatment with her husband and who regularly attends recovery group meetings, whether she thinks her twenty-year marriage to Ralph will survive, she replied, after a long pause, "I don't know. I know I want it to, and I know Ralph wants it to." Their relationship contained lying, distrust, resentment, and other bad feelings for so long that it is still a real struggle for them, two years later, to turn things around.

A woman who attended a combined self-help meeting for recovering sex addicts, their spouses, and divorced people, confirmed this problem:

The couples who had been married a long time and said that things are better than ever did not look happy! There just seems to have been too much pain to erase. The most enthusiastic members were probably the single people— they were truly getting a new start in their lives. I'm glad my husband and I found the group early in our marriage.

Couples who have been together for many years have deeply entrenched patterns of relating to one another. Even if both are willing to make changes in a recovery program, the old patterns are very difficult to alter.

A second major problem for married women is their tendency to monitor their husband's recovery program and to gauge their actions accordingly. This, of course, is a continuation of their coaddictive behavior. The single woman has an advantage because she is in a new environment where she can focus on her own recovery. In contrast, married women have the task of trying to make changes in their behavior and thinking, while living with the man they spent years trying to control. Chemical dependency counselors know how difficult it is for addicts to remain sober if their environment is unchanged, even if they are working hard to change their attitudes with the help of the Twelve Steps. For this reason counselors often advise alcoholics to stay away from drinking buddies, bars, and situations where drinking takes place. Sexual coaddicts have the difficult task of overcoming their relationship addiction while continuing the relationship with the man to whom they have been addicted.

For those of us in recovery who see hope for our marriage, it is natural to try to make it a success in any way we can. When we see our partner attending meetings, talking on the phone with other Twelve Step group members, and acting committed to change, our reaction is likely to be not to make any waves that might hurt his progress toward recovery. We might try especially hard not to get into arguments with him, not to make any demands, and to overlook any minor failings or transgressions on his part. If he wants to make love and we aren't in the mood, we very likely go along with him, particularly now that we know he is committed to monogamy. In early recovery, no matter how many meetings we attend and how committed we are to the principle that we cannot control our husband's behavior nor his addiction, we often find it difficult to avoid trying to help him in all the old coaddictive ways. Feeling bad or guilty about our efforts is useless. It is better to recognize our actions as inevitable; we will be able to let go more and more as the weeks and months go by. For now, it is enough for us to *recognize* that we are still trying to control him, since awareness of the problem is the first step toward change.

Another coaddictive behavior we often fall into in early recovery is monitoring our husband's progress. We feel the need to be informed to reassure ourselves that he is seriously involved in his recovery program. We might check on whether he went to his meetings, and we want to know about every temptation and how he handled it. What we really feel is that if we know everything that is going on in our husband's mind, we can control or at least influence what he is thinking. Although we may admit that this is illogical, it is hard for us to feel comfortable with not knowing what is going on. We probably will feel more and more comfortable later in our recovery.

Thus, for those of us who are starting our own recoveries, we often struggle with daily slips that we recognize but can't seem to prevent. It usually takes months to years in recovery programs before we truly believe that a man is but the icing on the cake of our lives; until then, the part of us that is terrified of abandonment will do almost anything to hold on to our husbands, and repeatedly act in ways that our healthier selves recognize as coaddictive. Eventually, we'll be able to recognize slips in our thinking before acting on them—even these mental lapses become less frequent.

So far I have discussed the problems a woman faces because she is still living with the man to whom she has been addicted. In addition, there are specific issues couples must face together as they restructure their relationship. These include

- celibacy;
- deciding how much to tell the spouse about our past and what to tell the children;

- setting limits and boundaries on each partner's behavior; and
- re-establishing trust.

Celibacy

Sex and celibacy, which is abstinence from sex, are very closely connected. As Gabrielle Brown, Ph.D., author of *The New Celibacy*, wrote:

> Just as silence is the basis for sound, for speech, for music, celibacy is the basis for sex. . . . Celibacy can be understood in the context of sexuality as the subtlest form of sexuality—potential but unexpressed.[1]

Celibacy can occur by default—because no attractive partner is available, or because one's personality prevents the person from comfortably engaging in any sexual activity—or it can happen by choice. We cannot choose to be celibate unless we can also choose to be sexual. When sexual activity is a compulsion, not a choice, celibacy clearly does not constitute a viable option. To learn that life without sex *is* possible is an important part of recovery.

An inpatient recovery program for sexual addiction requires each patient, upon admission, to sign a 90-day celibacy contract that prohibits sex with self or others. Maintaining celibacy gives the patient a measure of success, preventing him from using inappropriate sexual behavior to perpetuate the cycle of sexual dependency. It also allows him to practice intimacy outside a sexual relationship and to become aware of his repressed feelings. Finally, maintaining celibacy lets the sex addict learn more effective ways of dealing with pain and guilt.[2]

Some sex addicts in self-help programs based on the Twelve Steps of A.A. have also found that a period of celibacy can be very useful early in the recovery process.

For the person who has always believed sex is his most important need, it is a real educational experience to find out that he *can* survive without sex. "I didn't die," said one man with surprise about his experience with celibacy. Moreover, during a period of celibacy he can begin to view his spouse as a human being rather than as a means for his sexual gratification.

The sex addict who experiences celibacy, like the alcoholic who gives up the bottle, learns that he can manage without his "drug of choice." For his wife, however, there is a key difference in these two situations. In an alcoholic marriage, the decision of the alcoholic spouse to stop drinking does not force the other spouse to do the same. The wife of a recovering alcoholic may choose not to keep liquor in the house, but she may have a drink at a friend's house or at a restaurant. In contrast, the decision of one spouse to give up sex prevents the other from experiencing sexual intimacy.

Before recovery, our attention was focused on our husband's needs. Decisions were usually based on what would be good for him rather than us. In the sexual area, we generally ignored our own wishes in deference to those of our spouse. Perhaps out of fear of abandonment, we learned never to deny him sex. Should our recovering spouse now decide that he needs a period of "sexual detoxification," the message we may interpret is that, once again, *our* needs do not merit consideration. We might find ourselves feeling resentful that we were not included in the decision. Because we sincerely want our husband to succeed in his recovery program, we feel guilty about feeling resentful. We think, now that my husband is finally admitting his problem and doing something about it, I certainly can't rock the boat—I'll just have to do whatever is best for him. This perpetuates the previous pattern of the marriage.

Another likely outcome of a unilateral celibacy decision is that we will feel rejected and unwanted. One of our core beliefs may be that sex is the most important sign of love. When our husband withdraws sex, we might logically conclude that we are no longer loved. Our instinctive reaction will be to try to win him back sexually. This, of course, will only serve to sabotage his program. We may realize this and stop ourselves from trying to seduce our husband. Caught in the middle of conflicting feelings, we will feel powerless and out of control.

Sex in a marriage is a relationship issue. In order for us to feel comfortable about a period of celibacy, the decision must be a joint one. When this happens, many benefits can accrue to us and to the relationship.

1. *We find out that we're wanted for more than just our bodies and that we can get love without giving sex.*

For Patty, the petite, attractive 25-year-old blonde, sex has been an important element in all her relationships, including her current marriage to a man who had multiple affairs in both his previous marriage and the present one. Patty's little-girl manner and her take-care-of-me body language are what strike the observer first; it takes several minutes of conversation with her to realize that she is an intelligent, articulate person who is also a successful career woman.

When Peter started going to Twelve Step meetings, he came home and asked me about celibacy. I said, "No way!" I certainly wasn't going to do that; it was just too frightening to me. Eventually I agreed, but it scared me to death at first. I realized that to me sex had been security. If things had been horrible and then we made love, then I thought, Phew! He still wants me. It was my security. During that month of celibacy, a real bond came between us. We knew that it was more than just sex we wanted in the relationship; we wanted each other. We learned just to enjoy snuggling. We'd wake up in the morning and we'd hold each other. I found myself able to ask him, "Would

*you hold me? Would you give me a kiss?'' It was very
comfortable.*

A very different experience was had by Diane, the 30-
year-old school teacher, whose husband decided on his
own to avoid sex as a part of his recovery program. Looking back on that period, she recalls:

*I felt rejected, that there was something wrong with me,
you know, the old equating of love and sex. I think if it
had been an actual agreement I wouldn't have felt personally rejected or deprived.*

When husbands and wives agree mutually to a period
of celibacy and then continue to act lovingly toward each
other, they learn, through the husband's actions, that their
beliefs about sex were irrational. They learn that they are
worthwhile people, that they are lovable for themselves,
that sex is not the most important sign of love, and that
they don't need to control their spouses through sex.

2. *Celibacy forces us to adopt new coping strategies and
face problems directly.*

Linda, the 45-year-old socialite, had sexual relations
with her computer programmer husband two or three times
a day for most of their 25 years of married life. She rarely
enjoyed these encounters because she felt like an object
that was being used for her husband's sexual gratification.
Before they got into recovery, Linda would overlook her
husband's many affairs. Linda is slender, athletic, and ex-
pensively dressed. Her shiny black hair is brushed back
into an elegant chignon. She looks relaxed and self-
confident.

*I used to use sex. When Lawrence and I had an argu-
ment and he was angry at me, I knew I had a tool. I could
get him into bed, and as long as he made love to me,*

everything was going to be all right. And it was. When Lawrence suggested a period of celibacy and we stopped having sex, I didn't have this tool anymore. Instead, I had to talk with him about the problem and try to resolve things instead of substituting sex for a solution.

Also, part of me believed that the only reason Lawrence was staying with me was for all the sex I was giving him. During our months of celibacy I found out that wasn't true. It was a wonderful discovery. Now I know that my husband doesn't need that from me—that our marriage can still go on as a happy, loving relationship without all that sex.

3. A celibacy period can be the bridge to a new sexual relationship in which we feel more comfortable paying attention to our own needs.

Patty relates:

I've been learning that I've got to satisfy myself and he's not responsible for that. Both of us have experienced a real connectedness with each other. Before, I never knew where his mind was and I was always trying to figure it out. I never really enjoyed the physical part because my mind was so involved in trying to figure out what he was thinking and what he wanted. I felt so used before, I felt he really didn't want to be there. I always let him initiate sex. If he decided to have sex, then we did, and I never said no. Now I'm beginning to ask myself, "How do I feel about making love? Do I want to, or do I not want to?"

Linda, too, found a new freedom in the way she relates to her husband sexually.

When we ended our period of celibacy, it frightened me to death. I was afraid things would go back to the way they were before, but they haven't. One time when Lawrence wanted to make love I said no, and it was fine. He

*didn't insist and argue the way he used to, and my guilt
for saying no lasted only about 30 seconds. Now if I don't
feel like having sex, I know I don't have to.*

Linda has learned that it is safe to pay attention to her
own needs.

4. *A period of celibacy can allow us to work through
our own issues.*

Rita, a 38-year-old psychotherapist whose husband had
affairs with both men and women, has requested two periods of celibacy since they both went into recovery programs. The first time was immediately after she learned
of his affairs. A lot of publicity about AIDS was just coming out, and Rita was so fearful of contracting this disease
that she did not want to have sexual relations with her
husband. It took her some weeks to overcome this fear.

The second time Rita wanted a period of celibacy was
when, in the course of counseling, she remembered something she had long repressed: in childhood she had been
raped by her brother. Suddenly, when her husband touched
her sexually, she found herself confusing him in her mind
with her brother. She needed time out from the sexual
relationship to work through the rape in her counseling
sessions. That her husband was supportive of her requests
for celibacy helped to improve their marriage relationship.

5. *A period of celibacy in a relationship that is committed to growth can result in renewed intimacy and can
teach us new, deeper levels of relating.*

According to Linda:

*Lawrence and I used to hold hands now and then, but
he hated it. He never wanted to be hugged, never wanted
to be touched, never wanted to be kissed. He wanted sex,
but that was as far as the intimacy ever went. Now we're*

trying to touch more. When I walk by him, I'll pat him on the shoulder. It's a gradual process.

Not only Lawrence and other sex addicts, but many members of American society are uncomfortable with nonsexual touching. Most Europeans shake hands on meeting someone and on leaving, and the French and Italians hug and kiss each other routinely. In the United States, nonsexual hugging and kissing are common only among women friends and between parents and children or other relatives.

Touching is a basic human and animal need. In Harry Harlow's famous experiments with baby monkeys separated from their mothers, those who had a soft, fuzzy, surrogate mother in their cage to cling to for comfort developed normally, whereas those babies who had only a wire mesh surrogate grew up neurotic and were unable to form relationships with their peers. Human babies who are fed and diapered adequately but who are deprived of touching do not gain weight. Both animals and humans require touching as part of normal development.

Somehow in our society touching has become confused with sex. Many of us are therefore fearful that an innocent touch will be misunderstood as an invitation to sex. If our foot accidentally touches another's leg, then we will usually apologize. Many of us have never learned how to give or receive nonsexual touch. One of the benefits of a period of celibacy is that it gives us the freedom to explore nonsexual touching.

6. *A period of abstinence teaches that sex is optional.* Nancy, the 40-year-old mother of seven comments:

Our sexual relationship is very different now. He's there, making love with me. And we don't feel the pressure to have sex. If we start but then one of us isn't in the mood,

*we'll just drop it for now. Our spiritual life comes first,
and we're not ruled by sex so much anymore.*

Gabrielle Brown provides a good description of the way
a period of celibacy can put a relationship on a new basis:

Celibacy provides married couples with more choices
of expression—a kind of limitless market of possible
connections. It may be like "courting" all over again,
but without the fear of rejection or the limitation of future goals. If a husband brings flowers to his spouse as
a first step or prelude to a great night of sexual love,
the meaning of the flowers becomes lost in the chain of
events that follow. But flowers in times of celibacy are
a thing-in-themselves—perhaps the whole expression of
love for that day, not simply an offering to insure the
future.

Celibacy can give the couple the chance both to re-
establish presexual communication of tender feelings
and to open new channels of expression free from re-
strictive associative behavior. It can be a time for re-
newal of old feelings that occurred before sexual habits
set in, and it can be a time to discover other modalities
[ways] of loving. It can re-create and create the un-
bounded qualities of romance—the intensity, energy,
sweetness, simplicity, and careful attention of two people falling in love.[3]

Not all couples in recovery need or want a period of
celibacy. This is very much an individual choice. What is
important, however, is that a decision for celibacy needs
to be made mutually, not by one person or the other. If
one partner wishes a period of celibacy, the reasons should
be discussed and understood. Celibacy should not be used
by one partner as a way of punishing the other. Nor should
it be used to avoid dealing with problems in the marriage,
or as a way to avoid intimacy. When approached in a pos-

itive spirit, celibacy can be a period of spiritual growth and increased intimacy in the marriage.

Sex

When a man who uses sex to feel good marries a woman who believes sex is the most important sign of love, sex is likely to constitute a very important part of their relationship. By the time both partners are in enough emotional pain to seek treatment, about half the couples will be having significant problems in their sexual relationship. The remaining women are likely to say, "Our sex was so good, I don't understand why he had to have affairs." Entering a recovery program can cause major changes in a couple's sexual relationship. Some were discussed in the section on celibacy; others will be mentioned here.

Most married couples have unspoken rules about their sexual relationship. For example, some men are always the initiators. Many women never say no. In the recovery process, the rules that formerly governed many aspects of the couple's life together are replaced by new rules. In the sexual sphere, these rules may take some getting used to; things may get worse before they get better.

Judy, a 35-year-old social worker confided:

In my family, no one talked about sex. In my 16 years of marriage, George was always the aggressor. I never talked with him about my sexual feelings—I just didn't know how to talk about these things. Now George wants to know how I feel. He's trying to be more sensitive to my needs. He wants me to be more actively involved and to initiate our lovemaking. I just don't know what to say or do, but I want to learn because I really like the new George.

In the past, our sexual feelings often might have been enhanced by the fear and uncertainty in our relationship.

The unpredictability of our husband's behavior added excitement to our lovemaking. If we argued and then reconciled by making love, the excitement of the argument was experienced as part of the excitement of the sexual activity. For such couples, sex during recovery may be less intense than it was before.

Jessica, the intensive care unit nurse, remembers:

In the old days, sex with Joe was always very exciting. I expected that when he stopped having affairs and our life together straightened out, then the sex would be even better. But that's not what happened—we've grown closer in many ways and are now experiencing real intimacy, but our sex is just not as intense as before. It took me a while to realize that the intensity I used to feel was all mixed up with the craziness of my life. When I'd spent all day obsessed with thoughts of Joe, worrying whether he still loved me, naturally it was very exciting to fall into bed with him. I no longer feel that panic and uncertainty. Our lovemaking is calmer, more intimate. It's different from before. Joe and I are really there for each other. We're making love to each other, instead of just using sex to feel loved or to temporarily forget bad feelings.

Here is Joe's side of the story:

I used to do a lot of fantasizing in bed. My body would be making love to my wife, but my mind was miles away with some attractive girl who had recently crossed my path. Jessica thought I was a terrific lover, but she didn't realize it wasn't her I was really making love to. Things are different now. I don't allow myself to fantasize about other women—I want Jessica to be the woman in my mind as well as in my bed. This wasn't easy at first; I had to really retrain my mind to focus on Jessica. Fantasizing about other women may be okay for most men, but not for me. What it did was isolate me from Jessica. Now I feel much closer to her emotionally, and I feel a lot better about our lovemaking.

The key to a successful restructuring of the sexual relationship is a willingness to talk to each other about feelings. It is not easy for most couples to discuss sex, and it is especially difficult for many codependents who have grown up believing it's not okay to talk about feelings. Both in counseling sessions and in self-help meetings, people are encouraged to express feelings. As they hear others doing so, they begin to believe that the group is a safe place to risk emotional vulnerability. With communication about feelings, couples can deal with many sexual problems that may occur.

Several couples I interviewed agreed that their sexual relationship was better now than when the man was having affairs. They attributed this to the overall improvement in their relationship. They now felt less isolated, more connected, and more concerned with the other. As the level of trust in each other increased, so did the intimacy and sharing in their marriage. Sex became for them an enjoyable affirmation of their commitment to each other rather than the most important element in their relationship.

What Should a Man Tell His Wife About His Past?

When a man is having affairs, his wife often suspects it. What brings many couples into treatment, however, is a crisis in the marriage that occurs when evidence of the latest affair is so blatant that it can no longer be denied. The husband is then forced to admit the affair. Some wives at this point will ask for more information, and the husband must decide how much to reveal.

In recovery, too, there are times when a similar choice must be made. If a man has a one-night stand after two years of monogamy, should he tell his wife? What about if he is only considering a sexual escapade—does she need to know about that? The whole issue of "How much should I tell my wife?" is very complex.

Sexaholics Anonymous, a book about recovery used by the members of a self-help group, cautions the recovering addict to be very careful about confessing his sexual sins to his spouse. The book advises that newcomers to the program not discuss their sexual past with family members who do not already know of it until some time has elapsed, and even then only after discussing it first with group members. The book cautions that some marriages might otherwise not withstand the shock. Avoiding compulsive sexual behavior and working the Steps of the program will, it is hoped, cause improvement in behavior and attitude that the spouse will see and feel. "The best amends is a changed life over time."[4]

Hope and Recovery: A Twelve-Step Guide for Healing from Compulsive Sexual Behavior expresses the same point of view. The recovering addicts who authored this book advise waiting to tell the spouse until one has discussed it with the group, prayed about it, and felt it was the right time to do so.

> Some of us found that it was helpful to have our sponsors with us when we told our partners about our addiction. And if our partners also happened to be in recovery, it was helpful to have their sponsors present, too. . . . We wrote down exactly what we wanted to say to our partners and shared it with other addicts first.[5]

When affairs or the preoccupation with other women has been a recurring theme in the marriage, however, it may be advisable to give the spouse some information. For Alice, her husband's willingness to answer questions was a critical element in restoring trust in the relationship:

For my first two years of marriage, I lived on a roller coaster. My husband had wide mood swings which didn't seem to correlate with anything that was happening in our lives. At times when I would be feeling particularly happy with him and would tell him, he would respond in a deliberately hurtful way. Romantic vacations would be spoiled by his bad moods. Plans would be changed at the last minute. I kept trying to make sense of it all, and I kept feeling crazier and crazier.

I had no idea he was leading a separate life of affairs and fantasies and lies. One day when he tried to break an affair off, she threatened to tell me about it, so he told me first. I thought I was going to die; I could hardly breathe. But as I revived, I felt a tremendous need to put the pieces together. I asked for specific dates, for details on the ups and downs of their relationship. It was painful to hear the answers, and my husband kept trying to end the dialogue. But I insisted, and he answered everything I asked. There were things I didn't ask, because I didn't want to know.

The answers I got to my questions provided explanations for so many puzzling things that had happened, so many times I'd thought I was crazy. Now I knew why he had been so hurtful on a particular vacation. I had said, ''You're so good to me,'' and his guilt over the affair, which was at its peak at that time, made him unable to accept the compliment; he needed to prove to me on the spot that he wasn't good to me. . . . Now I knew that I hadn't been crazy after all, that I had been right those times when I'd had a strong gut feeling that something was wrong, that he had been lying when he'd told me, ''You're just imagining things.''

I realized that on one level I had been aware all along of what was happening with him. To have him tell me the truth was to acknowledge the validity of those feelings. Not to have told me would have meant to keep me wondering.

And another thing: Over the years I had begun to distrust him. Things just didn't add up. Not to have told me would have kept the distrust going. By answering all my questions, my husband began to rebuild trust in the rela-

tionship. This was a process that took many months. It is true that "the best amends is a changed life over time." But for me, the first step toward renewed trust after all the deceit was to receive honest answers from him. Evasiveness would have perpetuated the distrust.

Now, three years later, I still have no guarantees that my husband will not have another affair. But, based on that initial honesty and on the continued honesty since then, what I do know is that he will be honest with me. He will not assume he knows better than I do about what I should know. He will treat me as an adult, not as a little girl who needs protection. For me, honesty was crucial to the survival of our marriage during that crisis; I am glad he told me about his past.

In many addictive relationships, we rest the responsibility for our happiness in the hands of our spouse. We give him the power to make us happy or unhappy, and to make decisions about our emotional life. For the husband to decide what information we should have about his past is to perpetuate the old pattern, to agree that the husband is a better judge of what is best for us than we are ourselves. In individual cases this may be true, but in most cases I believe that the wife is the best judge of what is best for her in the relationship.

This sentiment was echoed by Rita:

When Ralph asked the other guys whether he should tell me about his past, everyone said, "No, don't tell her; I know a guy who told his wife, and she left him." The counselors in his treatment program wouldn't tell Ralph what to do; they wanted him to make the decision on his own, but they believed he needed to tell me the truth. So Ralph told me, and I'm glad he did. It validated my sanity. I could look back and say, "So that's why that happened when it did. I really wasn't crazy!" Everything seemed to

*fall in place for me. All the things I'd thought, I'd sus-
pected, were true.*

*I also believed that if I were going to rebuild this marriage
with Ralph, the only way I could do so was to know his dark
side as well as the good about him. I didn't believe then, and
I don't believe today, that anyone in his recovery group has a
right to know a secret about Ralph that I don't have the right
to know. What I've grown to understand in my own recovery
is that if there's a secret between us, there's a wall, and I don't
want to live with that anymore.*

An entirely different point of view is expressed by
Nancy, who would prefer to have a minimum of information.

*The first time Nick went out with this girl, he told me
every little detail, and I spent the next ten or fifteen years
just obsessing on it, thinking about it all the time. She was
one of my best friends going through school. And every
time I heard her name, my gut just turned over. Every time
I met someone who even looked like her, I had to fight off
feelings of hating her. A woman shouldn't have to bear the
burden of that.*

*I think Nick was a lot smarter this last time when he
had an affair. I don't know who it was, and I'm glad I
don't. If he needs to talk about it with someone, it should
be in a group or with a person who doesn't have anything
to do with her—because we codependents usually just use
that information to beat ourselves over the head with. And
I don't need to do that anymore.*

*I tried to get information out of him about the latest
affair. I asked him, but he refused to tell me. At the time
I thought he was just protecting her, but now I'm glad he
didn't tell me anything. I don't need particulars about
where or when or how. I need to know what it was that
was going on in our relationship that might have contributed to it, so that we can be helped to work better together*

as a couple. But I don't need to know if he liked this better or that better.

And I've come to realize that the sexual things that he did really didn't have all that much to do with me. You see, I'm a foodaholic, and when I go to the refrigerator and pig out on chocolate cake, I don't tell myself as I'm eating that I'm doing it to make Nick miserable. Or because I like this cake better than I like him. It was an obsession with him, it was a sickness with him. It didn't mean there was anything much wrong with me. He still loved me as best as he could, as best as any sexaholic could love anybody, and that's been a very good thing for me to understand, that it didn't have that much to do with me. So I don't need any of these particulars. I know that we want to know it, but I don't think it's helpful for us to know it. I think it's better for men to keep that information to themselves or to give it to someone in a group or to a psychologist that they're working with.

Nancy believes it is not healthy for her to know the details of Nick's past affairs; she would prefer to focus instead on their relationship together. Another recovering coaddict, a youthful-looking, athletic 40-year-old school administrator, said much the same thing:

When I am in my codependent state, I need to know. When I am healthy, I don't need to know. Part of needing to know is not letting go, and needing to be in control, which is the way I was running my life for a long time. Since my recent work on my codependency, I no longer need to know.

Patty agrees that obtaining information about her husband's affairs can be part of an effort to control him.

I've heard some women say they want to know all the details. I don't. Before I got into the program I wanted to

*know everything. I wanted to figure out what he was doing,
and I'd try to make him confess. But now that I'm in the
program I don't want to go back and learn more about
those affairs. I was devastated enough by what I thought I
knew at the time. Also, there are things that I don't want
him to know about, things I've told my [Twelve Step group]
sponsor that I don't think Peter has to hear about. So I
don't feel that he has to tell me everything.*

Sarah, a certified public accountant and an assertive person, now divorced and living alone with her two small sons, had several crises with her sexually addicted, alcoholic husband. He had confessed to an affair and promised to be faithful, only to begin lying again. She recalls:

*I needed to know a certain amount of information about
the affair. Maybe that was a part of my beating up on
myself, I don't know. I did want to know something about
it. But the bottom line was that I needed to know it was a
past issue. Then I could move on in the relationship, which
is what I tried to do. The problem was that he would always lie to me about it. I think that if the goal is to have
the relationship continue, then the woman should be told
only as much as she asked for. He should tell her only
what she needs to hear, and she is the best judge of that.
He shouldn't just dump on her. But on the other hand, if
he withholds when she asks, it's equally bad. She's asking
because she has a need to know.*

Some of the women I interviewed felt they needed certain details about their husband's past to sort out in their minds the craziness they had gone through. Some women felt they needed the secrets out in the open to make a fresh start. Other women believed it was in their best interest not to have more than the barest of facts; they recognized they would use detailed information to try to control their husbands' behavior and to make themselves feel worse.

Nearly every woman, however, felt it should be *her* decision how much to be told. Most women did not ask for information that they were not ready to hear.

I believe that if a relationship is to survive the crisis of disclosure of his affairs, a spirit of honesty and respect for each partner is essential. Treating one's wife with respect means letting her decide how much she needs to know and then giving her answers to the questions she asks.

Several women made a distinction between their need for information about the affairs the husband had *before* he entered a program of recovery and the information they would prefer *not* to know about now. One young woman met her husband after he had already begun to participate in a recovery group for sex addicts. She stresses the open communication and total honesty they had from the beginning of their relationship.

> When I first came into this relationship I decided I wasn't going to let any secrets go on. At first we went through a lot of disclosures. Everything had to be gone over in detail. Now, if my husband is having problems, he'll just say, "I'm having a real rough day with my urges." I don't have to know exactly how rough, or all the gory details; I just know how difficult it is.

For Alice, who wanted detailed information at the time of her husband's disclosure, the need to know has also diminished.

> I realize now that part of my past need to know had to do with a feeling I had that the more I knew, the fewer surprises there would be and that the more I knew, the more control I would somehow have over the situation. Part of my recovery has been learning to let go. Early in his recovery, Alan felt he had to be scrupulously honest with me about everything that was going on in his head. So he'd come home and tell me he'd met a very attractive

girl. He had forced himself to break off the conversation with her, and he'd felt sad all day at the lost opportunity. All these confessions did was make me feel bad. But I listened anyway, because I thought it was important that he felt he could confide in me. Besides, there was a part of me that was glad to have the opportunity to monitor his progress.

Now I've come far enough along in my own recovery to realize I don't have to listen to stuff that makes me feel bad. I've asked Alan to tell these things to his group or his sponsor. If he has some significant triumph that he wants to share with me, or some particularly traumatic event that is obviously influencing his mood, then I want to hear about it. I find it's good for me occasionally to be reminded that Alan has an ongoing struggle with the temptation to connect with other women. After all, sex addiction is like food addiction; unlike alcohol, you can't give up people or food altogether—you must learn to relate to them in a healthier way. Alan has become so healthy that it's easy for me to forget he's not "cured," and he fights these little battles on a daily basis. But I no longer have to monitor his recovery; I realize I have no control over his behavior. Either he's working his program, or he's not. If he decides it's too difficult, he'll tell me. Otherwise, I can assume he's doing okay, and I don't have to hear about all the temptations, setbacks, or bad feelings. He can tell it to his group.

Patty, the dentist's wife, agrees:

When we were first in the program, Peter would come home and tell me, "I had a problem with lust today." And I'd find my mind would start working—where? Was it at the office? Was it one of the patients? And I'd begin to obsess about it. I finally was able to say, "If you have a problem with that, right now I'm not able to handle it. Would you tell your sponsor or somebody else; I feel like

*you're dumping on me." He was just trying to be honest,
but it made me feel bad. So now he tells his sponsor, and
I don't have to know about it. If he tells me that he saw
someone today who really drove him crazy, it might trigger
the sickness back in me. So I trust him to take care of it.
If he lusted after somebody, I hope he's well enough in his
program that he can call his sponsor and tell him.*

In summary, some of us need to know more than others
do about our husband's past affairs. Most of us feel that
we should decide how much we should be told. And we
often find that the further along we get in our own recovery, the less we want to know about our husband's present
struggles. All we often really need to know is that our
husband has not exceeded the limits with which we are
willing to live.

Setting Limits

For many of us, one of our prominent characteristics is
that we have no clear boundaries; we are not certain where
we end and the outside world begins. We are, as Anne
Wilson Schaef put it, "externally referented."[6] We depend on others for information on how we feel, what we
think, and how much we are worth. Decisions are based
on what we think *he* wants, not on what *we* want.

A significant part of our recovery is to learn to pay
attention to our needs and to our feelings. We must learn
to be assertive about our wants and to deal constructively
with situations that make us feel bad. In order to do this,
we must first develop self-esteem so that we are willing to
risk another person's displeasure by asserting our rights.
As experienced people-pleasers, we need to learn that we
also deserve to be pleased.

Prior to recovery, many of us were so fearful of abandonment that we were willing to tolerate behaviors that
hurt us rather than risk confrontations with our husbands.

There seemed to always be mitigating circumstances we could use to explain and excuse the behavior. There seemed to always be reasons, however implausible, that we believed to avoid facing the truth.

As our self-esteem improves, however, we eventually no longer believe in keeping our man at any cost. When the possibility of living alone ceases to feel like a fate worse than death, we are ready to consider what is or is not acceptable to us in our relationship. This is the point at which we begin to consider the possibility of divorce if our husband is unwilling to become monogamous. We may choose to stay despite his affairs if we feel that the benefits outweigh the costs. One woman, for example, decided to remain married for another three years while she went back to college so she could be self-supporting. Another woman, who had been very poor in childhood and was now enjoying an affluent lifestyle, decided her financial needs were more important than her emotional needs. To a third woman, it was more important to provide a stable home for her children; divorce was unheard of in her family. Some may not agree with the reasons why these women decided to stay in the marriage, but what is important is that in each case the decision was based on something other than a desperate fear of abandonment.

When we are in recovery along with our spouses eventually we can develop some limits or boundaries for our relationship. Sometimes the limits are discussed, along with the consequences if the agreement was to be broken. In other marriages, the wife has internal limits, but they have not been discussed. For women whose husbands have had affairs, the limit is often another affair. Rita, who went through a one-month inpatient codependency treatment program, told her husband at the end of her treatment, "If you have another affair, I will leave you."

Nancy initially told me that she had no limits in her marriage.

*I haven't set any limits because in the past I told him,
"If you do this again, that's it; I'm leaving." And he'd do
it and we'd break up and then we'd get back together.*

Nancy had given her husband many ultimatums in the
past, and they hadn't worked. She had tried to control his
behavior with threats. She now perceived setting a limit
as just another way of trying to control his behavior. She
was confusing setting a limit with giving an ultimatum.

The difference was clarified by Jessica, the nurse:

*When I first learned about my husband's affairs, I went
through a great deal of emotional pain and a terrible loss
of trust in him. I don't ever want to experience such pain
again or to share him sexually with anyone else. I told him
that if he has another affair I can't continue in our marriage. One of my friends said, "I, too, have given my
husband ultimatums. But isn't that trying to control him?
Doesn't the program teach us that we cannot control another person's behavior?"*

*I explained to her that I'm not trying to control his be-
havior. What I'm doing is setting boundaries of behaviors
that are acceptable to me and those that aren't. My husband can choose how to behave, and I can choose whether
or not to live with that behavior. My husband's "first
drink" is not sexual intercourse: it's making that first connection with a new woman. Several deliberate decisions
then lead to the "tenth drink," the bedroom. He can
choose to risk the "first" or the "second drink"; but if
he proceeds to the "tenth drink," I will no longer be there
for him. This is my boundary; it is not an ultimatum.*

Another woman's husband used to have brief homosexual encounters. Now in a recovery program, he still has
occasional slips. She is hopeful her husband's slips will
eventually stop. She wants to stay in the marriage with
him because she sees progress. Meanwhile, for her own

protection, she has decided she cannot have sexual relations with him as long as he continues to have sex with other men. She is not trying to control his behavior; rather, she is trying to avoid the possibility of catching AIDS, herpes, and other diseases. She has set a boundary for herself, and she is comfortable with it.

Although Nancy has never discussed any boundaries with her recovering husband, she has a very definite internal limit:

If Nick had another affair, I would leave him. It wouldn't be worth it to be in a relationship with somebody like that anymore. I'm well enough now, and I know too much to ever go back into that kind of sickness. An affair isn't just a slip, it's a long, involved process. People have to set those kinds of things up, it goes on over a period of time. It would be unacceptable for him to go out on me and then tell me, "I had an affair because . . ." Anyway, at this point I would know long before it happened. It wouldn't be like it was before, because I could spot the signs right away. I guess an affair would be the limit for me. I'm not that dependent anymore. Before, I was sure that I would starve out there, that the kids would starve. That's what Nick kept telling me too. Now I have enough faith in my Higher Power that He would get me through.

It is interesting that Nancy mentions she would not have to wait for her husband to reveal an affair to her—she would know long before. The same sentiment was expressed by several other women, who stated that their limit would not be some particular sexual transgression by their husband, but rather if he should stop working his recovery program. They felt that would be a prelude to affairs and would be evident long before an affair occurred.

A young woman explained:

I don't have to set any limits. My husband told me that if he stops working his program I'd be a fool to stay. Our life is so different now than before, so much calmer and more reasonable; I see evidence every day that he's working his program. If he stopped, I'd know it right away and we would discuss our future before anything happened.

Patty would be willing to have an open mind about any transgressions as long as her husband was still sincere about working his recovery program.

When Peter and I were first married, I used to think that if he ever had an affair, I'd leave him. Well, he did and I didn't. Now I can't say what I'd do, but I know that I would be willing to be open enough to listen to him to find out where he was at in the situation. Was it a slip? Does he feel regret? Does he want to continue in the program? I don't know what I'd do.

I do know that I want a real relationship. Even if he never had another affair but we drifted apart and the relationship wasn't what I wanted, I would consider ending it. Whether he has an affair or not, I want more. I want us to be able to give to each other and grow together. The [Twelve Step] program has shown us that we can do that.

Some may say, "It's easy to decide in advance that you'd leave your husband if he has another affair or visits a prostitute, but how can you be sure you'd really go through with it?" The answer is, we can't ever be totally certain of anything until it happens. That's why some of us try not to think in terms of consequences.

Linda, whose husband used to have affairs with both men and women, says:

We've never made a contractual limit. Perhaps it's because I see a man who's trying down to his toenails to be the best that he can. He's working very hard in his pro-

*gram. Thank God that to this day there hasn't been a slip. I
don't know how I would react if there was. I don't know what
I would do. Until I cross that path I will never really know.
I might think I'd walk out in a heartbeat, or I might think I'd
be warm and understanding and loving and help him through
it—but I might do just the opposite. I try not to think in those
terms. If he comes home late from a meeting, I just don't
think about it. I know he's working his program, and I have
to be concerned with me and my program.*

Women who are at the beginning of their own recovery
are sometimes reluctant to set limits in their marriage. "I
set a lot of limits in the past and always broke them," said
one young woman. Another added, "I don't want to be
judged myself, so how can I judge another person?" Along
the same vein, a third woman revealed, "I didn't even
realize I wasn't setting limits in my marriage. Now I'm
trying first to set limits on my own behavior. But I'm constantly slipping, so how can I set any limits for my husband?" As these women progress in their own recovery
and as their coaddictive slips become less frequent, they
will most likely feel more comfortable in building expectations and accountability into their relationships.

When I first met Diane, the young teacher and mother
of a small child, she was a member of the walking
wounded. She had recently learned that the money that
kept mysteriously disappearing from their meager savings
account was being spent by her husband in pornographic
bookstores and on casual sexual encounters. Diane's religion, which was an important part of her life, taught her
that marriages are created in heaven and last a lifetime.
She did not understand her husband's behavior; she felt
hurt and confused, but she was sure that she would never
leave him—no matter what he did. She believed her husband's problems were somehow her fault and if she could
be more understanding or more attractive, his extramarital
sexual activities would cease. Dick had begun attending

a self-help group for sex addicts, but Diane did not understand why he thought of himself as an addict. In her own self-help group, Diane sat and listened but said very little; she obviously disapproved of the women who spoke of the possibility of leaving their marriages.

Two years later, Diane's views on the permanence of marriage have shifted.

> I don't like to confront and say *this* I will tolerate and *that* I won't. I'm always so scared of being like my mother, who was such a domineering, critical, tough woman. I guess I'm also scared with Dick, that if I'm too tough or too mean he'll just blow up, or who knows what horrible thing might happen—he might even leave. He doesn't react well to criticism. But I know I can't live with him anymore if he has casual sex. We haven't talked about what would happen if he went back out there again, but I envision a progression of steps, where I would confront him and say, "This can't go on." And if it went on then I would call in outside reinforcements—elders of the church, for instance—and insist on counseling. I'd ask for a contract that he would not do this or that, and if he did, then that would be the end of the marriage. I **would** do that, but never after one episode. I would have to see that he was genuinely **not** going to change, that this was **his** choice, that he was not going to try to get better. I would feel justified then in ending the marriage.

Diane now feels she has certain rights and expectations within her marriage.

This very important point was enunciated clearly by James C. Dobson, a Christian family counselor with a wide radio and television following. In his book, *Love Must be Tough*, Dobson addresses the traditional Christian wife who turns the other cheek when her husband misbehaves:

Infidelity is an addiction that can destroy a life as easily as drugs or alcohol. Once a man or woman is hooked on the thrills of sexual conquest, he or she becomes intoxicated with its lust for pleasure. This person needs every available reason to go straight—to clean up his life. He certainly does not need a spouse who says dreamily, ''I understand why you need the other woman, David. My goodness! I am so riddled with flaws that it's no wonder you went looking for someone else. You should see the list of my own stupidities that I'm keeping. . . . You just go on with your other friendships for a few years while I work on myself, and maybe you'll eventually feel like being a husband again. Spend our money foolishly, if you wish, and I'll get along somehow. . . .'' That approach is like buying booze for the drunk and drugs for the junkie. It is *weak* love! It is disastrous!''[7]

Dobson recommends a course of action he terms *tough love*. Pointing out that a wife's power to negotiate will never be greater than during the crisis of the husband's revelation, Dobson suggests she get her spouse's written commitment to participate in counseling immediately, not even waiting two or three weeks to get started. Also, he states, the wife

must make it clear that *never* again—and I mean *never*—will she tolerate sexual unfaithfulness. [Her husband] needs this motivation to go straight. He must know, and *believe* that one more romp with another lover and the sky will surely fall. [His wife] must convince him that she means business. If he wavers, even slightly, she should give him another month or two to sit somewhere wishing he could come home. Better that they continue at the door of matrimonial death now than go through the misery of infidelity again in a few years. Finally, [the wife] should insist on some major spiritual commitments within the family. This couple is going to need the healing powers of God and His grace if they are to rebuild what sin has eroded.[8]

When asked whether it's not true that marriage is supposed to be based on unconditional love, Dobson explains:

> I certainly believe in the validity of unconditional love, and in fact, the mutual accountability I have recommended is an expression of that love! For example, if a husband is behaving in ways that will harm himself, his children, his marriage, and the family of the "other woman," then confrontation with him becomes an act of love. The easiest response by the innocent partner would be to look the other way and pretend she doesn't notice. But from my perspective, that is tantamount to a parent's refusing to confront a fourteen year old who comes home drunk at 4 A.M. That mother or father has an obligation to create a crisis in response to destructive behavior. I'm trying to say that *unconditional love* is not synonymous with permissiveness, passivity, and weakness. Sometimes it requires toughness and discipline and accountability.[9]

Of several people he interviewed who tolerated their spouse's infidelities in order to try to save the marriage, Dobson says:

> A key ingredient in the erosion of their homes was a kind of marital permissiveness which proved to be fatal. Upon learning that their spouses were involved in affairs, their instinctive reaction was to understand, to explain, to forgive, or to ignore the adultery occurring under their noses. These good people were motivated by committed love in its purest form, and I admire them for their compassion under the most awful pressure.

Nevertheless, they each found "excuses" for the unfaithfulness of their partners, which permitted the disloyal behavior to continue unchecked.

Therein lies a fundamental problem. These loving, gracious people inadvertently shielded their wayward spouses from the consequences of infidelity. If there is *anything* that an adulterer does not need, it is a guilt-ridden mate who understands his indiscretion and assumes the blame for it. Such a person needs to be called to *accountability*, not excused by rationalization![10]

What Dobson is saying is that to turn the other cheek, to be forgiving no matter what, is to *enable* the addict, to protect him from experiencing the consequences of his behavior. Taking a loving but tough stance, on the other hand, encourages the addict's recovery while at the same time improves our self-esteem. Having clear rules about what is acceptable within the marriage often helps to put the relationship on a new basis of mutual respect and accountability.

A final aspect of limits and boundaries is that which applies to us as recovering coaddicts. In the past, we may have engaged in behaviors we were uncomfortable with in order to hold on to our man. As our self-esteem improves, we begin to be able to risk saying no if we don't want to do something. This may be a particular sexual activity we never liked but we went along with. Or it may be listening to our recovering husband describe his latest struggle with lust. Whatever it is, learning to say no and to establish limits on our own behavior is a part of the new self-respect we strive to acquire.

Re-establishing Trust

One of the biggest costs of affairs is the loss of trust we have as couples. Trust in one another involves predictability, dependability, and faith. A person who is predictable will behave the same way in the future as he has in the past. A dependable person is someone who can be relied on when it matters. Both predictability and dependability reflect past behavior. But since future behavior cannot always mirror the past, faith is the belief—based on past experience that our partner cares—that he will continue to be responsive and caring. According to Erich Fromm, author of *The Art of Loving*, "Faith is an indispensable quality of any significant friendship or love. 'Having faith' in another person means to be certain of the reliability and unchangeability of his fundamental attitudes, of the core of his personality, of his love."[11] The person may change his opinions, but his basic motivations remain the same.

When an affair comes to light, predictability, dependability, and faith vanish. We learn that our partner's past behavior has been very different from what he had led us to believe, and we therefore have no basis from which to predict his future behavior. We no longer feel we can depend on his concern for us. Moreover, not only can we no longer be certain of the unchangeability of his fundamental attitudes, but we suddenly realize we don't even *know* what his fundamental attitudes are. All the elements of trust are gone.

For the couple who decides to rebuild their marriage following disclosure of an affair, re-establishing trust is *the* major task. This is usually a slow process that takes months to years and requires much work on the part of both partners. Honestly, predictability, and dependability are the key elements which the man must consistently show to his partner in order to allow her to develop faith in him again. Involvement in a recovery program seems to facilitate the process of restoring trust.

Jessica, the nurse, recalls:

When I first learned about all his lies, I thought I could never trust him again. It's taken a long time to rebuild the trust. I'd say that the first step was his willingness to answer all my questions about his affairs. I could see he didn't want to tell me, but the fact that he was willing to be honest about these painful things made an impression on me even then.

*The **consistency** of his behavior is the second factor which permitted me to trust him again. He told me so many lies and half-truths in our early years together that even he doesn't know anymore whether he told me the truth or a lie about any particular event. One day I found out about yet another lie from those years and got upset. He told me, "I can't guarantee the truth of anything I told you before I got into the program, but I can promise you that I've been entirely honest with you ever since and will continue to be so." That was a couple of years ago, and I haven't had a single occasion since then to doubt his word. He is consistently caring and loving, totally different from the roller coaster life we used to lead before.*

The third factor that helps me trust him is his commitment to his self-help program. He goes to meetings, he talks with people on the telephone, he reads the literature. He does a lot of Twelfth Step work—when he meets someone whom he identifies as a fellow addict, he tells him about the program and about how his life used to be then and how it is now. I can see that he's so much more at peace with himself now than he used to be. He's told me, "I can't promise that I'll never have another affair. But I will tell you about it in advance. And if that happens, you won't have to leave me. I'll probably feel so bad that I'll leave first. On one level I'll be making a conscious choice; on another, I'll be acknowledging the power of the addiction."

So far he has given Jessica no reason to think that this will ever happen.

In addition to consistently honest behavior, a consistently *caring* attitude on the part of our partner can also contribute to restoring trust in the damaged relationship. According to Nancy:

At first I didn't have any trust. When I found out there was a woman in Nick's self-help group, I thought he could still have an affair with her. He's not that much to look at, but I guess I thought that every woman was falling all over herself trying to be with him.

It's been a gradual process. He's been very trustworthy. He made sure to be home when he was supposed to. He would always phone me or leave me a note if he had a change of plans. For a long time he took a lot of care to be on that straight and narrow, even if he had to go out of his way. And then there came a time that he didn't need to do that anymore. If he was going to be late, he didn't have to rush to a phone to let me know why he was going to be late; I was no longer sitting at home tapping my fingers and wondering where he was if he was five minutes late. As I got better, I didn't need all those reassurances anymore.

Nancy's husband recognized that his past behavior had contributed to her insecurity, and he bent over backward to give her no cause for concern. As her recovery progressed, this was no longer necessary. This account illustrates that rebuilding trust is a mutual process involving changes by both partners.

Another important element is open communication between partners. This is what Diane, the young religious woman, feels has made all the difference in the survival of her marriage. In the days when Dick was frequenting the pornographic bookstores and having casual sex, Diane and Dick never talked much about their problems. Both had grown up in families where problems were not discussed; each was afraid of rejection by the other if they did not appear strong.

After we had our big talk about his sexual activities, I felt I couldn't trust him. I didn't know if I could ever trust him. How could I trust him to be honest with me? How could I know if he was being truthful when he said he was no longer having sexual contact with other people? I had no way of knowing, and I felt absolutely no trust. But it's gradually coming back. Now I see that we can discuss things. When he slips, we can talk about it. He is seeing that people can talk about difficult things and still be connected, and not totally reject each other. Dick told me at the time that he couldn't trust me either. He felt he couldn't be himself without being criticized or judged. I guess I didn't feel emotionally that he could trust me. I think that's changing now.

Rebuilding trust takes time. A period of stress and distrust is inevitable. The Twelve Step program advises living "one day at a time." This does not mean we avoid necessary plans or not undertake projects that can't be completed today. It means not being overwhelmed by the problem, but deciding what can be done *today* and doing that. If we approach each day with honest, consistent, trustworthy behavior, this attitude builds upon the previous day, until a track record exists on which we can base new trust.

What to Tell Our Children and Our Parents

All addictions involve secrecy. We make attempts to keep secrets from our spouse, children, parents, neighbors, employers, or significant others. Much of the time we have only an illusion of secrecy. In alcoholic families, for example, Dad's drinking is often well-known by the neighbors and the employer despite the family's efforts to keep it a secret within the family. Certainly the drinking is no secret from the spouse.

When the addiction is affairs, secrecy is even more

common. Our husbands have probably tried to keep their affairs secret from us. If we know, we will almost always avoid telling the children. As discussed in earlier chapters, we often feel that our husband's affairs are somehow our fault; the fewer people know about it, the less chance there is that they will think badly of us. The philandering husband most certainly does not want the children or his parents to know.

Because addictions are considered a family disease, recovery is most effective if it involves the whole family. Alcoholism rehabilitation programs routinely include a "family week" when concerned others—spouses, children, or significant others—interact with the alcoholic and work on their own issues. Teenagers are encouraged to attend Alateen, an Al-Anon program for teenagers, where the impact of the parents' addiction and coaddiction on the children is discussed.

But what about recovery from sex addiction? What should the children be told? What should their own involvement be? Divorced parents, who generally have grievances against each other, have always struggled with the issue of what to tell children about the other parent. Couples who are recovering together have had to work out their own guidelines. Because of the sensitive nature of sex, a lot seems to depend on the age of the children. Most of the people I interviewed have chosen to talk openly to their teenagers, but not to younger children. In families where there is also chemical dependency, some parents have decided to emphasize to their children the recovery from alcohol and other drugs and not to discuss the affairs. Where there is no chemical dependency, the parents have felt more of a need to explain to the children why they are attending self-help groups and counseling sessions.

Couples who have talked openly with their teenage or older children have found it beneficial to their relationship with the children and often helpful to the children. Here is one family's story:

We've talked to our children individually a lot, but not collectively. A few weeks ago Nick took our oldest daughter out to dinner and talked with her about his sex addiction. Later she told me, ''That was the most wonderful night of my life. We just had the best talk!'' We've been trying to help her because she's in a bad situation with a boy. She's me all over again. She's codependent, she's addicted to this boy she's living with, and it's been awful! When I hear her talking about how badly he treats her, I feel so bad for her. So we've been trying to help her through. Her talk with Nick was wonderful; it allowed her to see her problems in the context of the family problems. I don't think that Nick has talked with the boys. But they've talked with me, they've asked me about certain things, and I was amazed to learn that some of the kids hated me more than they did him. They hated me because of the times I was always in bed, depressed, not taking care of them. They blamed me for a lot of the stuff that was going on. That was a real eye-opener.

For Nancy and Nick, talking with their children about their addiction and coaddiction opened the way for better understanding between parent and child and gave their oldest daughter insight into her own relationship addiction. Nancy is hopeful her daughter will recognize her own codependency sooner than Nancy did and will get help much earlier.

Earlier recognition by young adults of their own addiction or coaddiction can be a valuable outcome of the parents' sharing the family secret. Ralph, who had multiple affairs, shared his story with his two teenagers as part of his recovery process. Some months later the seventeen-year-old son told his mother that he recognized he was using sex compulsively. Had the parents not been so open with their son, it might have taken him another ten or twenty years to recognize that he had a problem with his sexual behavior.

When Alan and Alice's eighteen-year-old daughter, Tracy, chose as her first serious boyfriend an unreliable young man who broke as many dates as he kept and had two arrests for drunk driving before he was nineteen years old, Alan decided it was time to talk with her about his own recovery program from sex addiction. Alan had always been a hero to Tracy, and he feared she would begin to hate him if he told her he had been unfaithful to her mother. But Alan was very aware that addiction and coaddiction are family diseases; Tracy had been very much the "responsible child" in the family, and he could see her now beginning a lifelong pattern of addictive relationships with men.

Much to Alan's relief, Tracy did not reject him after he talked with her about his past and his program. On the contrary, she thought it was courageous of him to have told her, and she admired him for the changes he had been able to implement in his life. Alice talked with Tracy about her own previous addiction to Alan and, at Alice's recommendation, Tracy read Robin Norwood's book, *Women Who Love Too Much*. Tracy began attending Al-Anon and also started seeing a therapist who specialized in alcoholism and codependency counseling. After some months she was able to break off her relationship with her alcoholic boyfriend, although she is still struggling with feelings of loss. Alan and Alice are convinced that their openness with Tracy has been helpful to her in her own recovery.

Talking with the children about the parents' problems also serves to validate the children's own observations. Nancy explains:

Sometimes people think kids don't know what's going on, but they know! You have these arguments in the bedroom and somehow you think the kids aren't hearing it. It's insane! They're listening as hard as they can, wanting to hear what's going on.

In a dysfunctional family where feelings aren't discussed, the children may listen and absorb information for years, drawing their own conclusions without ever discussing it with their parents. Meanwhile, the children may be told that everything's fine. Discussing the "family secret" with them and allowing them to voice their own conclusions about what was happening in the family as they were growing up can help them realize they weren't crazy and can correct any misconceptions they may have formed.

Of course, telling our children about our past is risky; children do tend to be judgmental, and the relationship between parent and child may become strained as a result of the new information. This is what happened to Joe, whose wife divorced him many years ago because of his affairs. Two years into recovery and in a new marriage, Joe decided to tell his seventeen-year-old daughter, Laurie, about his sex addiction and his recovery program. Laurie had always felt very close to her father, whom she admired greatly. On the other hand, Laurie had a very stormy relationship with her mother and she could never seem to get along with her. When Joe told Laurie that he'd had affairs during both marriages, her first reaction was to express sympathy for what Joe's current wife, Jessica, had been through. Later that day she told Jessica, "I feel terrible now about how I've treated my mom all these years. I've always somehow assumed that the divorce was her fault, and not Dad's, and I've tried to punish her by being deliberately mean to her and trying to hurt her. Now I realize I've done her a terrible injustice." Laurie spent the next several weeks patching up her relationship with her mother. At the same time, she withdrew from her father, ignoring him when they happened to be in the same room. Eventually she told him how angry at him she was feeling. Although this was a difficult period for Joe, he still thinks telling Laurie was the right thing to do. Her relationship with her mother has definitely improved as a result of the disclosure, and Joe is optimistic that he and Laurie will be able to re-establish a bond, although he realizes that Laurie will no longer have the same idealized image of him that she had in the past.

Cara, a 32-year-old pharmaceutical representative, began having affairs after learning of her alcoholic husband's homosexual affairs. She and her husband now attend A.A. and Al-Anon, but each has continued to have affairs. When Cara shared her story with her teenage daughter, the daughter began confiding in a relative who happened to dislike Cara. As Cara explained, "She exposed me to the entire family. It caused a lot of friction between me and the rest of the family. I don't blame my daughter—she did what she had to do—but it really messed me up with the family."

There is always the risk, when sharing information with children, that other people we would prefer not to know will find out. This is even more of a problem with sex than with alcohol, since sex is such a personal matter. It is best to wait to talk with our children until we are truly convinced that our addiction or coaddiction is a disease, not a moral failing, and that we can handle the situation if others find out about it. Covering up the family secret is very much a part of the disease of addiction. Therefore, we should not share any information with our children about our progress in recovery from addiction or coaddiction if we want them to keep it a secret. Being open with our children is part of *our* recovery; allowing them to share with whomever they want is part of *their* recovery.

In addition to deciding how much to tell the children, couples in recovery sometimes also need to decide what to tell their parents. Often, the decision is to tell them nothing or very little. But if the couple feel that it is appropriate to share with parents, they may in return receive information that is helpful in their recovery. Diane's father and stepmother learned of her husband's addiction early on; they came to visit, noticed how unhappy Diane appeared, and asked for information. At the time, Diane knew only that Dick spent unexplained time away from home and he was unwilling to account for some of his expenditures; she suspected that he was having sexual contact with other people. Diane's parents urged her to get more information and to get help. The result was Diane's and Dick's first honest talk about his problem. Diane remembers:

As a result of getting a little prodding from my folks, we sat down and talked in a lot more detail than we ever had before. I insisted that he get tested for all these various diseases before we had any more sexual contact because I was suddenly afraid, and he agreed. It was a very good talk. He was able to open up and admit various things and I think it was because I was being nonjudgmental; I was just looking for information. I could do it because I felt supported, I didn't feel alone in it. I knew that if I looked at it and it was much more awful than I thought, my parents were there for me. It was not the end of the world. If it was the end of my marriage, I would survive; I would have some help in it.

Shortly thereafter Dick read Patrick Carnes' book *Out of the Shadows*, recognized himself in it, and found a self-help recovery program. Diane's father continued to be supportive. He told her that he himself had been involved with other women during his marriage and that both parents had been swingers during their early years together. He said, "I thought since you were having some problems in your marriage it might be helpful for you to know that I've had some problems in that area too." Diane's parents had gotten divorced when she was sixteen and she had never known why; she has very little recollection of her childhood. It was very helpful to her to have this new information about her parents.

Patty told her parents about her husband's affairs at the

time that she was considering ending the marriage. Now that she and Peter are both in self-help programs, she has tried to give her parents information about the meetings.

My family is very much into denial. They think that Peter and I are really funny, being in programs. They think you should be able to work things out for yourself. But they do see the change in the two of us. They've said to us, "You're so much better with each other, you're so much freer, and you laugh." My father's a practicing alcoholic and my mother has a terrible eating problem. She's one of the most unhappy people I've ever met. I've tried to get her to go to Al-Anon or to Overeaters Anonymous, but she won't go. My program has helped me deal with both my parents.

Patty's parents are not very interested in information about her recovery, but her ability to share with them has improved communication between them.

One word of caution: before deciding to share with your family members information about the affairs and about your recovery, it is crucial to understand your motives for doing so. Some acceptable motives are to become honest with your children or parents, to allow them to understand what was happening in the family, and to encourage open expression of feelings. But some people use their children inappropriately as confidantes, seeking allies in a struggle with the spouse and complaining about the marital partner's transgressions. Telling a child about the affairs may be used as a way of getting back at the spouse. The result can be increased disharmony in the family. In any case, the decision should not be taken lightly, as there is likely to be initial disappointment and anger toward either of the couple as the children learn that their parents do have clay feet.

In summary, recovery as a couple has unique challenges. But it also provides a wonderful opportunity for us to start over again with the same person in a relationship of increased intimacy, honesty, and communication. Working through problems together, sharing the experience of spiritual growth in a Twelve Step program, learning to communicate in the language of the recovery program, and making new friends who are also in recovery programs—all these shared experiences can create a new, powerful bond between us that might give us a better relationship than we ever had before. Moreover, we will both be in the marriage by choice and not because we need another person in order to feel whole. Says Alice: "I know now that I would be okay living alone, but I love Alan; he's my best friend and I like being with him. As long as the good outweighs the bad I'll continue to be in this relationship, enjoying the good times and working on the problems."

CHAPTER TEN

"I'm learning to be my own best friend"

Recovery as a Single Person

Recovery from coaddiction follows the same pathway as does recovery from any other addiction. There is first recognition of the problem. A "bottoming out" eventually results in a change in behavior. The bottom may occur for some of us when we can no longer deny to ourselves that our partner is having affairs. A particularly painful episode may make us decide that we are unwilling to take any more. For others, a crisis may occur when we threaten our husband once again with divorce and he decides to leave. Our change of behavior may consist of ending the relationship. A period of anger, mourning, and depression often follows. Gradually, new behavior patterns emerge as we forge a new life for ourselves. Attendance at Twelve Step meetings and counseling with a knowledgeable therapist may facilitate the process.

Here, in detail, is the story of Beverly, the wealthy mother of three who was married for fourteen years to a philandering husband.

The first time Brian admitted to me in a rather smug way that the reason he had been gone all night was be-

cause he was sleeping with someone else, I felt as if he had just taken away my "happily ever after" fantasy. I was furious. It's not that I hadn't accused him of having affairs before, but he had always denied it, and I had let myself be convinced. I guess you'd say it was a classic case of denial.

From that time on the process of pulling out of the denial and really admitting he was addicted and that I had a problem, too, was a very slow and painful one. At one point he confessed to me all the lies he had told me. I needed to have him tell me because I needed to know that my instincts were right. I had come to the point where I was so confused that he could tell me he took a shower at his office (not at a girlfriend's house) and even when I checked the tub in his office and there was dust in it and he still had wet hair, I doubted myself because he was so adamant.

Now I had to catch him in lies, even if he denied them. I had to learn to trust my instincts. That sounds so simple, but it's not when your whole world is upside down and you're feeling that maybe going back together wouldn't be so bad—at least you'd have him. But once that fantasy world of denial is broken you can only step back into it briefly.

He moved out and we had a few holiday reconciliations but gradually, over a four-year period before and after our divorce, we've separated emotionally as well as physically. I can now see him and talk to him and not get hooked into crazy behaviors, but it took a lot of failures to do it. I used to run after his car after he left the kids off. For a long time I wanted him to sleep with me "one more time." In retrospect I guess I wanted to feel like the most special person in his life and then it wouldn't hurt so much.

The next stage, after the period of pursuing him, was a feeling of tremendous anger and wondering if he ever loved me or if our entire marriage had been a romance novel that I had made up in my head. I asked him if he had ever felt close to me, felt intimate, and he said no. I was shocked.

Then I went through a stage that must be very similar to withdrawal from any addiction. I was unable to sleep. I felt pain all over my body and I would wake up realizing he was gone. I would wail for hours, I felt so alone.

There's a tremendous attraction to me to feel like I'm playing a part in a tragic novel. I like to be under stress. I'm not sure why but I do know that life used to depress me a lot and having conflict in it helped. This became clear when Brian left. With him around life was constantly on a roller coaster and I hardly had to do anything to cause the crisis. But with him gone, I began to see that I looked for a crisis to focus on. It usually ended in a fight with my kids that they didn't understand. I began to try to deal with my depression instead of avoiding it. I spent months in bed. When I felt insecure and afraid and angry, I felt cold and a bed made me feel warm. I still functioned for most of the day but I spent every afternoon in bed. It got to the point where my kids were embarrassed to have friends over because I was in bed all the time. I felt guilty and that made me stay in bed longer. It wasn't until I told myself that it was okay to stay in bed—at least I wasn't drinking or taking pills—that I finally got out of bed. In place of the bed, I have now been able to substitute an image in my head of a warm blanket being thrown over me by someone who genuinely cares about me. When I feel that stress is draining me, I use this image to get back on track.

I had built up a lot of anger over the years, and after I admitted I had no control over Brian's behavior I was very angry. I began going to an exercise program every morning to vent the anger. I often cried through portions of it, but it really helped release that energy. I also began to realize that I ate whenever I saw Brian, and I wanted to lose weight. Another motive for losing weight was to become so attractive that he'd want to come home again.

Because I didn't want to be home alone, I began to do volunteer work in every area available. The funny thing is that this had an unexpected benefit. I took on projects in areas I knew nothing about and I did them well. This helped my self-confidence, and I began to know who I was, something I had never experienced. I also found a lot of friends who were **my** *friends, not* **our** *friends. To learn that they actually liked me, and not because I was Brian's wife, was exhilarating. Eventually I didn't need the work frenzy. I began to realize being alone was a risk I needed to take, and each time it was less painful. I found out that when I needed a best friend in times of insecurity, that best friend could be me.*

When I reflect on times in my marriage when I felt incredibly insecure I realize I wanted to connect with someone else who could make me feel better, but I never did feel better. I used to talk to Brian all night while he tried to be supportive, but he really didn't understand how I felt and his not understanding increased my anxiety and desperate need to make him make me feel better. I can see now that when I turn to myself for this comfort, it's there.

By far the biggest change that's happened in me is I no longer fear abandonment from anyone I'm leaning on. I used to be so afraid of Brian's anger and disapproval for fear he would leave me, but that's not the case now. He used to come to pick up the kids and eat food from the refrigerator or borrow money—all things I resented in Brian but was too afraid to say no. Every time I accomplished something I wanted to let him know, hoping he would like me.

I went through a kind of purification process. I took everything out of the house that was his, and I took everything out I had bought to please him. It was a process of testing my own likes and dislikes and validating my own feelings. I would pick out an outfit I had in the closet and ask myself, what do I feel about this? To my utter surprise, all kinds of images would come to mind, such as, I bought this to please Brian and I hate it. I ended up with an empty shell of a house, and then, gradually, I filled it with things that made me feel good.

Many times I needed to talk to a friend, and I was lucky enough to have a good friend who listened any time, day or night. She has been through a divorce and we both have kids. She likes to laugh and yet she's very supportive. She also was very skeptical about sex being an addiction. I needed that, because I was trying to convince myself that it just wasn't me or a bad marriage. Every time I explained it to her I became more convinced myself. This became crucial because I finally believed that Brian was and always will be sexually addicted.

I'm still working on a healthy attitude toward a sex life for myself. . . . I became celibate, and I found so much clarity in not having to be sexual with anyone. It was a real relief just relaxing at home, something I'd never done before.

Putting myself first above everyone else was something I had never done before. At first I struggled with how self-ish it was until I saw how much better I felt and how my life pattern changed. I had to say to myself and my children that I deserve to do things for myself.

Beverly has had a long struggle. A sympathetic counselor and a self-help program have given her support in her recovery. Like many divorced women whose ex-husbands maintain contact with their children, she cannot avoid interaction with him. This has proven to be a further obstacle to her recovery, but she has finally managed to detach from him and is ready to consider dating other men. She has gone through a period of mourning, anger, depression, and finally acceptance, and has restructured her life in a healthier way.

Another recovering single person contrasts her present life with the way it used to be:

One of the main differences in my life now, compared to before I was in the program, is I don't have the complications of a relationship. That's important because, always before, a relationship got in the way of my other priorities. At this time I'm able to focus on me, I'm able to experience my feelings, and I'm able to spend time and thoughts with my kids. I'm not exhausted to the point of just being able to hang on. I'm able to give more quality time to my kids, more positive energy to my job. I feel much better about myself because I know I can say no. That's a protection I have that I didn't have before. I was always afraid that somehow, in spite of how I felt, I'd do something once again that I didn't want to do and I'd wonder why I was doing it. At this point it seems that I have more control over my behavior.

Married for many years to an alcoholic who had multiple affairs, Helene is now recovering from alcoholism and lives alone with her two teenage children. In response to a query about whether she still needs a man for validation, she told me:

It's not that I don't need a man for validation; I just don't need the sexual intimacy for validation. I've come to the realization that my validation has to come from inside me, not outside. And the validation itself is different. I need to accept I can do my best, I'm a capable and valuable human being without having someone say he needs me. But I still like the approval and the company of men; it just doesn't have to be one man for whom I'm special. I don't have to be the best in some person's eyes. But I still do need validation.

Helene's validation now comes from her knowledge that she is doing well on the job and as a parent, and from her friendships with men and women.

Grieving

Just as recovering addicts go through periods of mourning the loss of relationships with the addictive chemical or behavior, so we go through a grieving process as well. If we have ended our marriage or an intense relationship, we may grieve its loss. We might also grieve the loss of the intense feelings we experienced in relationships. In the past, these feelings may have been our only confirmation that we were really alive and could feel. As we remember them, the tremendous highs we occasionally experienced seem to more than have made up for the more common lows in our life. Now that we may find ourselves having to get along without experiencing either extreme of emotion, life may seem flat and uninteresting.

During this early time, a period of depression is common. Helene, the recovering alcoholic who subsequently recognized her propensity for relationships with addicted men, recalls that after she decided to stop seeing a sex addict, she went into an incredible depression. She said:

From the day that I broke up with my "white knight," all I could do was get up in the morning, go to work, come home, fix a sandwich, and go to bed. For about six weeks I wasn't capable of doing anything else. I did continue to attend A.A. meetings. Gradually I was able to involve myself in more normal activities, like spending time with my daughter after I got home instead of going to bed, and talking to people in a normal sort of way.

It was as if I was in suspended animation, like there was a part of me that had died, and the other part hadn't been born yet. It was a terrible time. And then, gradually, I was able to come alive a little bit at a time. But all the way through it, I realized that getting involved with another man was not going to fix it. Just like with my alco-

holism, having a drink wasn't going to fix it. That was clear to me, so I didn't do it. This was breaking another pattern, because always before, when I was feeling low, I looked to another person to make me feel better.

Having already experienced recovery from alcoholism, Helene had the strength to go through the pain and depression of the first weeks of recovery from coaddiction without turning to her "drug of choice"—a man.

Avoiding Another Addictive Relationship

Probably the biggest problem for the recovering single coaddict is how to avoid another addictive relationship. Robin Norwood, author of *Women Who Love Too Much*, stated at a lecture she gave in Tucson in 1986, "The people with whom we can have a nurturing, trusting relationship are not the same kinds of people with whom we can feel tremendous passion and intensity for." Meeting a "normal" man requires adjusting to a relationship that isn't so exciting. "Being in a relationship where the other person shows up—it *is* boring, compared to what it used to be."[1]

Accustomed to finding addicts exciting and "normal" men boring, and having already experienced the painful consequences of being in one or more addictive relationships, those of us who are single may decide simply not to date rather than risk repeating our mistake. Early in recovery, a period of not dating is often an excellent idea and is highly recommended by codependency counselors. Some of us who begin recovery need at least six to twelve months of not dating, spending time with ourselves and with friends, going to meetings, and learning where our priorities are and what we want to do with our lives.

When we resume dating, we must be very aware of the reasons we are attracted to a new man. A divorced 30-

year-old alcoholism counselor who is recovering from co-dependency reports:

If I'm very attracted to someone immediately, I see a red flag. It doesn't mean I'll stop seeing him, but I'll be very cautious. I'll ask questions about his history, family, use of chemicals, and his previous relationships. I'm going to suspect that this is either an addict or a raving co-dependent. It's unfortunate, but because that is what my whole history has programmed me for, I'm most likely to be attracted to another codependent.

She has learned that instant attraction is a danger sign.

Another suggestion is to postpone sexual involvement until the new relationship has had some time to grow. Many of us tend to substitute sex for social skills. It is easier to be sexual with a man than to work at getting to know him. Spending an evening in conversation takes communication skills—spending the same time in bed may involve a minimum of conversation. Many people have noted that a new relationship tends to come to a standstill in its development once the couple have begun to sleep together.

Based on her experience, the alcoholism counselor told me:

I believe there has to be a long period of dating someone before you sleep with him. Because of my propensity to be attracted sexually to dysfunctional men, I have to avoid sexuality in the first stages of a relationship in order to get to know the man. I need to make sure that he is good for me, that he values and respects me and that we've got a common value system. Otherwise I'm likely to find myself sleeping with someone I hardly know and don't like, but by the time I realize this I'm so entangled with him emotionally that it doesn't matter. Sleeping with someone early on interferes with getting to know him. I believe that what we do is romanticize and delude ourselves when sexuality is involved. People are willing to sacrifice a lot of cognitive data for sex.

I also believe that really stable relationships are built on friendship, not on sexuality, and if you introduce sexuality very early you're likely to have a relationship based on sexuality rather than on companionship. I really enjoy sex, but I don't want to be in a relationship where that's all that's going on.

Postponing sex is scary for those of us who have behaved in past relationships as if sex were the most important sign of love. We may fear that a man may not want to continue seeing us if we are not giving him sex. Part of our recovery process is to become involved in relationships that are not based primarily on sex. We need to learn that we are valued for ourselves and not just for what we give sexually.

Many of us are usually ready to enter into a sexual relationship soon after meeting a man. This was true of Sarah, the certified public accountant who found that the new man in her life had different ideas.

When I first became involved with him I would have been willing to prematurely jump into a deeper relationship than he was ready for. I'm very thankful that we didn't, because I've now had over a year of experimenting with the relationship to see what kind of person he really is. Our disease tells us to get in there and hang on, right away, to get the hook in and just grab because who knows what's going to happen next. What I'm learning is that it's better to get to know someone well first. I've found out that if I mess up it's not fatal to our relationship, that I'm not a bad person and that I'm worthy of being around. Whenever I mess up I flash into the old fear that he'll leave, but I'm learning that if I talk to him about it, he

responds by being closer and more understanding. I'm
learning a lot about trust, which I'd never known before.

Helene, the recovering alcoholic whose former husband
had several affairs, contrasts her present social life with
how it used to be.

When someone asks me out, I go to lunch with him or I
arrange to have an appointment so that I can spend only
an hour or two with him; that helps me take it slowly. In
the past, within 24 hours of meeting someone I made emo-
tional contact and was in bed with him. Now I've been
seeing a man for two months, and we finally held hands.
This is a real change for me. There's still part of me that
believes there's one right person for me. But I realize that
what I'm looking for is not really "the right one," it's the
connection. I believe that we coaddicts, just like addicts,
are looking for a connection—an emotional, sexual con-
nection that has fireworks. I'm still attracted to that type
of man, but I don't act on the attraction. I avoid men who
have an intensity which I recognize through eye contact.
These folks always have some enormous problem, usually
in terms of relationships. There's something about them
that is not functioning in a healthy way, and it's always
something I thought I could fix. When I meet such a man
now I essentially interview him, looking for the broken
*part. And I always find it—and then I **run**.*

Before even beginning a relationship with a man she
finds initially exciting, Helene tries to find out from him
whether he is a man she should avoid.

Like most relationship addicts, Helene finds that healthy
men are boring. She deals with this by directing her energy in other areas rather than in looking for a relationship. She is developing more skills at work, strengthening
her relationship with her children, and is becoming acquainted with women—which she never thought was valu-

able or interesting. She believes that she is not yet ready for an intimate relationship.

Speaking on the problem that recovering coaddicts have of finding normal men boring, Robin Norwood is optimistic. She says, "When you go through the boredom, and you learn to live with it, it transforms into peace and serenity."[2]

Making Friends

Occasional loneliness is a natural part of life for the single person. Part of the recovery process is to learn to relieve the feeling of loneliness in nonsexual ways. Making friends, attending self-help group meetings, and talking on the phone with other people often helps to take away our loneliness.

Learning to relate to men as people rather than as romantic objects is an important part of recovery as single people. According to Sarah, the certified public accountant now divorced from a man who still juggles several women at a time:

I think it's really important for women to develop and maintain close personal friendships with men. We need to learn what it's like simply to be a friend with a man, to share confidences and to learn to trust men as friends. As a single person, it's easy to become isolated. You may be working your program well by going to meetings, but there may be only women at the meetings—and it ends up that you only interact with other women. I think it's very important to learn to relate to men as friends, because that's a tool you need in a relationship. A man also needs to know how to be friends with a woman and not to mystify the relationship by making it male/female. Especially when we've been involved with a sexaholic, we tend to get very angry with men and think that they're all bad, that we don't need them in our lives. It's important to have both male and female friends during recovery.

Before recovery, we attribute enormous power to the current men in our lives. They are not just men—they are the people who have control over our happiness and our future. Their emotions determine ours; they are the people who make us whole. One of our tasks in recovery is to learn to see men as ordinary human beings. As Sarah points out, this is best accomplished by developing friendships with men.

Working on our friendships with other women is another good project for those first months of nondating. Although many of us feel sympathy and affinity for other codependent women and have close women friends, some of us see other women primarily as competition. If we are this type of woman, we surround ourselves with men friends and avoid women; we have found that we just don't like women. At self-help meetings or in group therapy we will get to know other women who have gone through experiences very similar to our own, and we will probably find ourselves seeing women in a new light. Several women told me, "In the past I looked at other women as competition—now I suddenly have women friends."

Learning new patterns of relating to men and women friends can form the groundwork for healthier interactions in subsequent romantic relationships. Many of us have been people pleasers, fearful of abandonment if we should reveal how we really feel about something. Through non-romantic friendships where there is not the huge emotional investment that there is in romance, we can learn that it is acceptable to make our feelings known to our friends and to say no to a request that we really don't want to do. Later, once we feel more comfortable with these new patterns of relating, we can transfer them to our romantic relationships.

Developing New Interests

Another way to overcome loneliness is to fill our lives with interesting activities. For some, taking a class on auto maintenance can serve the dual purpose of increasing a sense of self-competence and promoting new friendships. Reading books is an interesting pastime that provides new topics of conversation. One woman said, "I'm reading books I wouldn't touch before, books that deal with relationships, connections, and spirituality. Before, books were boring because I had no way of connecting. I didn't have any experience or interest; my spirituality was in connecting with a man."

Many activities that in the past we thought of as couple activities can be enjoyed just as much when done alone. All that's required is a positive attitude. Darlene, a businesswoman who is divorced from a philandering husband, recalls how her attitude made all the difference in determining whether or not she enjoyed a vacation.

A few years ago I was madly in love with an exciting, unpredictable man. We planned a trip to Mexico City but at the last minute he canceled out. I had already arranged to take the time off from work, so I decided to go anyway. I had a miserable time—all around me I saw nothing but happy couples walking arm in arm. Instead of enjoying all the fascinating things there were to see, I spent the whole time feeling sorry for myself, wishing that my friend were with me. I might as well have stayed at home and saved the cost of the trip.

A year later I had an opportunity to spend a couple of weeks in Europe. I had never traveled overseas alone and the thought was a little scary. Complex travel arrangements aren't my forte, so I decided to keep it simple. I spent a week in Paris and a week in Florence. I visited museums, shops, and churches. I took long walks through each city, enjoying the sights and taking lots of photo-

graphs. I found out there are definite advantages to being a solo tourist. For example, I could spend exactly as much time as I wished at a museum or a store, and I didn't have to take into account anyone else's wishes. I was so involved in my day-to-day activities that I never felt lonely. I really enjoyed being alone. It was one of the best vacations I've ever had. I know I could have had just as good a time in Mexico City if I'd had a better attitude.

Spiritual Growth

Many of us report feeling an inner void that we have tried to fill in the past with other people or with food or drink. The inner void may represent spiritual emptiness, and may be filled by working on our relationship with our Higher Power. Meditation, taking pride in our work, helping others, and living a life of integrity can make us more spiritual and less lonely.

Sarah, the CPA, describes her daily program:

If I'm working my program reasonably well, I usually do a half hour of exercise a day, I read something spiritual, and I think about my relationship with my Higher Power several times during the day. I may be driving down the street, but I may be sort of meditating. I go to a couple of self-help meetings a week. I get on the phone and check in with someone from the women's group at least every other day, and if there's a problem I may be on the phone several times a day; I just may need that sort of support. I also go to church once a week.

The big difference is, I have more peace than I used to have. I am better able to let go of things. I obsess less and I lose my serenity less often. It's still hard—the patterns are still there, but recognizing them and dealing with them faster seems to be the key to recovery for me. If I find myself obsessing, I've got the tools to deal with it.

By getting in touch with our Higher Power, we can enjoy aloneness and avoid loneliness. Accepting a Higher Power can diminish our sense of isolation and bring us closer to understanding ourselves and those around us.

Twelfth Step Work

Because many codependents tend to go into the helping professions, the working wife or ex-wife of a man who has affairs often has opportunities on the job to meet other women in a similar situation. The recovering physician, nurse, or counselor is likely in the course of her working day to have patients or clients who are dealing with spousal affairs; the divorce lawyer who is a recovering coaddict will undoubtedly have clients who are getting divorced because of their spouse's drinking or sexual activities. If she is willing to share her own story with appropriate patients or clients, the recovering professional person can assist such people to obtain help for themselves through a Twelve Step program, counseling, or both.

An attorney recounts her experience with such clients:

Usually it's a divorce client or they're separated and she doesn't want the kids to go see him because he's always got his girlfriend over there, or it's a series of girlfriends, or he doesn't watch the kids because he's been drinking too much. I'll then share with her my experience of being with a man who was an alcoholic and who wanted to be with a lot of other women. I tell her about Al-Anon and S-Anon [a Twelve Step program for families of sex addicts] and I'll give her meeting lists. I tell her about other resources, and recommend helpful books.

This attorney has learned that to carry the message to others, as the Twelfth Step of A.A. recommends, is a good way to reaffirm her own commitment to the Twelve Steps and to her own recovery.

Relapses

Setbacks in our recovery from coaddiction are inevitable. Lifetime patterns of reacting are difficult to change, and progress may consist of recognizing the relapse before much time has passed or much harm has been done. Early recognition that we have slipped back into the old way of thinking can result in quick, corrective measures.

According to Sarah:

Sometimes I find myself feeling very needy, victimized and frightened, wanting to hibernate or escape. If I'm not working my program, not doing the things that I know can improve my situation, then it may go on for a week or more. For example, I'm dating a man, and generally it's been very comfortable having no expectations. He said something a few weeks ago about engagement rings, and I was off and running. I began to think, maybe he plans to give me a ring for Christmas. I really let my imagination go. And then I found out that he was simply asking out of an interest. I felt very victimized, unhappy, and rejected. I wanted to split and run; not literally, but there was a sense of wanting to hide and lick my wounds. In my relationship with my former husband, I operated from that perspective all the time. When things were bad, I tried to do everything I could to please. I obsessed about him and continued to manipulate things to make it all turn out okay. And of course I didn't succeed.

*Now, I still do some of those things, but I don't **keep on** doing them. I recognize them for what they are, part of my disease. What I do instead is pick up the phone and call someone and tell them what's going on, that I'm feeling really crazy, and I get some feedback on it. And I go to meetings and do some meditation. I still have the characteristics, but I handle things a bit differently most of the time. And generally, the craziness doesn't last long, about a day or two at the most.*

Helene laughs as she remembers a recent slip involving an old boyfriend.

A couple of nights ago I was all dressed up and I looked fit to kill. I decided to go over to his house and show him what he'd lost. Every once in a while I slip. I got all the way over to his house and then realized I don't need this, so I left before he saw me. So at times my behavior has yet to catch up with where I am. I still tend to fantasize about him, but less often than before.

No matter how long we have been in recovery, it is likely that certain situations will still elicit a feeling of rejection. Men with addictive personalities might continue to appeal to us and we may find ourselves hooked before we know it. We might be tempted to make telephone calls or visits to former lovers who are best forgotten. But we will probably find, with time, these situations will occur less frequently. We may not be able to prevent our initial emotional reaction, but we will recognize it for what it is earlier. And we will be able to choose to deal with the situation in a healthier way so as to minimize the pain to ourselves.

The recovering person whose relationship has ended must actually live through her worst fear—the fear of being alone. Like the sex addict who learns in his recovery program that sex is optional, we, having survived alone, find out that having a man in our lives is also optional. We learn that life as a single person is not only possible, but enjoyable. We come to realize that an intimate relationship is a *choice*, not a necessity. Once we believe this, we are ready to make some better decisions regarding our subsequent relationships. No longer driven to connect with a fellow codependent who needs rescuing, we can take the time to learn if the new man is good for *us* before committing ourselves to another relationship.

We might always be initially attracted to addictive men,

but we will not be compelled to act on those initial feelings. We will put at least as much effort into our relationship with ourselves, our children, and with our nonsexual friends as we used to put into our relationship with the "special man." No longer afraid of appearing selfish should we make our needs known, we will regularly ask ourselves what is best for *us* and make our decisions accordingly.

This chapter is aimed at wives of sex addicts and at the counselors who may be working with us. It offers suggestions for helping our children not to become codependent. It also gives guidelines for identifying the relationship addict in general (the woman involved in an addictive relationship with an emotionally unavailable man), and the sexual coaddict in particular (the woman who is in an addictive relationship with a sex addict). And it summarizes the conclusions of the book.

Helping Our Children Grow Up Healthy

The realization that sex addiction, coaddiction, and codependency are family diseases leads to the question, "How can we prevent the next generation, our children, from becoming victims of the family illness?" Too often, by the time we recognize our own disease and get help, many of our children are teenagers or adults and already exhibit signs of codependency. When we recognize the signs in ourselves, it becomes easier to see them in our children. The most we can do at this point is to become as healthy as possible so that the family in which our children reside is more healthy. It is not helpful to bring to the child's attention his or her codependent traits; rather, we are better advised to share our experiences and what has been helpful to us. In this way the child may recognize his or her negative behavior and make changes or seek help—years earlier than otherwise.

When we communicate with our children and encourage them to share feelings and trust in other people, we promote healthy attitudes and self-esteem. When we show interest in our children's feelings and opinions and take their problems seriously, they will probably develop the belief that they are worthwhile people whose well-being is of concern to their parents. If this has not been our pattern of relating to our children, it is never too late to make a change. The older the children are, the harder it is likely to be to bring about changes in our relationship with them, but it is worth our while to make the effort.

An important lesson we can teach our children is to face problems rather than to avoid them. Dr. M. Scott Peck begins his perennial bestseller, *The Road Less Traveled*, with the statement, "Life is difficult." What makes life difficult is that the process of solving problems is painful. It is tempting to avoid problems rather than to face them directly and experience the unavoidable suffering that dealing with problems entails. Discipline, according to Peck, is the set of tools we need to solve life's problems. When we teach children discipline, we teach them the necessity to face problems directly and to experience the pain involved.

There are basic principles of discipline that parents need to teach their children: delaying gratification, accepting responsibility, telling the truth, and having flexibility. The opposites of these principles—delaying problem solving in favor of immediate gratification, avoiding responsibility by saying, "It's not *my* problem," and lying—are all ways to postpone facing problems. Unfortunately, most problems do not disappear. Lying about them often only worsens the situation. For example, a child may accidentally break a dining room chair. Fearful of his mother's disapproval, he places the chair in such a way that she doesn't realize it's broken—until the night she is having a dinner party and moves the chair. The child has postponed having to face the problem, but now most mothers are likely to be more upset at the child's deception and the inconvenient timing of the discovery than if the child had admitted the problem when it first happened.

The proper role of the parent is not to keep shielding a child from stress; rather, it is to remind the child that there is always something he or she can do about the stress, even if the only good choice is to tolerate pain for a while. Even young children have to experience some discomfort in order to grow. For example, children will not learn to walk if they are not allowed to fall, to get up, and to try again. Depending on the child's age, we, as parents, must protect them from certain stresses, but not from all. The alternative to coping with stress is to avoid it—by using alcohol or other drugs or other mood-altering behaviors. Such patterns of avoiding problems can lead to addiction in later years.

Self-discipline is the ability to withstand the pain or discomfort of pushing ahead when we really don't want to. When we allow children to accept responsibility for what they do and to experience the natural or the social consequences of their actions, we are teaching them self-discipline. Because we love our children, it is tempting to protect them from unpleasant experiences. They will grow up healthier, however, if they face both the positive and the negative outcomes of their actions.

Another aspect of a healthy childhood is play. Play is fun, and it's important in a child's life. It's freely chosen and spontaneous. The play attitude allows us to enjoy what we are doing without being compulsive about it. The more dysfunctional the family, the less play there is likely to be. If our interactions with our children do not include having fun with them, we should start now.

To become a healthy adult, the best model a child can have is nonaddicted parents. Recovery from our own coaddiction is the greatest investment in our child's future that we can make.

Are You a Relationship Addict?

If you are in a relationship in which your spouse's behavior is problematic, asking yourself some simple questions may help you determine whether you are addicted to him.

Do you feel responsible for his behavior?

Do you believe you cannot live without him?

Do you fantasize about his problems?

Do you make excuses for his behavior, blaming it on other people?

Do you believe that you can make him change?

Have you threatened to leave him and not followed through? Or have you left him and then returned although no changes occurred?

Are you afraid to confront him on his behavior for fear he will leave you?

A "yes" to any of these questions suggests that you may be in an addictive relationship.

There is probably an addictive element in every love relationship, according to Howard M. Halpern, author of *How to Break Your Addiction to a Person*, but this is not necessarily bad.

Halpern says:

> It can, in fact, add strength and delight to the relationship. After all, who is so complete, so self-contained, so "healthy" and "mature" that he doesn't need to feel good about himself through a close tie with

another person? In fact, one sign of a good relationship is that it puts us in touch with the best in ourselves. What makes a particular relationship an addiction is when these little addictive ''I need you'' elements expand to become the controlling force in your attachment. This creates an inner coercion that deprives you of several essential freedoms: the freedom to be your best self in the relationship, the freedom to love the other person through *choice* and caring commitment rather than being *compelled* by our own dependence, and the freedom to choose whether to stay with the other person or to leave.[1]

In other words, we are likely to be addicted to a person if we are in the relationship because of compulsion instead of by choice. If we remain in a relationship that is bad and in which we can't reasonably expect any improvement:

Are we still in it by choice? Or is it because we are addicted?

Some of us may choose to remain in an unhappy situation because of practical considerations. We may be totally dependent on our husband's income and unwilling to take a job while the children are small. We may need our husband's financial support while we acquire some training that will enable us eventually to support ourselves. Or we may have no job skills and see no prospects of acquiring any.

Some of us may choose to remain in a bad relationship because of religious or other beliefs about divorce. Our religion may frown on divorce, or perhaps no one in our family has ever gotten divorced and we cannot imagine ourselves being the first to do so. Or possibly, having seen our parents' marriage break up, we've decided children need a stable family more than anything else, and we commit ourselves to remaining married until the children grow up. Or, we may be so committed to the concept of marriage "till death do us part" that we simply cannot consider another alternative.

Many of us, however, remain in an unhappy relationship because of our addiction to our partner. Halpern lists several signs of addiction that we can look for in ourselves when deciding why we are remaining in the relationship.

1. Even though your objective judgment (and perhaps the judgment of others) tells you that the relationship is bad for you and you cannot expect any improvement, you take no effective steps to break with it.

2. You give yourself reasons for staying in it that do not hold water or that you are not really strong enough to balance the negatives in the relationship.

3. When you think about ending the relationship, you feel dread, even terror, and you cling to it even harder.

4. When you take steps to end it, you suffer acute withdrawal symptoms, including physical distress, that can only be relieved by reestablishing contact.

5. When the relationship is *really* over (or you fantasize that it has ended), you feel the lostness, aloneness, and emptiness of a person eternally exiled—often followed or even accompanied by a feeling of liberation.[2]

In a bad relationship, denial is common for a woman who is addicted to her partner. Although she may give herself reasons for staying, an objective observer would find that her reasons do not outweigh the emotional abuse that exists in the relationship. A woman who decides to leave a bad relationship usually does learn to cope.

If we stay in a bad relationship we may be hiding the real problems from ourselves, believing strongly that any relationship with our husband is better than no relationship. This is typical of the codependent, who looks to others for affirmation of her self-worth.

Howard Halpern advises that we ask ourselves whether the benefits of remaining in a relationship outweigh the costs, or vice versa.

If you decide to end an addictive relationship, Halpern recommends several steps. First, take advantage of your friends; call *them* instead of him. Let your friends listen to you; they'll help remind you that you can survive without this person, and persuade you that there are other people in your life who care for you. Second, seek a feeling of attachment to something greater than yourself, a Higher Power. Third, consider psychotherapy or counseling, but be sure you choose a therapist or counselor who will not foster emotional dependence on him or her, or you may find yourself switching addictions from your former partner to your therapist.

Some of Halpern's steps are similar to recovery from addiction with the help of A.A. and Al-Anon. I believe that the most effective approach to recovery from codependency is through the Twelve Step programs, supplemented by individual or group counseling or both, given by Twelve Step-oriented counselors.

Identifying the Sexual Coaddict

Relationship addiction is very common, but to help you decide more specifically whether your coaddictive pattern involves sex addiction, here are some more questions to ask yourself:

Is sex extremely important in your relationship?

Are you afraid to refuse your spouse sex for fear that he will seek it elsewhere?

Have you, in order to please your husband, participated in uncomfortable or degrading sexual activities or sexual activities that were against your moral code?

Have you been emotionally hurt or embarrassed by your spouse's sexual activity?

Have you covered up for him for his sexual activities?

Has his sexual behavior caused your family financial or legal problems?

Have you looked through his clothes or other possessions for evidence of affairs?

Have you caught a sexually transmitted disease from him—and then continued to have sexual relations with him?

Have you considered suicide because of his affairs?

Do you believe that life would not be worth living if he should leave you for another person?

Have you had more than one committed relationship in which your partner was unfaithful to you?

Were you sexually abused as a child?

In your family of origin, were affairs an issue?

If you answered "yes" to four or more of these questions, you may be a sexual coaddict. It is even more likely if you recognize that you share the core beliefs described in Chapter Two, especially that sex is the most important sign of love. The other core beliefs of the sexual coaddict are that she is not a worthwhile person, that no one would love her for herself, and that she can control other people's behavior.

Recovery Is a Process

The basic premises of this book have been:

- For some men, their affairs are not a matter of choice, but rather compulsive behavior similar to alcohol dependency.
- Men who are addicted to affairs tend to marry women who become addicted to them and who often will participate in their addiction.
- Underlying and preceding both the sexual addiction and

the coaddiction is a pattern of behavior termed codependency.

- Codependency often has its roots in a person's dysfunctional family of origin.

- Recovery from addiction and coaddiction is often best
accomplished by membership in a recovery program
based on the Twelve Steps of Alcoholics Anonymous.

- Recovery can be facilitated by counseling by a knowledgeable professional who incorporates the self-help
group into the treatment plan.

- For the woman married to a man addicted to affairs,
divorcing him will not always resolve her problems;
her underlying codependency will most likely lead her
into a relationship with another sex addict or emotionally unavailable man—unless she gets treatment for
herself.

- The woman whose husband recovers from his sex addiction also needs treatment for her coaddiction; sex
addiction, like alcoholism, is a family disease.

If you have been in one or more relationships with a
man addicted to affairs, the best way to recover from his
affairs is for you to get help for yourself. With the help of
a Twelve Step program and a knowledgeable counselor
you can become a whole person who does not depend so
extremely on another for her self-worth.

Recovery is a process, not a cure that can be accomplished once and then forgotten. Recovery is not a
straight line, and relapses are inevitable. The Twelve
Step programs tell us that what counts is progress, not
perfection. Because many of us are perfectionists who
tend to be hard on ourselves, it is easy to get discouraged if we find ourselves falling back into the old behaviors. One of the goals of recovery from coaddiction
is to learn to be good to ourselves, to be forgiving and
nurturing.

There will probably always be times when we will experience an initial gut-wrenching emotional reaction to someone's words or actions that will transport us right back to the bad old days. At such times it is helpful to remind ourselves that although we cannot control our initial feelings, we do have a choice about how to respond. We can examine our feelings and decide whether they are part of our old behaviors or whether they truly have relevance to our current situation; then, we can act accordingly. If we find ourselves feeling frightened, insecure, panicked, and lonely, we should not get discouraged nor fear that we are making no progress. These episodes are likely to occur with decreasing frequency as we continue in our recovery program. Moreover, our program gives us tools for dealing with these troubling times:

- Talking with friends or our sponsor on the phone.
- Attending Twelve Step meetings.
- Talking with and lending help to other women who are suffering more than we are—it will remind us how far along we have come in our recovery.
- Seeing a counselor who can help us.
- Increasing our connection with our Higher Power by meditating, reading spiritual materials, and seeking daily evidence of the presence of a Higher Power in our lives.

Five years ago I was a needy, vulnerable person, dependent for my sense of self-worth on a partner whose own circumstances prevented him from being emotionally available to me. Uncertainty, unpredictability, and a roller-coaster existence was the way I thought a normal relationship functioned. I felt like a victim when I learned I was not the only woman in his life. Today I am reminded of the person I used to be when I meet other women who are at the beginning of their journey to recovery. My own journey has taken me to a place that feels much safer and much more comfortable. Along the path I have met wonderful people, I have discovered a spiritual part of myself that I never knew existed, and I have incorporated into my life a program for living (the Twelve Steps) that I believe can be of help to everyone, whether or not there is a problem of addiction in the family.

I have learned that I am not alone. Those who practice their recovery program tell us that life can be better than we ever imagined it. I believe that this promise can be fulfilled for all of us.

THE TWELVE STEPS OF A.A.*

1. We admitted we were powerless over alcohol—that our lives had become unmanageable.

2. Came to believe that a Power greater than ourselves could restore us to sanity.

3. Made a decision to turn our will and our lives over to the care of God *as we understood Him*.

4. Made a searching and fearless moral inventory of ourselves.

5. Admitted to God, to ourselves, and to another human being the exact nature of our wrongs.

6. Were entirely ready to have God remove all these defects of character.

7. Humbly asked Him to remove our shortcomings.

8. Made a list of all persons we had harmed, and became willing to make amends to them all.

9. Made direct amends to such people wherever possible, except when to do so would injure them or others.

*The Twelve Steps are taken from *Alcoholics Anonymous*, published by A.A. World Services, Inc., New York, N.Y., pp. 59–60. Reprinted with permission.

10. Continued to take personal inventory and when we were wrong promptly admitted it.

11. Sought through prayer and meditation to improve our conscious contact with God *as we understood Him*, praying only for knowledge of His will for us and the power to carry that out.

12. Having had a spiritual awakening as the result of these steps, we tried to carry this message to alcoholics, and to practice these principles in all our affairs.

APPENDIX A

Definitions of Terms Used in the Book

Here is my understanding of some terms which I have used in this book.

Addiction: A self-destructive relationship with a mood-altering drug or behavior. To be addicted to a behavior is to continue that behavior even though it has negative consequences. The addictive behavior becomes more important than anything else in a person's life and is continued even at the risk of losing one's family, job, or health. In sex addiction, what defines an addiction is not the number of sexual encounters, but rather the compulsive nature of the behavior despite the costs. Every addiction has two critical elements—a behavior disorder, and a thinking disorder which denies and rationalizes the addictive behavior.

Coaddict: A spouse or significant other who becomes so involved in the life of the addict that he or she starts to participate in the thinking disorder of the addict. The coaddict is someone who has developed an unhealthy pattern of relating to others as a result of having been closely involved with an addict. The coaddict's feelings and behaviors include low self-esteem, a need to control and change others, and a willingness to suffer. The coaddict so fills her life with the relationship with the addict that she cannot tolerate the threat of losing the relationship. To maintain the relationship, she joins in his irrational behavior and enables his addiction.

Because the coaddict can be viewed as being addicted to her partner, she can also be described as a *relationship addict*. These terms are often used synonymously, but some workers in the addiction field prefer to use the term coaddict specifically to designate a person who joins the addict in his addiction—for example, engaging in group sex with the sex addict.

Coaddictive behavior: Behavior by which the coaddict attempts to change the addict, but which in reality facilitates the addiction. This may refer to *any* such behavior (for example, the sex addict's wife may avoid arguments in an attempt to be the perfect wife). Or more specifically, it may refer to participating in the addict's addiction in order to control him (for example, the sex addict's wife will decide never to deny him sex or will agree to sexual practices she doesn't like in order to prevent him from straying).

Codependency: A definite pattern of personality traits that *precedes* addiction and coaddiction and predisposes a person to one behavior or the other. The primary characteristic of codependency is looking to others for one's self-worth. Codependency develops before adulthood as a result of an individual's experience in his or her family of origin, where there was a set of oppressive rules that discouraged any expression of feelings as well as the direct discussion of personal problems.

Denial: Refusal to confront a problem directly. The denial may be done with full awareness, such as a woman pretending to her friends that she has a perfect marriage, when her life is chaotic; or it may be self-denial, such as when she convinces herself that a motel receipt in her husband's coat pocket was something he happened to pick up from the floor when he was walking down the hall of his office building.

Enabling behavior: Behavior that protects the addict from experiencing the consequences of his or her addictive behavior. For example, the wife who suspects an affair hides her pain from her husband and makes excuses to her friends for his behavior. By postponing the time when the addict realizes that his life is out of control and that he needs help, enabling helps to perpetuate his behavior.

Sex addict: A person who is addicted to the sexual experience and its surrounding behaviors. The behaviors can include obsessing about an actual or potential sexual partner, compulsive masturbation, excessive expenditures on pornography, patronizing prostitutes at the risk of health, multiple affairs, or other sexual behaviors that the addict intuitively knows are against his best interest. In the context of affairs, the sex addict is the person who is secretly and compulsively sexual with a series of partners, substituting sensations for feelings in a spiraling escalation of risk, without apparent regard for the destruction of important relationships involving family and friends.

APPENDIX B

Resources

Unless you live in a large city, it may be difficult to find meetings of some of the groups listed below. Many cities have a "Help on Call" or "Information and Referral" telephone service; a call may yield information on what is available in your area. The organizations listed below may be able to put you in contact with others in your community who have the same problem, and these organizations may be able to give you guidelines on starting your own group.

Alcoholics Anonymous World Services, Inc.
General Services Office
468 Park Avenue
New York, NY 10016

Al-Anon Family Group Headquarters, Inc.
P.O. Box 862 Midtown Station
New York, NY 10018-0862

Sexaholics Anonymous (for sex addicts)
General Services Office
Box 300
Simi Valley, CA 93062

S-Anon (for those who have been involved with sex addicts)
P.O. Box 5117
Sherman Oaks, CA 91413

Twin Cities Sex Addicts Anonymous (for sex addicts)
P.O. Box 3038
Minneapolis, MN 55403

Sex and Love Addicts Anonymous (for sex addicts)
P.O. Box 88, New Town Branch
Boston, MA 02258

National Association for Children of Alcoholics
31706 Pacific Coast Highway
South Laguna Beach, CA 92677

Children of Alcoholics Foundation, Inc.
200 Park Avenue
New York, NY 10166

APPENDIX C

Suggested Reading

Understanding Addiction

Carnes, Patrick, *Out of the Shadows: Understanding Sexual Addiction*. Minneapolis: CompCare Publications, 1983. Originally published as *The Sexual Addiction*, this is the classic book on the subject.

Hope & Recovery: A Twelve Step Guide for Healing from Compulsive Sexual Behavior. Minneapolis: CompCare Publications, 1987. This book describes the thinking and behavior of the sex addict and the road to recovery.

Johnson, Vernon. *I'll Quit Tomorrow*. New York: Harper & Row, 1973. Describes the intervention process—how to help the addict accept treatment.

Maxwell, Ruth. *The Booze Battle*. New York: Ballantine Books, 1976. How to live with, and help the addict.

Sex and Love Addicts Anonymous. Boston: Sex and Love Addicts Anonymous Fellowship-Wide Services, Inc., 1986. The basic text for one of the fellowships of sex addicts, this book describes the nature of the addiction and the recovery process.

Understanding Coaddiction and Codependency

Beattie, Melody. *Codependent No More.* Center City, Minn.: Hazelden Educational Materials, 1987.

Forward, Susan and Torres, Joan. *Men Who Hate Women and the Women who Love Them.* Toronto and New York: Bantam Books, 1986.

Norwood, Robin. *Women Who Love Too Much.* Los Angeles: Jeremy Tarcher, Inc., 1985. The classic book on women who marry addicts.

Norwood, Robin. *Letters from Women Who Love Too Much.* New York: Pocket Books, 1988.

Schaef, Anne Wilson. *Codependence: Misunderstood-Mistreated.* Minneapolis: Winston Press, 1986.

Shainess, Natalie. *Sweet Suffering: Woman as Victim.* New York: Bobbs Merrill, 1984.

Recovery

Burns, David. *Feeling Good: The New Mood Therapy.* New York: Signet Books, New American Library, 1980.

Dobson, James C. *Love Must be Tough.* Waco, Tex.: Word Publishing Co., 1983. A practical, very helpful guide to dealing with affairs, by a Christian minister.

Friedman, Sonia. *Men Are Just Desserts.* New York: Warner Books, 1983.

Halpern, Howard. *How to Break Your Addiction to a Person.* New York: Bantam Books, 1982.

Schaeffer, Brenda. *Is it Love or is it Addiction?* Center City, Minn.: Hazelden Educational Materials, 1987.

Smedes, Lewis B. *Forgive & Forget: Healing the Hurts We Don't Deserve.* New York: Pocket Books, Simon and Schuster, 1984. A thoughtful discussion about a problem most women face in the aftermath of their husbands' affair.

Wanderer, Zev and Cabot, Tracy. *Letting Go.* New York: Warner Books, 1978.

Spirituality

Johnson, Robert A. *WE: Understanding the Psychology of Romantic Love.* San Francisco: Harper & Row, 1983.

Peck, M. Scott. *The Road Less Traveled.* New York: Simon and Schuster, 1978.

In addition to the above books, I would also recommend the various publications of Al-Anon Family Groups. Some of these are:

Al-Anon Family Groups. New York: Al-Anon Family Group Headquarters, Inc., 1986.

One Day at a Time in Al-Anon. New York: Al-Anon Family Group Headquarters, Inc., 1986.

Al-Anon's Twelve Steps and Twelve Traditions. New York: Al-Anon Family Group Headquarters, Inc., 1985.

Living With Sobriety: Another Beginning. New York: Al-Anon Family Group Headquarters, Inc., 1985.

The Dilemma of the Alcoholic Marriage. New York: Al-Anon Family Group Headquarters, Inc., 1987.

NOTES

Preface

[1]*Alcoholics Anonymous: The Story of How More Than One Hundred Men Have Recovered from Alcoholism* (New York: Works Publishing Company, 1939).

[2]*Journal of American Medical Association* 113 (1939): 1513.

Chapter One

[1]"Sexaholic: Addict of Infidelity," *Arizona Daily Star* (5 May 1985) Section K, 1. Reprinted with permission of the Arizona Daily Star.

[2]Alfred Kinsey, et al., *Sexual Behavior in the Human Male* (Philadelphia: W.B. Saunders Co., 1948), 585.

[3]Morton Hunt, *Sexual Behavior in the 1970s* (New York: Playboy Press, 1974), 254.

[4]Shere Hite, *The Hite Report on Male Sexuality* (New York: Alfred A. Knopf, Inc., 1981), 142.

[5]Robert A. Johnson, *WE: Understanding the Psychology of Romantic Love* (San Francisco: Harper & Row Inc., 1983), xii.

[6]*When Your Happily Ever After Isn't* (Denver: Raj Publications, 1981), 3.

[7]Ibid., 12.

[8]Francine Klagsbrun, *Married People: Staying Together in the Age of Divorce* (New York: Bantam, 1985).

[9]Ibid., 23.

[10]Morton Hunt, *The Affair* (New York: New American Library, 1973), 39.

[11]Ibid., 33.

[12]Ibid., 46.

[13]Catherine Johnson, "The New Woman Infidelity Report," *New Woman* (November 1986), 73.

[14]Hunt, *Sexual Behavior in the 1970s*, 268.

[15]Patrick Carnes, "Counseling the Sexual Addict" workshop in Tucson, Ariz., 1986.

[16]Alfred Kinsey, et al., *Sexual Behavior in the Human Female* (Philadelphia and London: W. B. Saunders Co., 1953), 444.

[17]Hunt, *Sexual Behavior in the 1970s*, 269.

Chapter Two

[1]Patrick Carnes, *Out of the Shadows: Understanding Sexual Addiction* (Minneapolis: CompCare Publications, 1983), 92, 98. Originally published as *The Sexual Addiction.*

[2]Carnes, *The Sexual Addiction,* 4.

[3]Robin Norwood, *Women Who Love Too Much* (Los Angeles: J.P. Tarcher, 1985), 183.

[4]Patrick Carnes, "Counseling the Sexual Addict" workshop in Tuscon, Ariz., 1986.

[5]Carnes, *The Sexual Addiction,* 105–114.

[6]Anne Wilson Schaef, *Codependence: Misunderstood-Mistreated* (Minneapolis: Winston Press, 1986), 44.

[7]Norwood, *Women Who Love Too Much,* 130.

[8]Ruth Maxwell, *The Booze Battle* (New York: Ballantine Books, 1976), 45.

Chapter Three

[1]Bill W., letter quoted in *The Grapevine,* January 1958.

[2]Robert Subby, *Co-dependency, An Emerging Issue* (Hollywood, Fla.: Health Communications, Inc., 1984), p. 26.

[3]Ibid.

[4]Claudia Black, *It Will Never Happen to Me* (Denver: M.A.C. Printing and Publications Division, 1981).

[5]Subby, *Co-dependency,* 36.

[6]Arthur and Cynthia Koestler, *Stranger on the Square* (New York: Random House, 1984), 170.

[7]Subby, *Co-dependency,* 39.

[8]Lou Ann Walker, *A Loss for Words* (New York: Harper & Row, Inc., 1986), 21.

[9]Ibid., 22.

[10]Ibid., 104.

[11]Ibid., 181–183.

[12]Ibid., 187.

[13]Sharon Wegscheider-Cruse, *Another Chance: Hope and Health for The Alcoholic Family* (Palo Alto, Calif.: Science and Behavior Books, Inc., 1981), 84.

[14]Black, 53.

[15]Wegscheider-Cruse, *Another Chance,* 111.

[16]"Ask Al", *Arizona Daily Star* (2 January 1987) Section C,2.

Chapter Four

[1]Louis McBurney, "Avoiding the Scarlet Letter," *Leadership* (Summer 1985): 44–51.

[2]Erich Fromm, *The Art of Loving* (New York: Harper & Row, Perennial Library Edition, 1974), 8–10.

[3]Dr. James C. Dobson, *Love Must be Tough* (Waco, Tex.: Word Books, 1983), 122.

[4]Patrick Carnes, *Out of the Shadows: Understanding Sexual Addiction* (Minneapolis: CompCare Publications, 1983), 82–85.

[5]Patrick Carnes, statement on the Phil Donahue Show, 7 January 1987.

[6]Carnes, *Out of the Shadows,* 20.

Chapter Five

[1] Jean Harris, *Stranger in Two Worlds* (New York: Macmillan Publishing Company, 1986), 61.

[2] Ruth Maxwell, *The Booze Battle* (New York: Ballantine Books, 1976), 41–43.

[3] Arthur Koestler and Cynthia Koestler, *Stranger on the Square* (New York: Random House, 1984), 228.

[4] Ibid., 115.

[5] Ibid., 179.

[6] Ibid., 108.

[7] Ann Wickett, "Why Cynthia Koestler Joined Arthur," *Hemlock Quarterly* (January 1985): 4.

[8] Koestler, *Stranger on the Square*, 150.

[9] Ibid., 225.

[10] Ibid., 14.

[11] Harris, *Stranger in Two Worlds*, 122.

Chapter Six

[1] Betty Friedan, *The Feminine Mystique* (New York: Dell Publishing Co., 1963), 255.

[2] Ibid., 65.

[3] Betty Friedan, *The Second Stage* (New York: Summit Books, 1981), 56.

[4] Ibid., 80.

[5] Margaret Mayo, *Afraid to Love* (Harlequin Books, 1979).

[6] Marabel Morgan, *The Total Woman* (New York: Pocket Books, Simon and Schuster, 1973), 20.

[7] Ibid., 119.

[8] Ibid., 170.

[9] Ibid., 34.

[10] Ibid., 65.

[11] Ibid., 75.

[12] Ibid., 77.

[13] Ibid., 113.

[14]Ibid., 117.

[15]Ibid., 152.

[16]Ibid., 184.

[17]Friedan, *The Second Stage,* 53.

[18]Marabel Morgan, *The Electric Woman* (New York: Pocket Books, Simon and Schuster, 1985), 205.

[19]Anne Wilson Schaef, *Co-Dependence: Misunderstood-Mistreated* (Minneapolis: Winston Press, 1986), 70.

[20]Ibid., 72.

[21]Ibid., 81.

[22]Ibid., 85.

[23]Stephanie Brown, *Treating the Alcoholic* (New York: John Wiley and Sons, 1985), 208.

Chapter Seven

[1]Judith Thurman, *Isak Dinesen, The Life of a Storyteller* (New York: St. Martin's Press, 1983), 149.

[2]"Update: Acquired Immunodeficiency Syndrome—United States," *Morbidity and Mortality Weekly Report* 35. Reprinted in *Journal of the American Medical Association* 257 (23 January 1987): 433–37.

[3]G. J. Stewart et al., "Transmission of Human T-Cell Lymphotropic Virus Type III (HLTV-III) by Artificial Insemination by Donor," *The Lancet* (14 September 1985): 581.

[4]"Update: Acquired Immunodeficiency Syndrome—United States," 433–37.

[5]Robert R. Redfield et al., "Frequent Transmission of HLTV-III Among Spouses of Patients with AIDS-Related Complex and AIDS," *Journal of the American Medical Association* 253 (15 March 1985): 1571–1573.

[6]Nancy Padian et al., "Male-to-Female Transmission of Immunodeficiency Virus," *Journal of the American Medical Association* 258 (14 August 1987): 788–790.

[7]"Heterosexual Transmission of Human T-Lymphotropic Virus Type III/Lymphadenopathy-

associated Virus, *Morbidity and Mortality Weekly Report* 34, 37, 38, (1985). Reprinted in *Journal of the American Medical Association* 254 (18 October 1985): 2051–2052.

[8]"Antibody to Human Immunodeficiency Virus in Female Prostitutes," *Morbidity and Mortality Weekly Report 36* 11 (1987). Reprinted in *Journal of the American Medical Association* 257 (17 April 1987): 158.

[9]L. H. Calabrese and K. V. Gopalakrishna, "Transmission of HLTV-III Infection From Man to Woman to Man," *New England Journal of Medicine* 314 (April 1986): 987.

[10]Warren Winkelstein, Jr., et al., "Sexual Practices and Risk of Infection by the Human Immunodeficiency Virus: The San Francisco Men's Health Study," *Journal of the American Medical Association* 257 (16 January 1987): 321–325.

[11]Margaret A. Fischl et al., "Evaluation of Heterosexual partners, Children, and Household Contacts of Adults with AIDS," *Journal of the American Medical Association* 257 (6 February 1987): 640–644.

[12]George Lundberg, "The Age of AIDS: A Great Time for Defensive Living," *Journal of the American Medical Association* 253 (21 June 1985): 3440–3441.

[13]Marcus Conant et al., "Condoms Prevent Transmission of AIDS-Associated Retrovirus," *Journal of the American Medical Association* 255 (4 April 1986): 1706.

[14]Elizabeth Huen et al., "Hepatitis B Virus Transmission Between Heterosexuals," *Journal of the American Medical Association* 257 (16 January 1987): 314.

[15]Katherine M. Stone et al., "Primary Prevention of Sexually Transmitted Diseases," *Journal of the American Medical Association* 255 (4 April 1986): 1763–1766.

Chapter Eight

[1]J. M. Gorman and J. F. Rooney, "Delay in Seeking Help and Onset of Crisis Among Al-Anon Wives," *American Journal of Drug and Alcohol Abuse* 6 (February 1979): 223–33.

[2]Timmen L. Cermak, M.D., *Diagnosing and Treating Co-dependence* (Minneapolis: Johnson Institute Publications, 1986), 3.

[3]Ibid., 9–10.

[4]Ibid.

[5]Robin Norwood, *Women Who Love Too Much* (Los Angeles: Jeremy Tarcher, Inc., 1985), 184.

[6]Robert A. Johnson, *WE: Understanding the Psychology of Romantic Love* (San Francisco: Harper & Row, 1983), 52.

[7]Ibid., 55.

[8]Shere Hite, *Women and Love* (New York: Alfred A. Knopf, 1987), 501.

[9]Ibid., 495.

[10]Johnson, *WE*, 55.

[11]Robert A. Johnson, *SHE* (New York: Harper & Row Perennial Library, 1977), 32.

[12]Howard Halpern, *How to Break Your Addiction to a Person* (New York: Bantam Books, 1981), 263.

[13]S. H. Kardener et al., "A Survey of Physician's Attitudes and Practices Regarding Erotic and Nonerotic Contact with Patients," *American Journal of Psychiatry* 130 (September 1973): 1077–1081.

[14]N. Gattrell et al., "Psychiatrist-Patient Sexual Contact: Results of a National Survey, I. Prevalence," *American Journal of Psychiatry* 143 (October 1986): 1121–1126.

[15]J. L. Herman et al., "Psychiatrist-Patient Sexual Contact: Results of a National Survey, II. Psychiatrists' Attitudes," *American Journal of Psychiatry* 144 (February 1987): 164–168.

[16]Ibid.

[17]"American Psychiatric Association Drops Sexual Misconduct Liability Coverage," *American Medical News* (22 February 1985): 16.

[18]Bob Womack, "Support Groups Struggling to Establish Themselves," *Arizona Daily Star* (5 May 1985), Section K, 1.

[19]Dr. Ruth Westheimer, "Ask Dr. Ruth," *Arizona Daily Star* (22 June 1987), Section C, 3.

[20]Stephanie Brown, *Treating the Alcoholic* (New York: John Wiley & Sons, 1985), 22.

[21]Erich Fromm, *The Art of Loving* (New York: Harper & Row, Perennial Library Edition, 1974), 22.

Chapter Nine

[1]Gabrielle Brown, *The New Celibacy* (New York: Ballantine Books, a division of Random House Books, 1980), 33.

[2]Karen Angst, ed., "Sexual Dependency," *ECHO* (Summer 1985): 10.

[3]Brown, *The New Celibacy*, 167.

[4]*Sexaholics Anonymous* (Simi Valley, Calif.: Sexaholics Anonymous Literature, 1984), 87.

[5]*Hope and Recovery: A Twelve Step Guide for Healing from Compulsive Sexual Behavior* (Minneapolis: CompCare Publications, 1987), 97.

[6]Anne Wilson Schaef, *Co-dependence: Misunderstood-Mistreated* (Minneapolis: Winston Press, 1986), 42.

[7]James C. Dobson, *Love Must be Tough* (Waco, Tex.: Word Books, 1983), 56.

[8]Ibid., 78.

[9]Ibid., 81.

[10]Ibid., 122.

[11]Erich Fromm, *The Art of Loving* (New York: Harper & Row, Perennial Library Edition, 1956), 103.

Chapter Ten

[1]Robin Norwood, lecture in Tucson, Ariz., May 1986.
[2]Ibid.

Chapter Eleven

[1]Howard M. Halpern, *How to Break Your Addiction to a Person* (New York: Bantam Books, Inc.), 9. Italics added.
[2]Ibid., 10.

INDEX

"EASY DOES IT BUT DO IT"
with Hazelden Recovery Books

THE 12 STEPS TO HAPPINESS   by Joe Klaas
36787-1 $4.95

BARRIERS TO INTIMACY: For People Torn by Addictive and Compulsive Behavior   by Gayle Rosellini and Mark Worden
36735-9 $4.95

BACK FROM BETRAYAL: A Ground-Breaking Guide To Recovery For Women Involved With Sex Addicted Men   by Jennifer Schneider, M.D.
36786 $4.95

LIVING RECOVERY: Inspirational Moments for 12 Step Living   by Men and Women in Anonymous Programs
36785-5 $4.95

COMPULSIVE EATERS AND RELATIONSHIPS   by Aphrodite Matsakis, Ph.D.
36831-2 $4.95

These bestsellers are available in your local bookstore, or order by calling, toll-free 1-800-733-3000 to use your major credit card.

Price and order numbers subject to change without notice. Valid in U.S. only.

For information about the Hazelden Foundation and its treatment and professional services call 1-800-328-9000. In Minnesota call 1-800-257-0070. Outside U.S. call (612) 257-4010.